W9-COE-261

# GREAT PREACHING ON

# HEAVEN

# GREAT PREACHING ON

# HEAVEN

## COMPILED BY
## CURTIS HUTSON

SWORD of the LORD
PUBLISHERS
P.O. BOX 1099, MURFREESBORO, TN 37133

# *Preface*

We in these pages seek to better acquaint you with this strange and wonderful country, a country where there are no tears or heartaches, no sickness, pain or death. Those who live there never grow weary, carry no burdens, and never grow old. No one ever says goodby; and there are none of life's disappointments there.

In this country you will find that there is no sin, for no one does wrong. You will travel for thousands of miles and never see a cemetery or meet a funeral procession, for no one ever dies.

Nothing ever spoils there. Flowers never lose their fragrance; leaves are always green. There are no thunderstorms, no erupting volcanoes, no earthquakes. Upon those fair shores hurricanes and tidal waves never beat.

There are no germs or fevers, no pestilences of any kind. And it is always light, for there is no night there. No clouds ever darken the sky, no harsh winds ever blow.

There are no drunkards in this country, for no one ever drinks. None are immoral—men as well as women are pure. Prisons, jails and reformatories never darken its landscape. Doors have no locks, windows no bars, for thieves and robbers never enter there.

No lustful books are read; no sexy pictures shown. No taxes paid, no rent collected. And it is a country free from war and bloodshed.

Yes—and no cripples are to be seen; none are deformed or lame. Nor is anyone blind, deaf or dumb, for all are healthy and strong. No beggars are seen on the streets, for none are destitute.

Leprosy and cancer, palsy and tuberculosis are words never heard in this country! No asylums are there, for none are feeble-minded. Doctors are never needed, and hospitals are unknown.

What country is this? It is called Heaven, the Home of the saved, where God Himself shall be with us and be our God. "And God shall wipe away all tears from their eyes; and there shall be no more death, neither sorrow, nor crying, neither shall there be any more pain: for the former things are passed away" (Rev. 21:4).

Let these great men of God tell you what is yet in store for all who have trusted the Saviour!

Unsaved friend, do you not want to go to such a country? Then why not get ready now? It isn't difficult. All you have to do is trust Christ as your Saviour. Then when the journey of life is ended, you too can go to this wonderful country and dwell there forevermore.

Curtis Hutson
Editor, SWORD OF THE LORD

# *Table of Contents*

CURTIS HUTSON
1934-

# ABOUT THE MAN:

In 1961 a mail carrier and pastor of a very small church attended a Sword of the Lord conference, got on fire, gave up his route and set out to build a great soul-winning work for God. Forrest Hills Baptist Church of Decatur, Georgia, grew from 40 people into a membership of 7,900. The last four years of his pastorate there, the Sunday school was recognized as the largest one in Georgia.

After pastoring for 21 years, Dr. Hutson—the great soul winner that he is—became so burdened for the whole nation that he entered full-time evangelism, holding great citywide-areawide-cooperative revivals in some of America's greatest churches. As many as 625 precious souls have trusted Christ in a single service. In one eight-day meeting, 1,502 salvation decisions were recorded.

As an evangelist, he is in great demand.

At the request of Dr. John R. Rice, Dr. Hutson became Associate Editor of THE SWORD OF THE LORD in 1978, serving in that capacity until the death of Dr. Rice before becoming Editor, President of Sword of the Lord Foundation, and Director of Sword of the Lord conferences.

All these ministries are literally changing the lives of thousands of preachers and laymen alike, as well as winning many more thousands to Christ.

Dr. Hutson is the author of many fine books and booklets.

# I.

# *Bible Answers to Questions Most Often Asked About Heaven*

### CURTIS HUTSON

*"Let not your heart be troubled: ye believe in God, believe also in me. In my Father's house are many mansions: if it were not so, I would have told you. I go to prepare a place for you. And if I go and prepare a place for you, I will come again, and receive you unto myself; that where I am, there ye may be also."*—John 14:1-3.

When I was a small boy I heard the preacher say that when the Christian dies, he goes up to Heaven. I used to lie on my bed at night and wonder: If Heaven is a real place, where is it? If I were to die as a Christian, would I go to Heaven immediately? If I did, how long would it take me to make the trip? And when I got to Heaven, would I know my friends? Would they know me? What would I look like in Heaven? Would I have a body? Could I eat in Heaven? Would my loved ones know me? Would I know my loved ones? Would I know my grandmother and grandfather who had already gone to Heaven? These and many other questions went through my mind—death and Heaven were mysteries to me.

One of the greatest causes of sorrow, when our loved ones pass away, is a lack of knowledge concerning the dead. The Bible says in I Thessalonians 4:13, "I would not have you to be ignorant, brethren, concerning them which are asleep, that ye sorrow not, even as others which have no hope." A lack of knowledge is our chief cause of sorrow when we lose our loved ones.

I will try to answer several questions about Heaven.

## I. IS HEAVEN A REAL PLACE?

The Bible teaches that Heaven is a real, literal, physical place. Jesus said in John 14:2,3, "I go to prepare a place for you. And if I go and prepare a place for you, I will come again, and receive you unto myself; that where I am, there ye may be also."

I mention that Heaven is a place because some think that Heaven is a state of the mind. Jesus said:

*"Lay not up for yourselves treasures upon earth, where moth and rust doth corrupt, and where thieves break through and steal: But lay up for yourselves treasures in heaven, where neither moth nor rust doth corrupt, and where thieves do not break through nor steal."*—Matt. 6:19,20.

That could only be said of an actual, real, literal, physical place.

If I had time to read Revelation 21 and 22 you would see a beautiful description of the Holy City, the New Jerusalem, which is the eternal home of the saved. In those chapters the Bible says that Heaven has foundations, and the foundations are garnished with all manner of precious stones. It says the walls of the city are made of jasper. It says that there are three gates on the east, three on the west, three on the north, three on the south. It says the gates are made of pearl and every several gate is one pearl.

That could not be said of a state of mind; it could only be said of a real, literal place.

Revelation 21 and 22 give the measurements of the Holy City in cubits. If you take cubits and multiply them into feet, then divide them into miles, the Holy City, the New Jerusalem, would be fifteen hundred miles square. You could not measure Heaven unless it was a real, literal, physical place.

## II. WHAT KIND OF PLACE IS HEAVEN?

First, Heaven is a place of indescribable beauty and glory. The Bible says in I Corinthians 2:9, "Eye hath not seen, nor ear heard, neither have entered into the heart of man [or crossed man's mind], the things which God hath prepared for them that love him."

The Bible says there is no way to imagine the indescribable beauty of Heaven! When you read Revelation 21 and 22, you will have only a little glimpse of that beautiful place called Heaven.

One beautiful night a young boy was walking with his grandfather. The sky was deep blue, and it seemed like a million stars were on parade. The boy pulled at his grandfather's coattail and said, "Grandpa, Grandpa, if Heaven is so beautiful on the outside, what must the inside look like!"

The songwriter was correct when he wrote:

**How beautiful Heaven must be,**
**Sweet Home of the happy and free.**

Heaven is a place of indescribable beauty and glory. But Heaven, too, is a place of perfect rest. The Bible says in Revelation 14:13, "Blessed are the dead which die in the Lord from henceforth: Yea, saith the Spirit, that they may rest from their labours; and their works do follow them."

Most people never know what it is to experience complete and perfect rest, with no worries, no schedules to meet, no time clocks to punch, no alarm clocks in the morning.

When my mother died I was on soul-winning visitation. Some friends found me and told me that Mother had passed away. Hurrying home I entered the bedroom where she had been for several weeks due to illness. There lay my mother's body. When I looked at her, my first impression was, "Mother, this is the first time I've ever seen you relaxed." She always had a burden of some kind to carry; now she was resting from her labors.

Heaven is a place of indescribable beauty. It is a place of perfect rest. But Heaven, too, is a place of open vision.

A young couple had three small children. I was called to conduct the funeral of one of those little ones. A few months later the second child died. And in less than a year the third child was taken. All three had unrelated diseases. It was an unusual thing, and I had never had an experience like it.

As we walked away from the grave of their last child, the mother wept and said, "Explain to me why this happened. Why did God take every child we had while other families never lose one?"

I could not explain it, for I cannot see the end from the beginning. But God knows. Romans 8:28 is true. It is the Word of God. It is a fact. "All things [DO] work together for good to them that love God."

I said to that young couple, "You may not always be able to trace God, but you can always trust Him."

**My Father's way may twist and turn,**
**My heart may throb and ache;**
**But in my soul, I'm glad I know**
**He maketh no mistake.**

God knows what He is doing. I cannot explain everything now. I cannot see as God sees. But in Heaven I'll know as He knows. Heaven is a place of open vision, with no glass between; and there we will understand it all. First Corinthians 13:12 says, "Now we see through a glass, darkly; but then face to face: now I know in part; but then shall I know even as also I am known."

I read the story of a very young boy in England who, due to his father's death, had to drop out of school and go to work to make a living for his family. He was only ten or eleven years old. He sold papers to help his mother provide for other family members.

Each day after selling his papers, he would stop at a toy store on his way home to look at some beautifully painted toy soldiers in the window. The storekeeper had noticed this.

Then one day he missed the boy. He inquired of those in the street, "Has anyone seen the little paper boy who used to stop and look at the toy soldiers?"

Someone said, "Oh, haven't you heard? He was hit by an automobile the other day, and he is in the hospital unconscious."

The storekeeper was moved; he gathered up the little toy soldiers and took them to the hospital. He told the mother how the boy had looked wishfully at the soldiers every day, then he asked permission to give them to him. Though the boy was unconscious, the man placed the little soldiers across the foot of the bed. They stayed there several days.

One morning when the boy regained consciousness, the first thing he saw was the toy soldiers. He could hardly believe his eyes. He began moving forward, reaching with his little hands to touch the soldiers, getting closer and closer, until finally they were in his hands. With a smile he exclaimed, "Oh, look, Mother! Look! Here are the soldiers, and there is no glass between!"

## III. DO THE SAVED GO TO HEAVEN IMMEDIATELY?

The answer is yes. The Bible says in II Corinthians 5:8, "to be absent from the body" is "to be present with the Lord." There are only two places a Christian can ever be: in the body or with the Lord. In Philippians 1:23 Paul said, "I am in a strait betwixt two, having a desire to depart, and to be with Christ; which is far better." Depart and be with Christ.

Man is not a body; he is a soul. He has a body. The Bible says that God created man in His own image and breathed into his nostrils and he became a living soul (Gen. 2:7). My body is not me. It is mine.

My body is my possession. If I bump my head, I say, "I bumped *my* head." It is my head, my hands, my feet, my ears, etc. But this is also my watch and my coat. My coat is my possession, and my body is my possession. The body is simply the house in which I live. I am the soul and spirit on the inside. In I Thessalonians 5:23 Paul said, "I pray God your whole spirit and soul and body be preserved blameless unto the coming of our Lord Jesus Christ." When a man dies, his soul and spirit leave his body and go immediately to be with Christ.

In London, England, a tombstone has an unusual epitaph. A man named Solomon Peas gave instruction before he died to put these words on his tombstone:

> **Beneath these clouds and beneath these trees,**
> **Lies the body of Solomon Peas;**
> **This is not Peas; it is only his pod;**
> **Peas has shelled out and gone Home to God.**

When I read that, I wished my name were Solomon Peas: I would like those words on my tombstone.

When the Christian dies, he goes immediately to be with Christ: absent from the body; present with the Lord.

## IV. WILL WE KNOW EACH OTHER IN HEAVEN?

The Bible indicates we will. Jesus said, ". . . when ye shall see Abraham, and Isaac, and Jacob, and all the prophets, in the kingdom of God." Here the Bible teaches that we will know Abraham, Isaac and Jacob.

On the Mount of Transfiguration, Moses and Elijah appeared with Christ. Now keep in mind that Moses lived and died long before Elijah was born. But on the Mount of Transfiguration Moses knew Elijah, and Elijah knew Moses. Not only did they know each other, but they still had the same names.

Will we have our same name in Heaven? I don't know. I know Moses was still Moses, and Elijah was still Elijah; Abraham was still Abraham; Isaac was still Isaac, and Jacob was still Jacob. Maybe we will.

Will we know each other in Heaven? Yes. Moses knew Elijah, and Elijah knew Moses, though they had never met on earth. They not only knew each other, but they knew what would happen in the future. Luke 9 says they discussed the death that Jesus should accomplish in Jerusalem.

"Now we see through a glass, darkly; but then face to face: now I know in part; *but then shall I know even as also I am known.*"

I will know my mother in Heaven. I will know my dear grandfather who died when I was a little boy. I will know my grandmother who lived to be 99 years of age.

## V. WILL WE HAVE A BODY IN HEAVEN?

The Bible seems to indicate that we will. In Luke 16, when Lazarus died and was carried by angels to Abraham's bosom, the rich man looked across a great gulf and saw Lazarus in Abraham's bosom. And in the conversation with Abraham he asked that Lazarus dip his finger in water. That implies that Lazarus had a body.

In II Corinthians 5:1 Paul says, "For we know that if our earthly house of this tabernacle were dissolved, we have a building of God, an house not made with hands, eternal in the heavens." He goes on to say that in this tabernacle we groan, desiring to be clothed upon with our body or tabernacle which is from Heaven.

The Bible does indicate that there will be a body between death and resurrection. It is a body that will be occupied until Jesus comes and this body is raised.

Friends, the Bible teaches that Jesus is coming. When He comes, the bodies of Christians will be raised from the dead. First Thessalonians 4:16 says, "The Lord himself shall descend from heaven with a shout, with the voice of the archangel, and with the trump of God: and the dead in Christ shall rise first." Christians are going to come out of the graves.

The Bible says in Acts 24:15, ". . . there shall be a resurrection of the dead, both of the just and unjust."

In John 5:28,29 Jesus said, "Marvel not at this: for the hour is coming, in the which all that are in the graves shall hear his voice, And shall come forth; they that have done good, unto the resurrection of life; and they that have done evil, unto the resurrection of damnation."

In Job 19:25-27 Job said, "I know that my redeemer liveth, and that he shall stand at the latter day upon the earth: And though after my skin worms destroy this body, yet in my flesh shall I see God: whom I shall see for myself, and mine eyes shall behold, and not another."

The Bible teaches that when a man dies, his soul and spirit leave the body and go immediately to be with Christ. And based on II Corinthians 5, that soul and spirit occupy a temporary body while awaiting the resurrection of this body. I suppose the body of II Corinthians 5 is a temporary one that the believer occupies between death and resurrection; but when Jesus comes, the dead in Christ shall be raised first. And when this body is raised, it will be a body exactly like Jesus' body. "Beloved, now are we the sons of God, and it doth not yet appear what we shall be: but we know that, when he shall appear, we shall be like him; for we shall see him as he is," says I John 3:2. And Philippians 3:20,21 tells us, "For our conversation [or citizenship] is in heaven; from whence also we look for the Saviour, the Lord Jesus Christ: Who shall change our vile body, that it may be fashioned like unto his glorious body."

Here is the picture: the Christian dies; his soul and spirit leave his body and go immediately to be with Christ. His body is buried. The body goes back to dust. It may be a hundred years before Jesus comes. It may be a thousand years. On the other hand, it may be only a year or maybe a day. Nobody knows when.

But when Jesus comes, the Bible says He will come with a shout, with the voice of the archangel and with the trump of God; and the dead in Christ shall be raised first. The body of that Christian will be raised from the dead. The soul and spirit that have been with Christ since death will be brought back. "But I would not have you to be ignorant, brethren, concerning them which are asleep, that ye sorrow not, even as others which have no hope. For if we believe that Jesus died and rose again, even so them also which sleep in Jesus will God bring with him" (I Thess. 4:13,14).

When Jesus comes, the saints who have died will come back with Him. The body will be raised, and the soul and spirit will be reunited with the resurrection body, and in eternity the person will be with Christ. First Thessalonians 4:17 says, ". . . and so shall we ever be with the Lord."

Now I raise the question,

## VI. DO THE SAVED IN HEAVEN KNOW WHAT IS HAPPENING ON EARTH?

The answer is yes, as I will show you from a number of Bible verses. The saved in Heaven are conscious and awake. Some think that when a man dies he goes to sleep and knows nothing until the resurrection. The Bible does say that man sleeps, but "sleep" has reference only to the body.

First Thessalonians 4:13: "I would not have you to be ignorant, brethren, concerning them which are *asleep*." In John 11, Jesus spoke of Lazarus as being asleep. But that has no reference to the soul and spirit. There are other Bible verses that teach that those in Heaven are conscious and know what is happening on earth.

Here is a good rule to follow when interpreting the Bible: never use an obscure passage to contradict a clear one.

Let me show you several verses that teach that those in Heaven are conscious and awake.

Luke 15:7 and 10 tell us there is more rejoicing in Heaven over one sinner that repents than over ninety-nine just persons who need no repentance. The rejoicing is not by the angels, because angels do not know what salvation is. The only ones who can rejoice are those who know about salvation.

Up in Heaven, the saved look down on earth. They see friends and loved ones who accept Christ at Saviour, and they rejoice over their salvation.

We read in Revelation 6:9,10 when the fifth seal was opened, "I saw under the altar the souls of them that were slain for the word of God, and for the testimony which they held: And they cried with a loud voice, saying, How long, O Lord, holy and true, dost thou not judge and avenge our blood on them that dwell on the earth?"

Now these people in Heaven are those who had been martyred or slain. The Bible says they cried out with a loud voice. They were not asleep. Rather, they were talking to the Lord and asking Him how long before He did something about those who had martyred them.

Notice several things here. These people in Heaven could look back on earth, and seeing the people who had martyred them were getting by without punishment, they asked the Lord, "How long . . . dost thou not judge and avenge our blood on them that dwell on the earth?"

Notice something else. The Lord spoke back to them; then verse 11 says, "And white robes were given unto every one of them; and it was said unto them, that they should rest yet for a little season, until their fellowservants also and their brethren, that should be killed as they were, should be fulfilled."

Now do the saved in Heaven know what is happening on earth? Look at Hebrews 12:1: "Wherefore seeing we also are compassed about with so great a cloud of witnesses. . . ." These witnesses are those mentioned in Hebrews 11, which lists at least seventeen names; then Hebrews 12 begins, "Wherefore seeing we also are compassed about with so great a cloud of witnesses . . . ."

In the original manuscripts, there were no chapter-and-verse divisions. These were added by men. Spurgeon complained about those who chopped the Bible up into chapters and verses. I think his complaint is justified. Now if we stop at the end of Hebrews 11, we miss a very important truth, because Hebrews 12:1 teaches that those in Heaven know what is happening on earth. We are "compassed about" with such a great cloud of witnesses.

Do the saved in Heaven know what is happening on earth? Yes. How much do they know? I am not sure they see all the sin and sorrow, all the murder and wickedness; but I do know they know when unsaved people trust Christ as Saviour, for Luke 15:10 says they rejoice in the presence of the angels of God over one sinner who repents.

Man's existence is divided into three stages: the present, the intermediate and the eternal. The present is from the time a man is born until he dies. The intermediate is from the time a man dies until he is resurrected. The eternal is from the time a man is resurrected on through eternity. I say "through" because it is a common expression. Of course, there is no such thing as going through eternity. When a man is resurrected, from that point on is the eternal state.

I am living in the present. If I were to die right now, my soul and spirit would leave my body and go to be with Christ. My body would be buried. And that intermediate stage would be the time between death and resurrection, while we await the coming of Christ.

There are several theories concerning this intermediate time. Some say there is soul sleep, that people don't know what is happening. Our dear Catholic friends say there is a purgatory where unconfessed sins are purged before going on to Heaven. But the Bible says that between death and resurrection a man is with Christ, that he is conscious, that he has a body, and that he does know what is happening on earth.

Now there is another question asked:

## VII. WHERE IS HEAVEN?

When I was a little boy, I used to say "up to Heaven." When I got older, someone reminded me that if I died in China and went up I would be going an opposite direction from a man who died in America and went up. Since the world is round and China is on the other side of the world, that seems reasonable. But I have discovered from the Bible that Heaven is in a fixed location in the sides of the North beyond the highest star.

Here is an interesting passage: "Promotion cometh neither from the *east,* nor from the *west,* nor from the *south.* But God is the judge: he putteth down one, and setteth up another" (Ps. 75:6,7).

Isn't it strange that the word "north" is left out? Why? Because promotion does come from the North from God. "He putteth down one, and setteth up another."

In Isaiah 14:12-17 Lucifer, who became Satan, said, 'I will exalt my throne above God's throne.' He said, "I will ascend above the heights of the clouds." He said, 'I will go into the sides of the north.'

Heaven, then, is in a fixed location in the sides of the North. According to Isaiah 14, it is beyond the highest star. Satan said, "I will ascend into heaven, I will exalt my throne above the stars of God." If he is talking about literal stars, he is talking about going out beyond what we call the second heaven.

There are three heavens. Paul said in II Corinthians 12:2,4, "I knew a man in Christ above fourteen years ago, (whether in the body, I cannot tell; or whether out of the body, I cannot tell: God knoweth;) such an one caught up to the third heaven . . . . How that he was caught up into paradise, and heard unspeakable words, which is not lawful for a man to utter."

If there is a third Heaven, there is a second and a first heaven. The first heaven is the atmospheric one where the birds fly. Says II Peter 3:10, ". . . the heavens shall pass away with a great noise." He is speaking of the atmospheric heavens. Psalm 19:1 says, "The heavens declare the glory of God." This is talking about the second heaven—the starry or planetary heavens. And the third Heaven, the Paradise of God, where Christians go and where Jesus is, is somewhere out beyond the last star, beyond the second or starry heaven.

I am told that the farthest star man has been able to locate through his most powerful telescopes is 500 million light years away. Light travels a little more than 186,000 miles per second. That means if you could go 186,000 miles per second, it would take 500 million years to reach the last star that man has been able to locate; and Heaven is somewhere out beyond the highest star, in the sides of the North, according to Isaiah 14.

So when as a little boy I said, "up to Heaven," I was right, though I did not understand it. Any time you go North, you are going up. Everybody says "up North" and "down South." The North Pole is the top of the earth. So Heaven is up.

Heaven is real. It is in a fixed location in the sides of the North, beyond the highest star.

## VIII. WHO IS GOING TO HEAVEN?

Suppose I ask you, "Who is going to Heaven?" Some would say the man who reads his Bible and prays. Others would say the man who lives good and keeps the Ten Commandments. Still others would say the one who attends church faithfully or the one who has been baptized. I have even heard people say if one suffers enough here, he goes to Heaven when he dies.

When I was a small boy, there was a great fire in Atlanta, Georgia. The Winecoff Hotel burned, and many people lost their lives. Someone wrote a song (it was supposed to have been a gospel song) about the Winecoff Fire. One verse went like this:

**Surely there's a Heaven**
**For folks who die this way;**
**And we'll go Home to see them**
**In Heaven some sweet day.**

The implication is, since they suffered in a fire, they would go to Heaven. Yes, people have different ideas about how to go to Heaven.

When I worked at the Post Office, a lady came in and said, "Preacher, the way I see this business about Heaven is: we are all at the Post Office this morning. You came up Covington Highway and out Candler Road and you are here. So-and-So came through Panthersville, and he is here. I came through East Lake Park and I am here." She went on to describe how a number of people had all arrived at the Post Office, none having come the same way. When she finished, she said, "Now that is the way it is about Heaven. We are all working for the same thing, and as long as we are sincere we will all go to Heaven when we die." Then she asked, "What do you think about that?" I replied, "There is only one thing wrong with it: when we die, we are not going to the Post Office."

There are many ways to the Post Office, but only one way to Heaven. John 14:6 tells us, "I am *the* way, *the* truth, and *the* life: no man cometh unto the Father, but by me." And Acts 4:12: "Neither is there salvation in any other: for there is none other name under heaven given among men, whereby we must be saved."

Now who is going to Heaven? Let's see what the Bible says. In Revelation 7 we have a heavenly scene. There is an innumerable host, clothed in white robes. Verse 13 says, "And one of the elders answered, saying unto me, What are these which are arrayed in white robes? and whence came they?" John answered in verse 14, "Sir, thou knowest. And he said to me, These are they which came out of great tribulation, and have washed their robes, and made them white in the blood of the Lamb." These people in Heaven were there because they had washed their robes and made them white in the blood of the Lamb.

Friends, only those who have been washed in the blood are going to Heaven.

But what does it mean to be washed in the blood? There is no way we can take the blood of Jesus and put it into a basin and wash our hands. We have never seen that blood. Let me briefly explain.

Romans 3:23 teaches that all men are sinners. "For all have sinned, and come short of the glory of God." Verse 10 says, "As it is written, There is none righteous, no, not one."

Not all men have committed the same sins or the same number of sins, but all have sinned. Since all men are sinners, all men owe a penalty. Sin demands a price, says Ezekiel 18:4: "The soul that sinneth, it shall die." Says Romans 6:23: "The wages of sin is death . . . ." James 1:15: "Sin, when it is finished, bringeth forth death."

Now here is the picture: I have sinned. And being a sinner I owe a penalty. The penalty for sin is death. But that death is more than dying with a gunshot wound or cancer. That death is described in the Bible as the second death, the lake of fire. Look at Revelation 20:14: "Death and hell were cast into the lake of fire. This is the second death." If I pay what I owe as a sinner, I must go into Hell and stay there forever and ever and ever.

Now here is the bright side of the story. The Bible teaches that two thousand years ago God took every sin I ever have committed and all I ever will commit and placed those sins on Jesus. That is not just preacher talk but exactly what the Bible says in Isaiah 53:6, ". . . the Lord hath laid on him the iniquity of us all." Two thousand years ago God looked down through the telescope of time and saw every sin that I ever would commit, and He took those sins—one by one—and placed them over on Jesus. And I Peter 2:24 says, "Who his own self bare our sins in his own body on the tree." The Bible also says in II Corinthians 5:21, "He hath made him to be sin for us, who knew no sin; that we might be made the righteousness of God in him."

Now you can never change the fact that two thousand years ago God took every sin you have ever committed, all you ever will commit, if you live to be a thousand years old, and placed those sins on Jesus; and while Jesus was bearing our sins in His own body, God actually punished Him in our place to pay the debt we owe.

Someone said the Jews killed Him. But that is not so. Others say the Roman soldiers killed Him. They are wrong. The Bible says, "For God so loved the world, that *he* gave his only begotten Son." And Romans 8:32 says, "He that spared not his own Son, but delivered him up for us all . . . ." God actually punished Jesus in our place to pay the debt we owe so that when we die we won't have to pay it.

That sounds like everyone is saved, doesn't it? It sounds like everyone will go to Heaven, because He died for everyone. But everyone is not saved. The death of Jesus Christ on the cross is sufficient for all, but it is efficient only to those who believe.

Here is what happened. God transferred your sins to Christ, and on the cross Jesus Christ died for you. He shed His blood. Leviticus 17:11 tells us, "The life of the flesh is in the blood." Blood in the body means the man is alive. Shed blood speaks of death. When Jesus shed His blood, He gave His life for you. He paid what you and I owe. He suffered what we should have suffered.

That is what we mean when we sing:

**What can wash away my sin?**
**Nothing but the blood of Jesus.**

Hebrews 9:22 says, "Without shedding of blood is no remission." When Jesus died in our place, He shed His blood. That is what it means when it says they "have washed their robes, and made them white in the blood of the Lamb." It means they believe that Jesus Christ died for them, that He suffered their death and paid their debt and they are trusting Him as Saviour.

Now let me briefly sum up what I have said. We are sinners. We owe the sin debt. God transferred our guilt to Jesus. Jesus shed His blood. He died on a cross. He paid what we owe. That is what He meant when He cried out from the cross, "It is finished." Now for us to be washed in the blood, or to accept the payment, we must do it by faith. John 3:16 says, "For God so loved the world, that he gave his only begotten Son, that whosoever believeth in him should not perish, but have everlasting life."

The main hangup is over that little word "believe." Everybody says, "I have always believed in Christ. I'm not an atheist." But the Bible word "believe" does not mean to accept the historical fact that He was a person who lived and died. To "believe" means to trust, to depend, to rely on.

I have often illustrated faith by an airplane.

We go to the airport. You say to me, "Is that a plane?"

"Yes."

"Do you believe the plane will fly?"

"Yes."

"Do you believe the plane will take you to California?"

"Yes."

But I never make the trip. I must not only believe it is a plane, that it will fly, that it is going to California; but there must come a time and point when I make a decision that I will definitely trust that plane and that pilot with my physical life. When I get on the plane, I am depending on the pilot to take me to California. My physical life is in his hands.

That is what it means to believe on Christ. It means I admit that I am a sinner: I believe that I do owe the sin debt like the Bible says; I accept the fact that Jesus Christ has already died and that with His death He paid what I owe as a sinner, and finally it means that I will fully trust Him to get me to Heaven. Just like I put my physical life in the hands of a pilot to take me across America, so I must put my eternal life in the hands of Jesus to take me to Heaven.

If you can pray this prayer honestly and sincerely, I promise you that when you die you will go to Heaven: "Dear Lord Jesus, I know that I'm a sinner. I do believe You died for me, and here and now I do trust You as my Saviour. From this moment on, I am fully depending on You to get me to Heaven."

If you will trust Him, I promise that you have everlasting life. And you can know that when you die you are going to Heaven.

How can you know it? In John 3:36, Jesus said, "He that believeth on the Son hath everlasting life." God said it. He cannot lie. Hebrews 6:18 says it is impossible for God to lie. If you are trusting Him completely for salvation, you have everlasting life, and you have God's Word for it. If you will, write and tell me you have trusted Him. I have some free literature I would like to send you that will help you as you set out to live the Christian life. All you need do to receive your free literature is simply fill out the decision form on the next page and send it to me.

## DECISION FORM

Dr. Curtis Hutson
THE SWORD OF THE LORD
P. O. Box 1099
Murfreesboro, Tennessee 37133

Dear Dr. Hutson:

I have read your sermon on Heaven. I do want to go to Heaven when I die. I know that I am a sinner and do believe that Jesus Christ died for me. The best I know how I trust Him as my Saviour. From this moment on, I am depending on Him to get me to Heaven.

Please send me the free literature that will help me as I set out to live the Christian life.

Date _____

Name _____

Address_____

City_____State_____Zip_____

## *The Other Side*

This isn't death; it's glory!
It isn't dark; it's light!
It isn't stumbling, groping,
Or even faith—it's sight!

This isn't grief; it's having
The last tear wiped away.
It's sunrise; it's the morning
Of my eternal day!

It isn't even praying;
It's speaking face-to-face;
It's listening, and it's glimpsing
The wonders of His grace.

This is the end of pleading
For strength to bear my pain;
Not even pain's dark memory
Will ever live again.

How did I bear the earth life
Before I came up higher,
Before my soul was granted
Its every deep desire,

Before I knew this rapture
Of meeting face-to-face
The One who sought me, saved me,
And kept me by His grace!

Martha Snell Nicholson

## II.

# *Heaven—the Home of the Saved*

## JOE HENRY HANKINS

(Sermon preached at Central Baptist Church, Chicago, Illinois, February 24, 1946.)

*"Let not your heart be troubled: ye believe in God, believe also in me. In my Father's house are many mansions: if it were not so, I would have told you. I go to prepare a place for you. And if I go and prepare a place for you, I will come again, and receive you unto myself; that where I am, there ye may be also. And whither I go ye know, and the way ye know. Thomas saith unto him, Lord, we know not whither thou goest; and how can we know the way? Jesus saith unto him, I am the way, the truth, and the life: no man cometh unto the Father, but by me."*—John 14:1-6.

*"After this I beheld, and, lo, a great multitude, which no man could number, of all nations, and kindreds, and people, and tongues, stood before the throne, and before the Lamb, clothed with white robes, and palms in their hands; And cried with a loud voice, saying, Salvation to our God which sitteth upon the throne, and unto the Lamb. And all the angels stood round about the throne, and about the elders and the four beasts, and fell before the throne on their faces, and worshipped God, Saying, Amen: Blessing, and glory, and wisdom, and thanksgiving, and honour, and power, and might, be unto our God for ever and ever. Amen."*—Rev. 7:9-12.

When I read a thing like that in the Bible, I wonder how people who are afraid to say, "Amen," regardless of what kind of sermon is being preached or what kind of service is being held, are going to act in Heaven. We have gotten so sedate and so stylish, even we Baptists, that you can hardly get a holy grunt out of a Baptist crowd any more, much less a good Amen!

*"And one of the elders answered, saying unto me, What are these which are arrayed in white robes? and whence came they? And I said unto him, Sir, thou knowest. And he said to me, These are they which came out of great tribulation, and have washed their robes, and made them white in the blood of the Lamb. Therefore are they before the throne of God, and serve him day and night in his temple: and he that sitteth on the throne shall dwell among them. They shall hunger no more, neither thirst any more; neither shall the sun light on them, nor any heat. For the Lamb which is in the midst of the throne shall feed them, and shall lead them unto living fountains of waters: and God shall wipe away all tears from their eyes."*—Rev. 7:13-17.

*"And I saw a new heaven and a new earth: for the first heaven and the first earth were passed away; and there was no more sea."*—Rev. 21:1.

## A New Heaven

God is going to make a new Heaven some day. We read also in verse 5 of this same 21st chapter of Revelation that He is going to make all things new. The word translated "new" literally means "renewed" or "renovated."

Why is it necessary for God to make a new Heaven and a new earth? God is a holy God, and God does not propose to live with sin. He cannot; and God has sworn by Himself that He is going to purge this universe of sin, and everything that sin has touched. When God gets through, there will not be a mark, a stain, a blot of sin left—not a scar nor a trace. Every pollution of sin will be thoroughly purged.

"What!" you say. "Has sin ever touched Heaven? Has sin polluted Heaven?" Yes! God tells us in His Word that once there was war in Heaven when Satan and his angels rebelled against God. Sin, in other words, has lifted its ugly head and made its slimy trail right up to the very throne of God. And God is going to make a new Heaven. When God starts in to purge sin out of His universe, every person that ever lived who holds on to his sin and has not been washed of that sin in the blood of Jesus Christ, will be purged out with it.

My friend, hear me! If sin is so loathsome to God that He would make a new Heaven because sin had touched Heaven, then dismiss from your mind the thought that anybody ever will live with God who has not been purged from his sins in the blood of Jesus Christ. God is not only going to be rid of sin, but He is also going to be rid of everything sin has ever touched: "Behold, I make all things new."

*"And I John saw the holy city, new Jerusalem, coming down from God out of heaven, prepared as a bride adorned for her husband. And I heard a great voice out of heaven saying, Behold, the tabernacle of God is with men, and he will dwell with them."*—Rev. 21:2,3.

Tabernacle means "dwelling place." This new Jerusalem will be the capital city, and Heaven will be moved down here upon the earth. Then will be fulfilled the promise of the Scripture that the righteous shall inherit the earth.

Brother, listen! I know lots of people who sell their souls for a little bit of this world, which they can keep for only a very short time, a very few years. I will take mine after awhile. And when I come into my own and when God's people inherit the earth, inherit all things, it will be ours for eternity.

Oh, "Lay not up for yourselves treasures upon earth, where moth and rust doth corrupt, and where thieves break through and steal" and where you have to lie down and die and leave them! I have something in Heaven with God, an inheritance incorruptible, undefiled, and that fadeth not away. Give me that, and you take the world.

We used to sing, "Take the world, but give me Jesus." That is my sentiment. I tell you, it is great to be a Christian!

Now let us read on:

*". . . and they shall be his people, and God himself shall be with them, and be their God. And God shall wipe away all tears from their eyes; and there shall be no more death, neither sorrow, nor crying, neither shall there be any more pain: for the former things are passed away.* [He is talking about Heaven—the home of God's redeemed, the place of many mansions.] *And he that sat upon the throne said, Behold, I make all things new. And he said unto me, Write: for these words are true and faithful. And he said unto me, It is done. I am Alpha and Omega, the beginning and the end. I will give unto him that is athirst of the fountain of the water of life freely. He that overcometh shall inherit all things; and I will be his God, and he shall be my son."*—Rev. 21:3-7

We read again in Revelation, chapter 22:

*"And he shewed me a pure river of water of life, clear as crystal,*

*proceeding out of the throne of God and of the Lamb. In the midst of the street of it, and on either side of the river, was there the tree of life, which bare twelve manner of fruits, and yielded her fruit every month: and the leaves of the tree were for the healing of the nations."*

Isaiah says that the inhabitants of that land will never say one to the other, "I am sick."

Praise God for what He has for His children! We will never sit by the side of another sickbed or weep by the side of another deathbed. We will never have to watch as the breath grows short and the eyes of loved ones grow dim. There will be no death there. What would you take for a hope like that?

*"And there shall be no more curse: but the throne of God and of the Lamb shall be in it; and his servants shall serve him: And they shall see his face; and his name shall be in their foreheads. And there shall be no night there; and they need no candle, neither light of the sun; for the Lord God giveth them light: and they shall reign for ever and ever."—Vss. 1-5.*

Heaven, the home of God's redeemed!

## Where Is Heaven?

But where is Heaven? Does the Bible locate it for us more than just to say it is up? Yes. In chapter 14 of Isaiah, verses 12 to 14, we read about the casting of Satan out of Heaven:

*"How art thou fallen from heaven, O Lucifer, son of the morning! how art thou cut down to the ground, which didst weaken the nations! For thou hast said in thine heart, I will ascend into heaven, I will exalt my throne above the stars of God: I will sit also upon the mount of the congregation, in the sides of the north: I will ascend above the heights of the clouds; I will be like the most High."*

In other words, "I am going to usurp the throne of God, sit where God sits on the mount of the congregation, in the sides of the north." That is where Heaven is.

Again you will find in Psalm 48:2:

*"Beautiful for situation, the joy of the whole earth, is mount Zion, in the sides of the north, the city of the great King."*

God gave Moses instructions about the blood of the sacrifice: Pour it out on the north side of the altar toward the Lord.

Heaven is in the North. When the Bible says Heaven is up, it is exactly right, because from any point on earth the only direction that is always up is north. It is no accident that wherever you find men—from here to the South Pole—they always say, "Up north," and, "Down south." That is the speech of men. And then it is no accident that scientists call the North Pole the top of the world. Why couldn't they just as easily have designated the South Pole as the top? It hangs right out in the middle of space. The North Pole is called the top of the world because it points toward the North Star. Yonder on the sides of the north sits the One who made the universe. Neither is it an accident that the whole universe revolves around the North Star. If you could focus a camera on the north star that would take in all the heavens around and let that focus stand long enough, you would find that every star, every planet, every constellation, every solar system would make a complete circle around the North Star.

The Scripture says:

*"For by him were all things created, that are in heaven, and that are in earth, visible and invisible, whether they be thrones, or dominions, or principalities, or powers: all things were created by him, and for him: And he is before all things, and by him all things consist* [hold together].*"* —Col. 1:16,17.

### The Three Heavens

What about the first, second and third heavens? In the first chapter of Genesis we read, "And God said, Let the waters bring forth abundantly the moving creature that hath life, and fowl that may fly above the earth in the open firmament of heaven" (vs. 20). That is the first heaven. The Bible uses the exact language that we use. We speak of the birds of the heavens. We speak of the heavens being overcast with clouds. We say that the heavens are filled with airplanes. And God says that the birds fly in the open firmament of heaven.

In Psalm 19:1,2 we read: "The heavens declare the glory of God; and the firmament sheweth his handywork. Day unto day uttereth speech, and night unto night sheweth knowledge." Then verse 4 says, "Their line is gone out through all the earth, and their words to the end of the world. In them hath he set a tabernacle for the sun." You and

I speak every day about the stars of the heavens. That is the second heaven mentioned in the Bible.

But the third Heaven mentioned in the Scriptures is the place where God dwells. Paul said:

*"I knew a man in Christ above fourteen years ago, (whether in the body, I cannot tell; or whether out of the body, I cannot tell: God knoweth;) such an one caught up to the third heaven. And I knew such a man, (whether in the body, or out of the body, I cannot tell: God knoweth;) How that he was caught up into paradise, and heard unspeakable words, which it is not lawful for man to utter."*—II Cor. 12:2-4.

Here Paul tells us that the third Heaven and Paradise are one and the same. Well, where is Paradise? Jesus said to the thief on the cross, "To day shalt thou be with me in paradise." When He breathed out His last, He said, "Father, into thy hands I commend my spirit." In other words, He said, "I am coming to You." So Paradise is where the Father is.

Revelation 2:7 tells us that the tree of life is in the midst of the Paradise of God. Revelation 22:1,2 tells us that the river of life flows out of the throne of God and the Lamb, and the tree of life is on either side of the river. So Paradise is Heaven, where God is now. And the third Heaven is the same place.

## Do the Saved Go to Heaven Immediately Upon Death?

Then the next question we answer is this: Do the saved go to Heaven immediately at death? Yes. How do I know? God said so. Hear the Word of the Lord, not mine. "For we know that if our earthly house of this tabernacle were dissolved, we have a building of God, an house not made with hands, eternal in the heavens" (II Cor. 5:1). And further we read, "Therefore we are always confident, knowing that, whilst we are at home in the body, we are absent from the Lord: (For we walk by faith, not by sight:) We are confident, I say, and willing rather to be absent from the body, and to be present with the Lord" (II Cor. 5:6-8).

Does that sound like purgatory? Does that sound like soul-sleeping? Does that sound like any kind of an intermediate state? "Absent from the body, and . . . present with the Lord"!

That is why Paul said: "For I am in a strait betwixt two, having a desire to depart, and to be with Christ; which is far better" (Phil. 1:23).

Where is Christ? Hear it! "Who is he that condemneth? It is Christ that died, yea rather, that is risen again, who is even at the right hand of God" (Rom. 8:34). Paul said, "Depart, and be with Christ"; and again, "Absent from the body . . . present with the Lord."

Just before Stephen was stoned he looked into Heaven and said, "Behold, I see the heavens opened, and the Son of man standing on the right hand of God" (Acts 7:56). And then when he sank down in death, he said, "Lord Jesus, receive my spirit."

Yes, my friend, if the Bible is clear on anything, it is clear on the fact that when a child of God closes his eyes in death, he opens them on the face of Christ that very instant. The fact of the matter is that God has permitted many of His saints to see the Lord before they crossed over, just about the time of the crossing; and they have left their testimony behind.

My mother said that just before her father passed away, he called the children around to tell them goodby. They began to cry, as they naturally would; and Grandpa said, "Don't cry. Why would you cry? Here is Jesus, and here is Mother with Him. And they are not crying; they are happy. They have come to take me Home." Many a child of God has left that testimony as he crossed over.

O my friend, isn't it wonderful to be a Christian! The hour of death, that to the lost world is the greatest enemy of all mankind, has no sting for the child of God, for we can say:

*"O death, where is thy sting? O grave, where is thy victory? The sting of death is sin* [the only thing that makes men afraid of death]; *and the strength of sin is the law. But thanks be to God, which giveth us the victory through our Lord Jesus Christ."* —I Cor. 15:55-57.

Triumphant in the hour of death!

When the time of his crossing had come, Dwight L. Moody asked his daughter who stood by, "Is this death?"

She said, "Yes, Father."

He said, "No; this is my coronation day!"

A woman said to me, "If you go to Heaven immediately when you die, what is the use of a judgment?" Well, she would never have asked that question had she understood the Bible teaching on the judgments. God does not teach anywhere that any judgment is to determine where I am going to spend eternity. There is but one time when that is decided and one person who decides it. You decide that while you live, and on one basis, and one only: what you do with Jesus.

Judgment has nothing to do with determining where you will spend eternity. You decide that yourself. Nobody else can do it. If you go to Hell, it will be because you made the wrong choice yourself. "For God so loved the world [you included], that he gave his only begotten Son, that whosoever believeth in him should not perish, but have everlasting life." The invitation is, "Come unto me, all ye that labour and are heavy laden, and I will give you rest" (Matt. 11:28). And the assurance is, "Him that cometh to me I will in no wise cast out" (John 6:37).

## Will We Know Our Loved Ones There?

The next question is: Will we know our loved ones in Heaven? Yes. Will my mother be mother to me in Heaven? Yes. Love never dies. It is eternal. It is from God. Besides, the Bible assures me that I will know my loved ones there. In II Samuel 12:18-23 we are told that David prayed for his baby seven days and seven nights—fasted, wept and prayed—but the baby died. His servants said, 'We can't tell him. Since he has grieved so over that baby while he was sick, and refused food, fasted, prayed and wept for seven days, what will happen when he hears that the baby is dead?'

Seeing them whispering to each other, David knew that the baby had died; so he asked them the point-blank question, "Is the child dead?"

They answered, "He is dead." Instead of going all to pieces, he got up from the ground, wiped away his tears, changed his clothes, went to the house of God and worshiped, then into his own house, asked for food, and ate what was set before him.

They wondered how he could do this.

David said, "But now he is dead, wherefore should I fast? can I bring him back again? I shall go to him, but he shall not return to me."

God put that in the blessed holy Book because He knew that David would not be the last parent who would follow a loved one or a little baby out yonder to the City of the Dead, and God wanted that mother or that father to know that you can go to that one again, that you can hold that dear one again.

To me, one of the most blessed things about Heaven is the reunion that is to be ours with our loved ones!

Jesus said, "Many shall come from the east and west, and shall sit down with Abraham, and Isaac, and Jacob, in the kingdom of heaven"

(Matt. 8:11). Yes, the same Abraham who walked the hills of Judea; the same Isaac whom he took up yonder on Mount Moriah that day; the same Jacob who made his pillow out of those stones and saw the ladder reaching to Heaven and saw the angels ascending and descending.

Jesus said to the Sadducees:

*"And as touching the dead, that they rise: have ye not read in the book of Moses, how in the bush God spake unto him, saying, I am the God of Abraham, and the God of Isaac, and the God of Jacob? He is not the God of the dead, but the God of the living: ye therefore do greatly err."*—Mark 12:26,27.

When Moses and Elijah stood beside Jesus on the Mount of Transfiguration, nobody had to tell Peter, James and John who they were; they recognized them immediately. They were still the same Moses and Elijah who had lived here upon the earth. It was the same Moses who had led the children out of Egypt, across the Red Sea and through forty years in the wilderness. It was the same Elijah who was taken up to Heaven in the chariot of God. The same Moses who walked up Nebo with God that day, and God buried him there, was recognized by men who had never seen him, nor seen a photograph of him.

In chapter 4 of I Thessalonians Paul is writing to the members of that church. They had evidently thought, from what Paul said, that no Christian would die until Jesus came back. But as time went on and some of them died, they wondered if they would see them any more, wondered if there was any hope. They had died before Jesus came— now what about it? Paul wrote:

*"But I would not have you to be ignorant, brethren, concerning them which are asleep, that ye sorrow not, even as others which have no hope.* [Don't think because they have fallen asleep there is no hope.] *For if we believe that Jesus died and rose again, even so them also which sleep in Jesus will God bring with him. For this we say unto you by the word of the Lord, that we which are alive and remain unto the coming of the Lord shall not prevent them which are asleep. For the Lord himself shall descend from heaven with a shout, with the voice of the archangel, and with the trump of God: and the dead in Christ shall rise first: Then we which are alive and remain shall be caught up together with them in the clouds,* [Brother, we will all go up together! Loved ones sleeping in the grave will be raised, and *together* we will

go to meet the Lord. Oh, what a reunion that will be!] *to meet the Lord in the air: and so shall we ever be with the Lord. Wherefore comfort one another with these words."*—I Thess. 4:13-18.

Get comfort from this, you who are sorrowing over the death of your loved ones. You will have a homecoming, a reunion one day. How much clearer could God make it?

One of these days I expect to walk down the golden streets of the new Jerusalem with my precious mother. Heaven used to seem to me a long way off, but since Mother has gone there it seems so much more real, and a lot closer. Sometimes Heaven seems so close I can almost reach up and touch it, since Mother is there. One day we will be reunited, never to be separated again!

## What Will We Do in Heaven?

The Scripture says, "Therefore are they before the throne of God, and serve him day and night in his temple" (Rev. 7:15). I had never known real joy until I cut loose from everything and gave my life to the Lord to serve Him. You know, I feel sorry for Christians who dabble around the edge, live with one foot in the world and one in the church. They have never known what it is to really live, never known real joy.

If you want to be happy; if you want real joy in your life, cut loose from the world and launch out into the deep with God, and be lost in the fullness of His wonderful love. "They shall mount up with wings as eagles; they shall run, and not be weary; and they shall walk, and not faint" (Isa. 40:31).

It is great to serve the Lord! The Devil can't make you happy. When will God's people learn that the world does not have anything for a Christian? When will people learn that it is feeding on ashes, as Isaiah said? When will they learn that it is a broken cistern that holds no water?

Oh, drink deep at the fountain of His grace! Cut loose from the shoreline and serve the Lord with gladness and singleness of heart. One of the greatest joys about Heaven is that I will be able to serve Him to my heart's content.

In Heaven there will be singing, and I expect to join in that. When the saints of God start singing, the angels are going to take a back seat! John says, "And I heard as it were the voice of a great multitude, and as the voice of many waters, and as the voice of mighty thunderings"

(Rev. 19:6). That mighty crescendo of praise rises and swells until the whole heavens resound with that chorus of the people of God singing, "Unto him that loved us, and washed us from our sins in his own blood" (Rev. 1:5).

If one could get to Heaven without being saved, he could not sing that song, because "no man could learn that song but the hundred and forty and four thousand, which were redeemed from the earth" (Rev. 14:3). Oh, it is going to be great when the singing starts! I think David is going to be the choir director. I do! Because he is the greatest singer and the greatest choir director God ever had. I am going to sit down and watch him.

I never had a chance to learn to play anything, but I have it in my soul. Nobody ever appreciated music more or loved it more than I do. When I hear an organist play those wonderful handfuls of notes at a time and in perfect harmony, I can hardly help but be envious. I want to do it so much! When I hear a violinist pick up a violin, a master, and pull that bow across the strings, it is just next to Heaven to me! I want to do it so much that I hurt inside. I did not have a chance to learn. But when I get to Heaven I am going to ask God to let me play on everything He has up there! He will do it! Of course He will! John said, "I heard the voice of harpers harping with the harps" (Rev. 14:2). When I read that, I want to jump up and say, "Glory to God! Isn't it great to be a Christian!"

That is the way I feel in my soul when I think about what God has for His children. Talk about shouting! I have been so happy here in this world that my soul has overflowed, and I am not ashamed of it. I am glad I love the Lord enough, that He is real enough to me, that He sends such joy of His Holy Spirit into my heart that it runs over sometimes.

### Who Will Be in Heaven?

Then, who will be there? "What are these which are arrayed in white robes? and whence came they?" If we would ask you that question, some of you would say, "Why, that's the crowd that lived the best they could, and treated everybody right, paid their honest debts, were good citizens, behaved themselves. That is the way I'm going."

That isn't the answer John got.

And if you would ask some others who that crowd is, they would say, "Why, that's the crowd that belonged to our church, because we are the only ones going to Heaven. If you don't come this way, you'll never get there."

But that is not the answer John got.

Somebody else would say, "Why, that's the crowd that was baptized a certain way and held out faithful to the end." But that is not the answer John got. "Who are these?" "These are they which came out of great tribulation, and have washed their robes, and made them white in the blood of the Lamb" (Rev. 7:14). Every one of them was arrayed in a white robe, and every robe was washed in the blood of Jesus.

When Jesus told the parable of the wedding feast, He said,

*"And when the king came in to see the guests, he saw there a man which had not on a wedding garment: And he saith unto him, Friend, how camest thou in hither not having a wedding garment? And he was speechless. Then said the king to the servants, Bind him hand and foot, and take him away, and cast him into outer darkness."*—Matt. 22:11-13.

No one can get in without the wedding garment, and it washed in the blood of Jesus. Settle that forever. If the Word of God is clear on anything, it is clear on that.

In chapter 21 of Revelation He said, "And there shall in no wise enter into it any thing that defileth, neither whatsoever worketh abomination, or maketh a lie: but they which are written in the Lamb's book of life." How can God make it any clearer?

In that wonderful chapter 14 of John, when He was describing the home of many mansions, Jesus said, "No man cometh unto the Father, but by me." Did you hear what He said? "No man cometh unto the Father, but by me."

In chapter 10 of John, when Jesus is talking about the sheepfold, He said, "I am the door: by me if any man enter in, he shall be saved." He also said, "He that entereth not by the door into the sheepfold, but climbeth up some other way, the same is a thief and a robber."

Friend, suppose you *could* get there some other way; why would you want to? Isn't Jesus good enough? Jesus, the Son of God, who loved you enough to die for you, made His soul an offering for sin for you, shed the last drop of His blood for you. I repeat: suppose you could get there some other way; why would you want to? If I knew there were one hundred ways, I wouldn't exchange Jesus for any of them.

## What Kind of a Place Is Heaven?

The last question is: What kind of a place is Heaven? Well, I think it is just exactly the kind of place God tells us it is. Look in chapter 21 of Revelation. I believe that its streets are paved with pure gold. I believe that one day I will look upon those jasper-studded walls. I believe that I will see those gates of one solid pearl. I believe that it is a place of real mansions.

Somebody may say, "Why, preacher, don't you think that language is figurative and that Jesus is just trying to tell us of the beauty of the place by using those beautiful ways to describe it?"

Then, why did Jesus say, "If it were not so, I would have told you"? In other words, "If it were not exactly this way, I would have told you so." And then why did God stop John twice when he was writing the description of that place to interpose these words, "Write: for these words are true and faithful"?

The Holy Spirit knew, and Jesus knew, that a lot of smart alecks would think they knew more about it than Jesus did, and He wanted the people of God to be absolutely certain that He was telling them the literal truth.

It is a real place, with real people, a real Saviour, a real God. Praise the Lord!

But to me, the most wonderful thing about Heaven is that it is home. Home! When I am away in a meeting and it comes time to go home, I can hardly wait. I have had the nervous jitters all day, because at one-thirty in the morning I am going to get on a plane and go home. There is no use for me to go to bed tonight. There is no use for me to try to sleep on that plane. I am going home!

John Howard Payne who wrote, "Be it ever so humble, there's no place like home," touched the deepest chord in the human heart.

Were you ever a long way from home and homesick enough to die? I know just exactly how those boys over yonder in the Philippines feel. I know why they have been making those protests. It is not because they are not loyal Americans! They just don't want to be away from home. After World War I, I was over there until July, 1919. I was homesick enough to die. On the fifteenth day of July, in Paris, I got a telegram which read: "Report in Brest on the morning of the seventeenth to sail for home on ship so and so"—an American ship.

Do you think I reported at Brest on the morning of the seventeenth?

I was down there about daylight on the morning of the sixteenth! I didn't mean to miss that boat! I was going home! I didn't think it would sail on the sixteenth, but I thought I might get to see it. And just to see it would be like a tonic.

All day long I paced up and down that long shed at Brest looking for that boat. It didn't come in, and I did not sleep any the night of the sixteenth of July, 1919—not a wink. The next morning, the seventeenth, I was out there by daylight, pacing up and down that long boardwalk, back and forth, looking out over the harbor. I would see a ship coming in. I would look at it and look at it. After a while I would see a French flag, and I would start walking again. Another would come in, and I would see a British flag, and I would start again. That was the longest day I ever spent in my life.

About four o'clock that afternoon I saw a ship coming up over the horizon. I put my hand up over my eyes and looked and strained every nerve to see and watch that ship until it got close enough for me to see Old Glory. I had thought all my life that we had the prettiest flag on earth, and I still think so, but it was never as pretty as it was that afternoon; for that was the ship coming to take me home! When they pulled her in and let down the gangplank, nobody had to beg me to get on! Why, bless your life, I was halfway up by the time the gangplank hit! I was going home!

The strangest thing to me is why people have to be begged to take Christ and go to Heaven. A thing I will never be able to understand is why we have to plead, pray, weep, persuade and beg people to be saved, when salvation is offered in Christ as a free gift to everybody who will take it, and guarantees a passage to Heaven and home and eternal fellowship with God and loved ones and the saints in Glory!

That ship was a slow one. It took fourteen days to cross the ocean. On the morning of the fifteenth day I was awakened by a band playing "Home, Sweet Home." The music was floating in at the porthole of that ship. Out of the bunk I went and into my uniform and up on deck. It was just getting daylight. As I looked out I could see the shore of the homeland. The band had come out in a little boat to meet us.

When they finished "Home, Sweet Home" over on the other side of the ship another band began playing, "My Country, 'Tis of Thee." I saw those sun-tanned soldiers standing there reach up and take off their caps and weep for joy like a bunch of little children. We had come home!

We landed at Philadelphia. I got on the *Pennsylvanian*—the slowest train I ever rode in my life! People can talk about the slow train through Arkansas all they want to; but it is like greased lightning by the side of the *Pennsylvanian*. It stopped more times, and they were the longest stops I ever witnessed!

Finally it crawled into St. Louis. I got on the *Missouri-Pacific* and started down to Arkansas. When that *Missouri-Pacific* pulled out of Little Rock, I knew it was just forty-two miles to home. I could not keep my seat any longer. I walked up and down that coach, back and forth, looking out the window at every tree, at every house—at everything, to see if I could not see something familiar.

When we got on down to Pine Bluff, a great big Negro porter stuck his head in the door and yelled, "Pine Bluff!" Brother, that was the sweetest music I ever heard! When the train pulled on down to the station, I said to the conductor—I had known him from boyhood—"Won't you pull up that platform and let me out on the steps? I know it is against the rule, but my mother and dad and my wife and my sister and my brother are down there at the station to meet me."

He said, "Go ahead and help yourself." I got hold of the rod, got out on that step, swung myself out and looked down the track. Soon I saw them. When we pulled in and got even with them, I swung loose and took the whole bunch in my arms. I was home! Home!

Listen, unsaved friend! The old ship of Zion is alongside tonight. She's sailing for Home. Home! We are inviting you to come aboard. Jesus is the Captain of that ship. She has weathered every storm of the ages. She has never lost a passenger. Come aboard. She is going Home!

## I Am Now in Heaven

I am now in Heaven—the gates have opened wide—
And now I have the privilege of walking by His side.
The angel choir is singing, and the music is so sweet;
I'll join them just as soon as I have worshiped at His feet.

I am now in Heaven, and the blood-washed throng is here.
I recognize a lot of them—there's not a single tear.
There's joy beyond description and reunions by the score;
There'll be no separations, for we'll be here evermore.

I am now in Heaven—please wipe away your tears!
I've fought the battle, run the race—I'm rid of all my fears.
There is no pain or sorrow here; the heartaches now are past;
I've read and sung of Heaven, and now I'm here at last!

I am now in Heaven, and, oh, the place is grand!
No one could ever tell me all the beauties of this land.
Since I cannot describe it, you'll have to come and see
That it was worth the trials to live here eternally!

                                        Becky Coxe

WALTER BROWN KNIGHT
1897-

## ABOUT THE MAN:

Having been a news correspondent in his early years, Walter B. Knight was ever alert for new stories and illustrations. So he is best known for his many books of illustrations.

Knight wrote his first book, *3,000 Illustrations for Christian Service*, when he was fifty; and each subsequent book has become a best seller in its field. *Master Book of New Illustrations* can be found in the White House Library, being one of fifty books selected by the Christian Booksellers' Association to be presented to the late President Lyndon B. Johnson. Others are: *Knight's Treasury of Illustrations, Knight's Up-to-the-Minute Illustrations, More of Knight's Timely Illustrations*, and who knows how many more!

He was a good preacher, too, as evidenced by his timely message in this volume. He is now in his eighties but still working for Jesus.

# III.

# *Heaven At Last*

WALTER B. KNIGHT

A father and mother lost three little children in one week by diphtheria. Only the little three-year-old girl escaped. On Easter morning the father, mother, and child were in Sunday school. The father was the superintendent. He led his school in worship and read the Easter message from the Bible without a break in his voice. Many in the school were weeping, but the faces of the father and mother remained serene and calm.

"How can they do it?" men and women asked each other as they left the church.

A fifteen-year-old boy, walking home with his father, said, "Father, I guess the superintendent and his wife *really believe it*, don't they?"

"Believe what?" asked the father.

"The whole, big thing, all of it—EASTER—you know!"

"Of course," answered the father, "all Christians believe it!"

"Not the way they believe it," said the boy, and he began to whistle.

How fear-allaying, sorrow-dispelling, and hope-bringing are these triumphant words of the death-conquering Saviour: "I am he that liveth, and was dead; and, behold, *I am alive for evermore*" (Rev. 1:18a). How rayless and starless the night of death would be but for the Saviour's triumph over death! Because He lives, we, too, live radiantly and victoriously in the present life, and shall live eternally in the life to come! When our loved ones slip away from us to be forever "with the Lord," we sorrow, to be sure, but in our sorrow, we are comforted and sustained in knowing that we shall see them again!

Death to the children of God is no "King of Terrors!" To the believer, death means only to be 'absent from the body—at home with the Lord!' (II Cor. 5:8).

After the Saviour's victory over death, the apostles seldom used the word "death" to express the close of a Christian's earthly life. The terms used were: "sleep," "at home with the Lord," "depart," or, "loose the moorings," as a vessel about to set out to sea!

It is the custom of some native African Christians to refer to their dead who "die in the Lord," not as having *departed*, but as having *arrived!*

> **On the jasper threshold standing,**
>   **Like a pilgrim safely landing,**
> **See the strange, bright scenes expanding,**
>   **Ah! 'tis Heaven at last!**
>
> **What a city, what a glory,**
>   **Far beyond the fairest story,**
> **Of the ages, old and hoary,**
>   **Ah! 'tis Heaven at last!**
>
> **Christ Himself the living splendor,**
>   **Christ the sunshine, mild and tender,**
> **Praises to the Lamb we render,**
>   **Ah! 'tis Heaven at last!**

When Dr. Rees preached last in North Wales, a friend said to him, "You are whitening fast, Dr. Rees." The old gentleman did not say anything. When he got into the pulpit, he said:

> There is a wee white flower that comes at this season of the year. Sometimes it comes up through the snow and frost. We are all glad to see the snowdrop, because it proclaims that winter is over and summer is at hand.
> A friend has reminded me that I am whitening fast. But heed not that brother. It is to me a proof that my winter will soon be over; that I shall have done presently with the cold east winds and the frosts of earth, and that my summer, *my eternal summer,* is at hand!

> **No chilling winds, nor pois'nous breath,**
>   **Can reach that healthful shore;**
> **Sickness and sorrow, pain and death,**
>   **Are felt and feared no more!**

"For, lo, the winter is past, the rain is over and gone; The flowers appear on the earth; the time of the singing of birds is come, and the voice of the turtle is heard in our land."—Song of Sol. 2:11,12.

Contemplating the end of his earthly journey and being "sustained and soothed by an unfaltering trust," Paul expressed the ardent wish of his glowing heart thus: "For I have a desire to depart, and to be *with Christ;* which is *far better*" (Phil. 1:23).

It will take the unending eons of eternity to fully disclose how much better it is for God's children to pass to the Home "not made with hands, eternal in the heavens," than to remain in earth's night with its sorrow and suffering! There they will behold the King in His beauty, and be forever with the Lord! As God's children stand at the opal gates of death, the Living One, Jesus, will unlock the gates, and will accompany them through the valley of the shadow of death. His presence will illumine the valley, and render them unafraid!

*"At evening time it shall be light."* —Zech. 14:7b.

How different it is with those who come to journey's end without God and without hope!

An old Indian chief was told of the Saviour. The missionary tried to persuade the chief to accept Christ as his *ONLY* hope of eternal life. Said the old chief, "The Jesus road is good, but I have followed the Indian road all my life, and I will follow it to the end!"

A year later, the old chief stood on the borderline of death. As he was seeking a pathway through the darkness, he said to the missionary, "Can I turn to the Jesus road now? *My road stops here. It has no path through the valley!"*

How grateful we are that, even in death, penitent hearts may turn to the gracious Saviour for "the gift of God [which] is eternal life through Jesus Christ our Lord" (Rom. 6:23). Even eyes glazing in death may "behold the Lamb of God, which taketh away the sin of the world" (John 1:29b).

**Look and live, my brother, live,**
**Look to Jesus NOW and live;**
**'Tis recorded in His Word, Hallelujah!**
**It is only that you look and live!**

*"Look unto me, and be ye saved, all the ends of the earth: for I am God, and there is none else."* —Isa. 45:22.

A miser, whose ruling passion was strong even in death, exclaimed, "Put out that candle, Marie!"

"But, Uncle, suppose you want something?"

"Put it out," he gasped. "One does not need light to die!"

Now for the contrast: One of God's servants lay dying. Said his mother tenderly, "Is Jesus with you in the dark valley?"

"Dark valley!" exclaimed God's child. "It's not dark! It's getting *brighter and brighter,* Mother. Oh," he murmured, "it's so bright now that I have to shut my eyes!"

As in life, so also in death, the promise is *sure:* "He that followeth me shall not walk in darkness, but shall have the light of life" (John 8:12b).

How bright is the future for God's children: "Eye hath not seen, nor ear heard, neither have entered into the heart of man, the things which God hath prepared for them that love him" (I Cor. 2:9).

Many of God's "precious promises" have to do with our victory over death and our entrance into Glory to be "at home with the Lord!" Let us meditate upon three keenly anticipated delights which await us at life's setting sun:

## I. WE WILL BEHOLD THE KING IN HIS BEAUTY AND BE LIKE HIM!

Whether we go to be with the Lord in death, or whether the Lord comes for us, the promise is *sure:* "Thine eyes shall see the King in his beauty" (Isa. 33:17). What joy unspeakable and full of glory will be ours when we awaken with His likeness and see Him as He is!

"For now we see through a glass, darkly; but then *face to face*" (I Cor. 13:12a).

> **Only faintly now I see Him,**
> **With the darkling veil between,**
> **But a blessed day is coming,**
> **When His glory shall be seen!**

What transformation our "body of humiliation" will undergo when we see Him! Then our body will "be fashioned like unto his glorious body, according to the working whereby he is able even to subdue all things unto himself" (Phil. 3:21). John said, "Beloved, now are we the sons of God, and it doth not yet appear what we shall be: but *we know* that, when he shall appear, *we shall be like him:* for we shall *see him as he is*" (I John 3:2).

A little boy was born blind. A skilled surgeon performed a delicate operation on the boy's eyes. The operation was a success. For days and weeks his eyes were covered with bandages. The time was nearing when the bandages were to be removed.

Said the nurse to the lad, "My boy, tomorrow we are going to remove the bandages from your eyes. When the bandages are removed, whom do you want to see FIRST?"

Without a moment's hesitation, the lad exclaimed, "I want to see FIRST the doctor who gave me my sight!"

We want to see FIRST the One who gave us our spiritual sight!

> **Oh, the dear ones in glory,**
> **How they beckon me to come,**
> **And our parting at the river I recall;**
> **To the sweet vales of Eden,**
> **They will sing my welcome Home,**
> **But I long to meet my Saviour FIRST of all!**

Till we behold the King in His beauty; till we are completely conformed to the image of Christ, let it be our fixed purpose to be like Him NOW in word and in deed. As we, by faith, fix our spiritual gaze upon Him, we become like Him: "But we all, with open face beholding as in a glass the glory of the Lord, are changed into the same image from glory to glory, even as by the Spirit of the Lord" (II Cor. 3:18).

Observe that it is the vision of the glorified, risen Christ, the Christ at God's right hand with limitless power in Heaven and on earth, which changes us from glory to glory. It was the glorified Christ whom Stephen saw. It was the Lord "high and lifted up" whom Isaiah saw. It was the living, exalted Christ whom Paul saw.

Never would we detract from the atoning death of Christ on the cross. If the cross, however, had ended all, and if there had been no resurrection, our faith would be "vain"; we would yet be in our sins, and "they also which are fallen asleep in Christ are perished" (I Cor. 15:17,18).

Michelangelo walked through a great art gallery with some of his artist friends. Turning with indignation he said to them, "Why do you keep filling gallery after gallery with endless paintings of Christ upon the cross, Christ dying, most of all Christ hanging dead? Why do you concentrate upon that passing episode, as if that were the LAST word and the final scene, as if the curtain dropped upon that hour of disaster? At worst, that only lasted for a few hours. But to the end of unending eternity, *Christ is alive! Christ rules and reigns and triumphs!*"

With joy we sing:

> **I serve a RISEN Saviour,**
> **He's in the world today;**
> **I KNOW that He is living,**
> **Whatever men may say!**

In the teaching and preaching of the apostles, Christ's victory over death was *central*. They had seen Him! They had handled Him! Boldly, they confronted the very men who had condemned Him to death, and said, "But ye denied the Holy One and the Just, . . . And killed the Prince of life, whom God hath raised from the dead; whereof we are witnesses" (Acts 3:14,15).

In speaking of His triumph over death, let us do it with joy and certainty. "For I *know* that my redeemer liveth, and that he shall stand at the latter day upon the earth" (Job 19:25).

Reichel was conducting the final rehearsal of his great choir to render *The Messiah*. The choir had sung through to the point where the soprano soloist takes up the refrain, "I know that my Redeemer liveth!" The soloist's technique was perfect. She had faultless breathing, accurate note placement, flawless enunciation. After the final note, all eyes were fixed on Reichel to catch his look of approval. Instead, he silenced the orchestra, walked over to the singer, and asked sorrowfully, "My daughter, do you *really know* that your Redeemer liveth? Do you?"

"Why, yes," she answered, flushing, "I think I do."

"Then sing it!" cried Reichel. "Tell it to me so that I will *know*, and all who hear you will *know* that you *know* the joy and power of it!"

Then he motioned the orchestra to play it again. This time, the soloist sang the truth as she *knew* it and had *experienced* it in her own soul. All who heard wept under the spell of it. The old master approached her with tear-dimmed eyes, and said, *"You do know, for you have told me!"*

## II. WE WILL BE WITH OUR LOVED ONES AGAIN!

Some of us have more loved ones on the other side of the river of life than on this side. Paul spoke of the whole family of God in Heaven and earth. Death has separated us from the "dear ones in Glory!" The separation, however, is only temporary. We ardently believe that, ere long "the Lord himself shall descend from heaven with a shout . . . and the dead in Christ shall rise first: Then we which are alive and remain shall be *caught up together with them"* (I Thess. 4:16,17). We will not only see them, but we also will know them.

David's heart was comforted in knowing that he would see again his child in Glory. Said he, "I shall go to him, but he shall not return to me" (II Sam. 12:23b). Peter, James, and John *knew* Moses and Elijah on the Mount of Transfiguration without the formality of an introduction!

When he knew that his earthly pilgrimage was soon to be over,

F. B. Meyer called for a pencil and paper and wrote this touching note to his wife:

> To my surprise, I have just been told that my days and hours are numbered. It may be that before this reaches you, I shall have gone into the Palace of the King! Do not trouble to write. *We shall meet in the morning!*

A physician was a strong, stalwart Christian. From his sunny nature radiated good cheer to his patients. He had enough sunshine also for the frail little wife who needed all the vigor of his personality to sustain her. When the doctor suddenly passed away, friends said, "It will kill her! This will be the end of her!"

But the faith in God which the two had shared together did not fail her. By the doorway of the living room she hung the card that the doctor sometimes left, during short absences, on his office door. It read: *"Gone Out—Back Soon!"*

The doctor's widow cherished the blessed hope of being again with her loved ones when Christ comes WITH His saints to reign on the earth.

A father and a son were shipwrecked. Together they clung to floating debris, until the son was washed off and vanished from the father's sight. The father was rescued in the morning in an unconscious condition. Several hours later, he awoke in a fisherman's hut, lying in a warm, soft bed. In agony of soul, he remembered his son! But, as he turned his head, he saw his son lying beside him and his heart was filled with joy!

One by one, our hearts cease their throbbing. One by one, we are being swept away by the billows of time.

> **There is no flock howsoever tended,**
> **But one dead lamb is there;**
> **There is no fireside howsoever defended,**
> **But has its vacant chair!**

When Christ comes and resurrects the bodies of God's children "who sleep in the dust of the earth," we shall be with our loved ones again! "The bright and cloudless morning when the dead in Christ shall rise" is SURE to come.

Of that blessed day the Lord Jesus said, "The hour is coming, in the which all that are in the graves shall hear his voice, And shall come forth; they that have done good, unto the resurrection of life" (John 5:28,29a).

On the headstone over a little mound in a cemetery occurs the word,

"Freddy!" as if someone called, and underneath occur the words, "Yes, Lord!" as if someone answered.

He who calls His sheep by name will some day call by name all the blessed dead who have entered life trusting in Him who is "the resurrection and the life!"

Robert G. Ingersoll, the well-known atheist of other years, told this story:

> I was never nonplused but once. I was lecturing one night and took occasion to show that the resurrection of Lazarus was probably a planned affair to bolster the waning fortunes of Jesus. Lazarus was to take sick and die. The girls were to bury him and send for Jesus. Lazarus was to feign death till Jesus should come and say, "Lazarus, come forth!" To emphasize the situation, I said, "Can anyone here tell me why Jesus said, 'Lazarus, come forth'?"
>
> Down by the door, a pale-faced, white-haired man arose and, with a shrill voice said, "Yes, Sir, I can tell you! If the Lord had not said, 'Lazarus,' the whole graveyard at Bethany would have come forth!"

## III. WE WILL REST FROM OUR LABORS

Of the righteous dead, the Bible says, "Blessed are the dead which die in the Lord from henceforth: Yea, saith the Spirit, that they MAY REST FROM THEIR LABOURS; and their works do follow them" (Rev. 14:13). Of this future rest, the Bible says, "There remaineth therefore a rest to the people of God" (Heb. 4:9).

God's servants oftentimes become weary IN His work, but not weary OF His work. As they "bear one another's burdens"; as they "bear the infirmities of the weak," making the sorrows of others their own, they, like the Saviour, become weary and exhausted. Of Him it is written, "Jesus . . . being wearied with his journey, sat thus on the well" (John 4:6). Of the rest which remaineth for the people of God, Isaiah said, "And his rest shall be glorious" (Isa. 11:10b).

Till we enter into this future rest, let us accept the Saviour's gracious word of invitation, "Come unto me, all ye that labour and are heavy laden, and I will give you rest" (Matt. 11:28).

> **I came to Jesus as I was,**
> **Weary and worn and sad,**
> **I found in Him a resting place,**
> **And He has made me glad!**

*"In returning and rest shall ye be saved; in quietness and in confidence*

*shall be your strength."* —Isa. 30:15b.

"Until the day break, and the shadows flee away," until He comes again for His own, let us "set [our] affection on things above, not on things on the earth"; let us "lay up . . . treasures in heaven, where moth nor rust doth corrupt, and where thieves do not break through nor steal"; let us go "without the camp" with Him, bearing His reproach. Let us daily talk of His wondrous love and care; let us do our *best* to bring the lost ones to His feet!

Ere long, the day of God's grace will be finished. Then will come the "day of vengeance of our God!"

> **Soon will the season of rescue be o'er,**
> **Soon will they drift to eternity's shore,**
> **Haste then, my brother, no time for delay,**
> **But throw out the Life-line and save them TODAY!**

It is later, dispensationally, than we think! "The night is FAR spent, the day is at hand" (Rom. 13:12).

As we scan the world horizons through the telescope of the "sure word of prophecy," we are constrained to exclaim, "The coming of the Lord draweth nigh!"

*"For yet a little while, and he that shall come will come, and will not tarry."* —Heb. 10:37.

"But the day of the Lord *will come* as a thief in the night; in the which the heavens shall pass away with a great noise, and the elements shall melt with fervent heat, the earth also and the works that are therein shall be burned up. Seeing then that all these things shall be dissolved, what manner of persons ought ye to be *in all holy conversation and godliness,* Looking for and hastening . . . the coming of the day of God" (II Pet. 3:10-12a).

Are YOU ready to meet Him in death? Are YOU ready to meet Him when He comes for His own?

*"Be ye also ready: for in such an hour as ye think not the Son of man cometh!"*

> **Ready to speak, ready to warn,**
> **Ready o'er souls to yearn;**
> **Ready in life, ready in death,**
> **Ready for His return!**

(Used by permission of Moody Press.)

## Earth and Heaven

There is a land that to the eye seems fair;
Yet strange to say, a poison haunts the air.
Within its border sin and sorrow reign,
And death grasps all within its massive chain,
AND THAT IS EARTH.

But there's a land where sorrow is unknown,
Where seeds of pain and death have not been sown.
Its atmosphere is always bright and clear;
No soul is ever faint and weary there,
BUT THAT IS HEAVEN.

There is a land where hearts are often broken
And parting words—alas! too oft are spoken;
Where briny tears are very often shed
By mourners as they gaze upon their dead,
AND THAT IS EARTH.

But there's a land where tears will never fall,
Where peace and joy sit smiling upon all.
Within its gates no dead are ever found;
No warrior's grave is marked by grassy mound,
AND THAT IS HEAVEN.

S. Britton.

THOMAS DeWITT TALMAGE
1832-1902

## ABOUT THE MAN:

If Charles Spurgeon was the "Prince of Preachers," then T. DeWitt Talmage must be considered as one of the princes of the American pulpit. In fact, Spurgeon stated of Talmage's ministry: "His sermons take hold of my inmost soul. The Lord is with the mighty man. I am astonished when God blesses me but not surprised when He blesses him." He was probably the most spectacular pulpit orator of his time—and one of the most widely read.

Like Spurgeon, Talmage's ministry was multiplied not only from the pulpit to immense congregations, but in the printed pages of newspapers and in the making of many books. His sermons appeared in 3,000 newspapers and magazines a week, and he is said to have had 25 million readers.

And for 25 years, Talmage—a Presbyterian—filled the 4,000 to 5,000-seat auditorium of his Brooklyn church, as well as auditoriums across America and the British Isles. He counted converts to Christ in the thousands annually.

He was the founding editor of *Christian Herald,* and continued as editor of this widely circulated Protestant religious journal from 1877 until his death in 1902.

He had the face of a frontiersman and the voice of a golden bell; sonorous, dramatic, fluent, he was, first of all, an orator for God; few other evangelists had his speech. He poured forth torrents, deluges of words, flinging glory and singing phrases like a spendthrift; there was glow and warmth and color in every syllable. He played upon the heart-strings like an artist. One writer described him as the cultured Billy Sunday of his time. Many of his critics found fault with his methods; but they could not deny his mastery, nor could they successfully cloud his dynamic loyalty to his Saviour and Lord, Jesus Christ.

# IV

# A Highway From Earth to Heaven

## T. DeWITT TALMAGE

You have heard of the Appian Way. It was three hundred and fifty miles long. It was twenty-four feet wide, and on either side of the road was a path for foot passengers. It was made out of rocks cut in hexagonal shape and fitted together. What a road it must have been! Made of smooth hard rock, three hundred and fifty miles long. No wonder that in the construction of it the treasures of a whole empire were exhausted. Because of invaders and the elements and Time—the old conqueror who tears up a road as he goes over it—there is nothing left of that structure except a ruin.

But I have to tell you of a road built before the Appian Way, and yet it is as good as when first constructed. Millions of souls have gone over it. Millions more will come.

> The prophets and apostles, too,
> Pursued this road while here below;
> We therefore will, without dismay,
> Still walk in Christ, the good old way."

*"An highway shall be there, and a way, and it shall be called The way of holiness; the unclean shall not pass over it; but it shall be for those: the wayfaring men, though fools, shall not err therein. No lion shall be there, nor any ravenous beast shall go up thereon, it shall not be found there; but the redeemed shall walk there: And the ransomed of the Lord shall return, and come to Zion with songs and everlasting joy upon their heads: they shall obtain joy and gladness, and sorrow and sighing shall flee away."*—Isa. 35:8-10.

### The King's Highway

In the diligence you dash on over the St. Bernard pass of the Alps, mile after mile, and there is not so much as a pebble to jar the wheels. You go over bridges which cross chasms that make you hold your breath; under projecting rock; along by dangerous precipices; through tunnels adrip with the meltings of the glaciers; and, perhaps, for the first time, learn the majesty of a road built and supported by governmental authority. Well, my Lord the King decided to build a highway from earth to Heaven.

It should span all the chasms of human wretchedness; it should tunnel all the mountains of earthly difficulty; it should be wide enough and strong enough to hold fifty thousand millions of the human race, if so many of them should ever be born. It should be blasted out of the "Rock of Ages," and cemented with the blood of the cross, and be lifted amid the shouting of angels and the execration of devils.

The King sent His Son to build that road. He put head and hand and heart to it, and after the road was completed waved His blistered hand over the way, crying: "It is finished!"

Napoleon paid fifteen million francs for the building of the Simplon Road, that his cannon might go over for the devastation of Italy; but our King, at a greater expense, has built a road for a different purpose, that the banners of heavenly dominion might come down over it, and all the redeemed of earth travel up over it.

Being a King's highway, of course, it is well built. Bridges splendidly arched and buttressed have given way and crushed the passengers who attempted to cross them. But Christ, the King, would build no such thing as that. The work done, He mounts the chariot of His love; and multitudes mount with Him; and He drives on and up the steep of Heaven, amid the plaudits of gazing worlds! The work is done—well done—gloriously done—magnificently done.

## A Clean Road

Many a fine road has become miry and foul because it has not been properly cared for, but my text says the unclean shall not walk on this one. Room on either side to throw away your sins. Indeed, if you want to carry them along you are not on the right road. That bridge will break; those overhanging rocks will fall; the night will come down, leaving you at the mercy of the mountain bandits; and at the very next turn of the road you will perish. But if you are really on this clean road of which I have been speaking, then you will stop ever and anon to wash in the water that stands in the basin of the eternal Rock.

## A Plain Road

"The wayfaring man, though a fool, shall not err therein." That is, if a man is three-fourths an idiot, he can find this road just as well as if he were a philosopher. The imbecile boy, the laughingstock of the street, and followed by a mob hooting at him, has only just to knock once at the gate of Heaven, and it swings open; while there has been many a man who can lecture about pneumatics, and chemistry, and tell the story of Farraday's theory of electrical polarization, and yet has been shut out of Heaven. But if one shall come in the right spirit, seeking the way to Heaven, he will find it a plain way.

He who tries to get on the road to Heaven through the New Testament teaching will get on beautifully. He who goes through philosophical discussion will not get on at all.

If you wanted to go to Albany, and I pointed you out a highway thoroughly laid out, would I be wise in detaining you by a geological discussion about the gravel you will pass over, or a physiological discussion about the muscles you will have to bring into play? No. After this Bible has pointed you the way to Heaven, is it wise for me to detain you with any discussion about the nature of the human will, or whether the atonement is limited or unlimited? There is the road—go on it. It is a plain way.

## A Safe Road

Sometimes the traveler on those ancient highways would think himself perfectly secure, not knowing there was a lion by the way, burying his head deep between his paws; and then, when the right moment came, under the fearful spring the man's life was gone; and there was a mauled carcass by the roadside. But, says my text, "No lion shall be there." The road spoken of is also

## A Pleasant Road

God gives a bond of indemnity against all evil to every man that treads it.

I pursue this subject only one step further. I do not care how fine a road you may put me on, I want to know where it comes out. My God declares it: "The redeemed of the Lord come to Zion." You know what Zion was. That was the King's palace. It was a mountain fastness. It was impregnable. And so Heaven is the fastness of the universe. No howitzer has long enough range to shell those towers. Let all the batteries of earth and Hell blaze away; they cannot break in those gates. Gibraltar was taken; Sebastopol was taken; Babylon fell, but these walls of Heaven shall never surrender either to human or satanic besiegement. The Lord God Almighty is the defense of it. Great capital of the Universe! Terminus of the King's highway!

## Visions of Heaven

Ezekiel, with others, had been expatriated; and while in foreign slavery, standing on the banks of the royal canal which he and other serfs had been condemned to dig by the order of Nebuchadnezzar—the royal canal called the river Chebar—the illustrious exile had visions of Heaven. Indeed, it is almost always so that the brightest visions of Heaven come not to those who are on a mountaintop of prosperity, but to some John on desolate Patmos, or to some Paul in Mamertine dungeon, or to some Ezekiel standing on the banks of a ditch he had been compelled to dig—yea, to the weary, to the heartbroken, to those whom sorrow has banished.

Oh, what a mercy it is that all up and down the Bible God induces us to look out toward other worlds! Bible astronomy in Genesis, in Joshua, in Job, in the Psalms, in the prophets, major and minor, in St. John's apocalypse, practically says, "Worlds! worlds! worlds!" What a fuss we make about this little bit of a world, its existence only a short time between two spasms, the paroxysm by which it was hurled from chaos into order and the paroxysm of its demolition!

And I am glad that so many texts call us to look off to other worlds, many of them larger and grander and more resplendent. "Look there," says Job, "at Mazaroth and Arcturus and his sons!" "Look there," says St. John, "at the moon under Christ's feet!" "Look there," says Joshua, "at the sun standing still above Gibeon!" "Look there," says Moses, "at the sparkling firmament!" "Look there," says Amos, the herdsmen, "at the Seven Stars and Orion!"

Don't let us be so sad about those who shove off from this world under Christly pilotage. Don't let us be so agitated about our own going off this little barge or sloop or canal boat of a world to get on some Great Eastern of the heavens. Don't let us persist in wanting to stay in this barn, this shed, this outhouse of a world, when all the King's palaces already occupied by many of our best friends are swinging wide open their gates to let us in.

Oh, how this widens and lifts and stimulates our expectation! How little it makes the present, and how stupendous it makes the future! O Lord God of the Seven Stars and Orion, how can I endure the transport, the ecstasy, of such a vision! I must obey His Word and seek Him. I will seek Him. I see Him now, for I call to mind that it is not the material universe that is most valuable, but the spiritual, and that each of us has a soul worth more than all the worlds which the inspired herdsmen saw from his booth on the hills of Tekoa.

## Longing for Home

An old Scotchman, who had been a soldier in one of the European wars, was sick and dying in one of our American hospitals. His one desire was to see Scotland and his old home, and once again walk the heather of the Highlands, and hear the bagpipes of the Scotch regiments.

The night that the old Scotch soldier died, a young man, somewhat reckless but kindhearted, got a company of musicians to come and play under the old soldier's window; and among the instruments there was a bagpipe. The instant the musicians began, the dying old man in delirium said: "What's that, what's that? Why, it's the regiments coming home. That's the tune, yes, that's the tune. Thank God, I have got home once more!" "Bonny Scotland and Bonny Doon," were the last words he uttered as he passed up to the highlands of the better country.

Hundreds and thousands are homesick for Heaven: some because you have so many bereavements, some because you have so many temptations, some because you have so many ailments, homesick, very homesick, for the fatherland of Heaven. At our best estate we are only pilgrims and strangers here. "Heaven is our home." Death will never knock at the door of that mansion, and in all that country there is not a single grave.

How glad parents are in holiday times to gather their children home again! But I have noticed that there is almost always a son or a daughter absent—absent from the home, perhaps absent from the country, perhaps—absent from the world. Oh, how glad our heavenly Father will be when He gets all His children home with Him in Heaven! And how delightful it will be for brothers and sisters to meet after long separation! Once they parted at the door of the tomb; now they meet at the door of immortality. Once they saw only through a glass darkly; now it is face to face; corruption, incorruption; mortality, immortality. Where are now all their sins and sorrows and troubles? Overwhelmed in the

Red Sea of Death, while they passed through dry-shod.

Gates of pearl, capstones of amethyst, thrones of dominion do not stir my soul so much as the thought of home. Once there, let earthly sorrows howl like storms and roll like seas. Home! Let thrones rot and empires wither. Home! Let the world die in earthquake struggle and be buried amid procession of planets and dirge of spheres. Home! Let everlasting ages roll in irresistible sweep. Home! No sorrow, no crying, no tears, no death. But home, sweet home; beautiful home; everlasting home; home with each other; home with God.

## Reunion: A Shipwrecked Father and Son

I heard of a father and son who among others were shipwrecked at sea. The father and the son climbed into the rigging. The father held on, but the son after awhile lost his hold in the rigging and was dashed down. The father supposed he had gone hopelessly under the wave. The next day the father was brought ashore from the rigging in an exhausted state and laid in a bed in a fisherman's hut; and after many hours had passed, he came to consciousness and saw lying beside him on the same bed his boy.

Oh, my friends! what a glorious thing it will be if we wake up at last to find our loved ones beside us! The one hundred and forty and four thousand, and the "great multitude that no man can number"—some of our best friends among them—we, after a while, to join the multitude. Blessed anticipation!

The reunions of earth are anticipative. We are not always going to stay here. This is not our home. Oh, the reunion of patriarchs, and apostles, and prophets, and all our glorified kindred, and that "great multitude that no man can number!"

Does it not seem that Heaven comes very near to us, as though our friends, whom we thought a great way off, are not in the distance, but close by? You have sometimes come down to a river at nightfall, and you have been surprised how easily you could hear voices across the river. You shouted over to the other side of the river, and they shouted back.

It is said that when George Whitefield preached in Third Street, Philadelphia, one evening time, his voice was heard clear across to the New Jersey shore.

When I was a little while chaplain in the army, I remember how at eventide we could easily hear the voices of the pickets across the Potomac, just when they were using ordinary tones.

And as we stand by the Jordan that divides us from our friends who are gone, it seems to me we stand on one bank and they stand on the other; and it is only a narrow stream, and our voices go and their voices come.

## Glories of Heaven

Oh, that I might show you the glories with which God clothes His dear children in Heaven! I wish I could swing back one of the twelve gates that there might dash upon your ear one shout of the triumph— that there might flame upon your eyes one blaze of the splendor. Oh, when I speak of that good land, you involuntarily think of someone there that you loved—father, mother, brother, sister, or dear little child garnered already. You want to know what they are doing this morning.

I will tell you what they are doing. Singing. You want to know what they wear. I will tell you what they wear. Coronets of triumph. You wonder why oft they look to the gate of the Temple, and watch and wait. I will tell you why they watch and wait and look to the gate of the Temple. For your coming. I shout upward the news, for I am sure some of you will repent and start for Heaven. Oh, ye bright ones before the throne, your earthly friends are coming. Angels, posing mid-air, cry up the name. Gatekeeper of Heaven, send forward the tidings. Watchman on the battlements celestial, throw the signal!

If a soldier can afford to shout, "Huzza!" when he goes into battle, how much more jubilantly he can afford to shout, "Huzza!" when he has gained victory! If religion is so good a thing to have here, how bright a thing it will be in Heaven! I want to see that young man when the glories of Heaven have robed and crowned him. I want to hear him sing when all huskiness of earthly colds is gone, and he rises up with the great doxology. I want to know what standard he will carry when marching under arches of pearl in the army of banners. I want to know what company he will keep in a land where they are all kings and queens forever and ever.

If I have induced one of you to begin a better life, then I want to know it. I may not in this world clasp hands with you in friendship; I may not hear from your own lips the story of temptation and sorrow, but I will clasp hands with you then when the sea is passed and the gates are entered.

We can, in this world, get no just idea of the splendors of Heaven. John tries to describe them. He says "the twelve gates are twelve pearls," and "the foundations of the wall are garnished with all manner of precious stones." As we stand looking through the telescope of St. John, we see a blaze of amethyst and pearl and emerald and sardonyx and chrysoprase and sapphire, a mountain of light, a cataract of color, a sea of glass, and a city like the sun.

John bids us look again; and we see thrones—thrones of the prophets, thrones of the patriarchs, thrones of the angels, thrones of the apostles, thrones of the martyrs, throne of Jesus—throne of God. And we turn around to see the glory, and it is thrones! thrones! thrones!

Skim from the summer waters the brightest sparkles, and you will get no idea of the sheen of the everlasting sea. Pile up the splendors of earthly cities, and they would not make a steppingstone by which you might mount to the city of God. Every house is a palace. Every step is a triumph. Every covering of the head is a coronation. Every meal is a banquet. Every stroke from the tower is a wedding bell. Every day is a jubilee, every hour a rapture, and every moment an ecstasy.

## Heavenly Hosts

David cried out, "The chariots of God are twenty thousand." Elisha saw the mountains filled with celestial cavalry. St. John said, "The armies which are in heaven followed him on white horses." There must be armed escorts sent out to bring from earth to Heaven those who were more than conquerors. There must be crusades ever being fitted out for some part of God's dominion—battles, bloodless, groanless, painless; angels of evil to be fought down.

John bids us look, and we see the great procession of the redeemed passing. Jesus on a white horse leads the march and all the armies of Heaven following on white horses. Infinite cavalcade passing, passing; empires pressing into line, ages following ages. Dispensation trampling on after dispensation. Glory in the track of glory. Europe, Asia, Africa, North and South America, pressing into lines. Islands of the seas shoulder to shoulder. Generations before the flood following generations after the flood; and as Jesus rises at the head of that great host and waves His sword in signal of victory, all crowns are lifted, and all ensigns slung out, and all chimes rung, and all hallelujahs chanted, and some cry, "Glory to God most high!" and some, "Hosanna to the son of David!" and some, "Worthy is the Lamb that was slain"—till all exclamations of endearment and homage in the vocabulary of Heaven are exhausted, and there comes up surge after surge of "Amen! Amen! and Amen!"

## Heavenly Awards

There are old estates in the celestial world that have been in the possession of its inhabitants for thousands of years. Many of the victors from earth have already got their palaces, and they are pointed out to those newly arrived. Soon after our getting there we will ask to be shown the apostolic residences, and ask, "Where does Paul live, and John?" and ask to be shown the patriarchal residences, and shall say, "Where does Abraham live, or Jacob?" and ask to be shown the martyr residences, and say, "Where does John Huss live, and Ridley?"

We will want to see the boulevards where the chariots of conquerors roll. We will want to see the gardens where the princes walk. We will want to see Music Row, where Handel, and Haydn, and Mozart, and Charles Wesley, and Thomas Hastings, and Bradbury have their homes; out of their windows, ever and anon, rolling some sonnet of an earthly oratorio or hymn transported with the composer. We will want to see Revival Terrace, where Whitefield, and Nettleton, and Payson, and Rowland Hill, and Charles Finney, and other giants of soul-reaping are resting from their almost supernatural labors, their doors thronged with converts just arrived, coming to report themselves.

But brilliant as the sunset, and like the leaves for number, are the celestial homes yet to be awarded, when Christ to you, and millions of others, shall divide the spoil. What do you want there? You shall have it.

An orchard? There it is; twelve manner of fruit, and fruit every month.

Do you want river scenery? Take your choice on the banks of the river, in longer, wider, deeper roll than Danube, or Amazon, or Mississippi if mingled in one, and emptying into the sea of glass, mingled with fire.

Do you want your kindred back again? Go out and meet your father and mother without the staff or the stoop, and your children in a dance of immortal glee.

Do you want a throne? Select it from the million burnished elevations.

Do you want a crown? Pick it out of that mountain of diamonded coronets.

Do you want your old church friends of earth around you? Begin to hum an old revival tune, and they will flock from all quarters to revel with you in sacred reminiscence. All the earth for those who are here on earth at the time of continental and planetary distribution, and all the heavens for those who are there.

That heavenly distribution of spoils will be a surprise to many. Here enters Heaven the soul of a man who took up a great deal of room in the church on earth, but there forsooth he is put in an old house once occupied by an angel who was hurled out of Heaven at the time of Satan's rebellion.

Right after him comes a soul that makes a great stir among the celestials, and the angels rush to the scene, each bringing to her a dazzling coronet. Who is she? Over what realm on earth was she queen? In what great Duesseldorf festival was she the cantatrice? Neither. She was an invalid who never left her room for twenty years; but she was strong in prayer; and she prayed down revival after revival, and pentecost after pentecost, upon the churches; and with her pale hands she knit many a mitten or tippet for the poor; and with her contrivances she added joy to many a holiday festival; and now, with those thin hands so strong for kindness, and with those white lips so strong for supplication, she has won coronation and enthronement and jubilee. And Christ says to the angels who have brought each a crown for the glorified invalid, "No, not these; they are not good enough. But in the jeweled vase at the righthand side of My throne there is one that I have been preparing for her many a year, and for her every pang I have set an amethyst, and for her every good deed I have set a pearl. Fetch it now and fulfill the promise I gave her long ago in the sickroom, 'Be thou faithful unto death, and I will give thee a crown.'"

## The Health of Heaven

Look at the soul standing before the throne. On earth she was a life-long invalid. See her step now, and hear her voice now. Catch, if you can, one breath of that celestial air. Health in all the pulses—health of vision; health of spirits; immortal health. No racking cough, no sharp pleurisies, no consuming fevers, no exhausting pains, no hospitals of wounded men. Health swinging in the air; health flowing in all the streams; health blooming on the banks. No headaches, no sideaches, no backaches. That child that died in the agonies of croup, hear her voice now ringing in the anthem! That old man that was bowed down with the infirmities of age, see him walk now with the step of an immortal athlete—forever young again! That night when the needle-woman fainted away in the garret, a wave of the heavenly resuscitated her forever—for everlasting years, to have neither ache nor pain nor weakness nor fatigue.

And then remember that all physical disadvantages will be exchanged for a better outfit. Either the unstrung, worn-out, blunted, and crippled organs will be so reconstructed that you will not know them, or an entire new set of eyes and ears and feet will be given you. Just what it means by corruption putting on incorruption we do not know, save that it will be glory ineffable; no limping in Heaven; no straining of the eyesight to see things a little way off; no putting of the hand behind the ear to double the capacity of the tympanum; but faculties perfect, all the keys of the instrument attuned for the sweep of the fingers of ecstasy.

## Heaven Rights All Wrongs

In the midst of the city of Paris stands a statue of the good but broken-hearted Josephine. I never imagined that marble could be smitten into such tenderness. It seems not lifeless. If the spirit of Josephine be disen-tabernacled, the soul of the Empress had taken possession of this figure. I am not yet satisfied that it is stone. The puff of the dress on the arm seems to need but the pressure of the finger to indent it. The figure at the bottom of the robe, the ruffle at the neck, the fur lining on the dress, the embroidery of the satin, the cluster of lily and the leaf and rose in her hand, the poise of her body as she seems to come sailing out of the sky, her face calm, humble, beautiful, but yet sad—attest the genius of the sculptor and the beauty of the heroine he celebrates. Looking up through the rifts of the coronet that encircles her brow, I could see the sky beyond, the great heavens where all the women's wrongs shall be righted, and the story of endurance and resignation shall be told to all the ages. The rose and the lily in the hand of Josephine will never drop their petals, beautiful symbol of the fact that Heaven rights all wrongs.

## No Sorrow There

This is a planet of weeping we are living on. We enter upon life with a cry and leave it with a long sigh. But there God wipeth away all tears from all eyes. Oh, this is a world of sorrow! But, blessed be God! there will be no sorrow in Heaven. Not one black dress of mourning, but plenty of white robes of joy; hand-shaking of welcome, but none of separation. Why, if one trouble should attempt to enter Heaven, the shining police of the city would put it under everlasting arrest. If all the sorrows of life, mailed and sworded under Apollyon, should attempt to force that gate, one company from the tower would strike them back howling to the pit. Room in Heaven for all the raptures that ever knocked at the gate, but no room for the smallest annoyance, though slight as a summer insect. Doxology, but no dirge. Banqueting, but no "funeral-baked meats." No darkness at all. No grief at all. Our sorrows over. Our journey ended. It will be as when kings banquet. And just as the snow of winter melts, and the fields will brighten in the glorious springtime, so it will be with all these cold sorrows of earth; they shall be melted away at the last before the warm sunshine of Heaven. When the clock of Christian suffering has run down, it will never be wound up again. Amid the vineyards of the heavenly Engedi, that will be restoration without any relapse; that will be "The Saints' Everlasting Rest!"

## The Bible, the Only True Guidebook

I have not heard yet one single intelligent account of the future world from anybody who does not believe in the Bible. They throw such a fog about the subject that I do not want to go to the skeptic's heaven, to the transcendentalist's heaven, to the worldly philosopher's heaven. I would not exchange the poorest room in your house for the finest heaven that Huxley or John Stuart Mill or Darwin ever dreamed of. Their heaven has no Christ in it; and a heaven without Christ, though you could sweep the whole universe into it, would be no heaven.

Oh, they tell us there are no songs there; there are no coronations in Heaven. But that would not satisfy me. Give me Christ and my old friends—that is the Heaven I want, that is Heaven enough for me. O garden of light, whose leaves never fail! O banquet of God, whose sweetness never palls the taste and whose guests are kings forever! O city of light, whose walls are salvation, and whose gates are praise! O palace of rest, where God is the monarch and everlasting ages the length of His reign!

## Theology

What are our departed Christian friends who found their chief joy in studying God, doing now? Studying God yet! No need of revelation now, for unblanched they are face to face. Now they can handle the omnipotent thunderbolts, just as a child handles the sword of a father come back from victorious battle. They have no sin, nor fear, consequently.

Studying Christ, not through a revelation, save the revelation of the scars—that deep lettering which brings it all up quick enough. Studying the Christ of the Bethlehem caravansary, the Christ of the awful massacre with its hemorrhage of head and hand and foot and side— the Christ of the shattered mausoleum—Christ, the sacrifice, the star, the sun, the man, the God.

## Society

What a place to visit in, where your next-door neighbors are kings and queens, you yourselves kingly and queenly.

If they want to know more particularly about the first Paradise, they have only to go over and ask Adam.

If they want to know how the sun and the moon halted, they have only to go over and ask Joshua.

If they want to know how the storm pelted Sodom they have only to go over and ask Lot.

If they want to know more about the arrogance of Haman, they have only to go over and ask Mordecai.

If they want to know how the Red Sea boiled when it was cloven, they have only to go over and ask Moses.

If they want to know the particulars about the Bethlehem advent, they have only to go over and ask the serenading angels who stood that Christmas night in the balconies of crystal.

If they want to know more of the particulars of the crucifixion, they have only to go over and ask those who were personal spectators while the mountains crouched and the heavens got black in the face at the spectacle.

If they want to know how the Huguenots suffered at the hands of their persecutors, they may learn the story from thousands who were victims of Henry II.

If they want to know more about the sufferings of the Scotch Covenanters, they have only to go over and ask Andrew Melville.

If they want to know more about the old-time revivals, they have only to go over and ask Whitefield, and Wesley, and Livingstone, and Fletcher, and Nettleton, and Finney. Oh! what a place to visit in!

If eternity were one minute shorter, it would not be long enough for such sociality. Think of our friends who in this world were passionately fond of flowers, turned into Paradise! Think of our friends who were very fond of raising superb fruit, turned into the orchard where each tree has twelve kinds of fruit at once, and bearing fruit all the year round!

What are our departed Christian friends in Heaven, those who on earth found their chief joy in the gospel ministry? They are visiting their old congregations. Most of those ministers have got their people around them already.

When I get to Heaven I will come to all the people to whom I have administered in the Gospel, and to the millions of souls to whom, through the kindness of the printing press, I am permitted to preach every week in this land and other lands—letters coming from New Zealand and Australia and the uttermost parts of the earth, as well as from near nations, telling me of the souls I have helped—I *will visit them all.* I give them fair notice.

## Occupation

Plenty of occupation in Heaven! I suppose Broadway, New York, in the busiest season of the year, at noonday, is not so busy as Heaven is all the time. Grand projects of mercy for other worlds! Victories to be celebrated! The downfall of despotisms on earth to be announced! Great songs to be learned and sung! Great expeditions on which God shall send forth His children! *Plenty to do, but no fatigue!*

## New Jerusalem Church

After awhile our names will be taken off the church book, or there will be a mark in the margin, to indicate that we have gone up to a better church and to a higher communion—a perfect church where all our preferences will be gratified. Great cathedral of eternity, with arches of amethysts, and pillars of sapphire, and floors of emerald, and windows aglow with the sunrise of Heaven! What stupendous towers, with chimes angel-hoisted and angel-rung! What myriads of worshipers, white-robed and coroneted! What an Officiator at the altar, even "the great High Priest of our profession!" What walls, hung with the captured shields and flags, by the church militant, passed up to the church triumphant!

Hark! the bell of the cathedral rings—the cathedral bell of Heaven. There is going to be a great meeting in the Temple. Worshipers all coming through the aisles. Make room for the Conqueror—Christ standing in the Temple. All Heaven gathering around Him. Those who loved the beautiful come to look at the Rose of Sharon. Those who loved music come to listen to His voice. Those who were mathematicians come to count the years of His reign. Those who were explorers come to discover the breadth of His love. Those who had the military spirit on earth sanctified, and the military spirit in Heaven, come to look at the Captain of their salvation. The astronomers come to look at the Morning Star. The men of the law come to look at Him who is the Judge of quick and dead. The men who healed the sick come to look at Him who was wounded for our transgressions.

All different, and different forever in many respects, yet all alike in admiration for Christ, in worship for Christ, and all alike in joining in the doxology: "Unto him who washed us from our sins in his own blood, and made us kings and priests unto God, to him be glory in the church throughout all ages, world without end!"

## Music

The Bible says so much about the music of Heaven that it cannot all be figurative. The Bible over and over again speaks of the songs of Heaven. If Heaven had no songs of its own, a vast number of those of earth would have been taken up by the earthly emigrants. Surely the Christian at death does not lose his memory. Then there must be millions of souls in Heaven who know "Coronation," and "Antioch," and "Mount Pisgah," and "Old Hundred," and they can easily learn the "New Song." And the leader of the eternal orchestra need only once tap his baton, and all Heaven will be ready for the hallelujah.

Cannot the soul sing? How often we compliment some exquisite singer by saying: "There was so much soul in her music." In Heaven it will be all soul, until the body after awhile comes up in the resurrection, and then there will be an additional Heaven. Cannot the soul hear? If it can hear, then it can hear music.

Grand old Haydn, sick and worn out, was carried for the last time into the music hall, and there he heard his own oratorio of the "Creation." History says that as the orchestra came to the famous passage, "Let there be light!" the whole audience rose and cheered; and Haydn waved his hand toward Heaven and said: "It comes from there." Overwhelmed with his own music, he was carried out in his chair, and as he came to the door, he spread his hand toward the orchestra as in benediction. Haydn was right when he waved his hand toward Heaven and said: "It comes from there."

Music was born in Heaven, and it will ever have its highest throne in Heaven; and I want you to understand that our departed friends who were passionately fond of music here are now *at the headquarters of harmony*. I think that the grand old tunes that died when your grandfathers died have gone with them to Heaven.

## Sweet Sabbath Song

When the redeemed of the Lord shall come to Zion, then let all the harpers take down their harps, and all the trumpeters take down their trumpets, and all across Heaven let there be chorus of morning stars, chorus of white-robed victors, chorus of martyrs from under the throne, chorus of ages, chorus of worlds, and let there be but one song sung, and but one name spoken, and but one throne honored—that of Jesus only.

What doxologies of all nations! Cornet to cornet, cymbal to cymbal, harp to harp, organ to organ! Pull out the tremolo stop to recall the suffering past! Pull out the trumpet stop to celebrate the victory!

O song louder than the surfbeat of many waters, yet soft as the whisper of cherubim!

Then shall be heard the great anthem of the ages, rolling out and rolling on, in tones "loud, as of numberless, yet sweet, as of blest spirits uttering joy"—the oratorio of the skies, in full orchestra, swelling the praises of God and the Lamb, forever and ever.

(From: *Gems from Talmage,* A Collection of Timely and Eloquent Extracts by Rev. T. DeWitt Talmage, D. D.; published by New York: Hurst & Company.)

# V.

# *Sundown*

*Blessed End of Sorrow, of Weakness,
of Failure, of Sad Parting*

T. DEWITT TALMAGE

*"At eventime it shall be light."*—Zech. 14:7.

While "night" in all languages is the symbol for gloom and suffering, it is often really cheerful, bright and impressive. I speak not of such nights as come down with no star pouring light from above, or silvered wave tossing up light from beneath—murky, hurtling, portentous, but such as you often see when the pomp and magnificence of Heaven turn out on night parade; and it seems as though the song which the morning stars began so long ago were chiming yet among the constellations, and the sons of God were shouting for joy. Such nights the sailor blesses from the forecastle, and the trapper on the vast prairie, and the belated traveler by the roadside, and the soldier from the tent, earthly hosts gazing upon heavenly, and shepherds guarding their flocks afield, while angel hands above them set the silver bells aringing: "Glory to God in the highest, and on earth peace; good will toward men."

What a solemn and glorious thing is night in the wilderness! Night among the mountains! Night on the ocean! Fragrant night among tropical groves! Flashing night amid arctic severities! Calm night on Roman Campagna! Awful night among the Cordilleras! Glorious night 'mid sea after a tempest!

Thank God for the night! The moon and the stars which rule it are lighthouses on the coast, toward which I hope we all are sailing, and blind mariners are we if, with so many beaming, burning, flaming glories to guide us, we cannot find our way into the harbor.

My text may well suggest that, as the natural evening is often luminous, so it shall be light in the evening of our sorrows—of old age—of the world's history—of the Christian life.

*"At eventime it shall be light."*

## Youth and Mature Middle Age Pass Away

This prophecy will be fulfilled in the evening of life. For a long time it is broad daylight. The sun rides high. Innumerable activities go ahead with a thousand feet, work with a thousand arms. The pickaxe struck a mine, the battery made a discovery, the investment yielded its twenty per cent, and the book came to its twentieth edition. The farm quadrupled in value, and sudden fortune hoisted to high position. Children were praised and friends without number swarmed into the family hive, and prosperity sang in the music, and stepped in the dance, and glowed in the wine, and ate at the banquet. All the gods of music and ease and gratification gathered around this Jupiter holding in his hands so many thunderbolts of power.

But every sun must set, and the brightest day must have its twilight.

Then comes old age. Blessed old age, if you let it come naturally. You cannot hide it. You may try to cover the wrinkles, but you cannot cover the wrinkles. If the time has come for you to be old, be not ashamed to be old. The grandest things in all the universe are old—old mountains, old rivers, old seas, old stars, an old eternity. Then do not be ashamed to be old, unless you are older than the mountains and older than the stars.

Glorious old age, if found in the way of righteousness! How beautiful the old age of Jacob, leaning on the top of his staff; of John Quincy Adams, falling with the harness on; of Washington Irving, sitting, pen in hand, amid the scenes he himself had made classical; of John Angell James, to the last proclaiming the Gospel to the masses of Birmingham; of Theodore Frelinghuysen, down to feebleness and emaciation, devoting his illustrious faculties to the kingdom of God!

*At eventime it was light!*

## Honor the Aged

See that you do honor to the aged. A philosopher stood at the corner of the street day after day, saying to the passersby, "You will be an old man; you will be an old man." "You will be an old woman; you will be an old woman." People thought he was crazy. I do not think that he was.

Smooth the way for that mother's feet; they have not many more steps to take. Steady those tottering limbs; they will soon be at rest. Plow not up that face with any more wrinkles; trouble and care have marked it full enough. Thrust no thorn into that old heart; it will soon cease to beat. "The eye that mocketh its father, and refuseth to obey its mother, the ravens of the valley shall pick it out, and the young eagles shall eat it."

The bright morning and hot noonday of life have passed with many. It is four o'clock! five o'clock! six o'clock! The shadows fall longer, and thicker, and faster. *Seven o'clock! eight o'clock!* The sun has dipped below the horizon; the warmth has gone out of the air. *Nine o'clock! ten o'clock!* The heavy dews are falling; the activities of life's day are all hushed; it is time to go to bed. *Eleven o'clock! twelve o'clock!* The patriarch sleeps the blessed sleep, the cool sleep, the long sleep. Heaven's messengers of light have kindled bonfires of victory all over the heavens. *At eventime it is light!* LIGHT!

## Out of This World's Darkness Into Heaven's Light

Finally, my text shall find fulfillment at the end of the Christian's life. You know how short a winter's day is, and how little work you can do. Now, my friends, life is a short winter's day. The sun rises at eight and sets at four. The birth angel and the death angel fly only a little way apart. Baptism and burial are near together. With one hand the mother rocks the cradle; with the other she touches a grave.

I went into the house of one of my parishioners on Thanksgiving Day. The little child of the household was bright and glad, and with it I bounded up and down the hall. Christmas Day came, and the light of that household had perished. We stood, with black book, reading over the grave, "Ashes to ashes, dust to dust."

But I hurl away this darkness. I cannot have you weep. Thanks be unto God, who giveth us the victory; at eventime it shall be light!

I have seen many Christians die. I never saw any of them die in darkness. What if the billows of death do rise above our girdle, who does not love to bathe? What though other lights do go out in the blast, what do we want of them when all the gates of Glory swing open before us, and from a myriad voices, a myriad harps, a myriad thrones, a myriad palaces, there dash upon us "Hosannah! Hosannah!"

"Throw back the shutters and let the sun in," said dying Scoville M'Collum, one of my Sunday school boys.

You can see Paul putting on robes and wings of ascension as he exclaims, "I have fought the good fight; I have finished my course; I have kept the faith."

Hugh M'Kail went to one side of the scaffold of martyrdom and cried, "Farewell, sun, moon, and stars! Farewell, all earthly delights!" then went to the other side of the scaffold and cried, "Welcome, God and Father! Welcome, sweet Jesus Christ, the Mediator of the covenant! Welcome, death! Welcome, glory!"

A minister of Christ in Philadelphia, dying, said in his last moments, *"I move into the light."*

They did not go down doubting and fearing and shivering, but their battle-cry rang through all the caverns of the sepulchre, and was echoed back from all the thrones of Heaven, "O death! where is thy sting? O grave! where is thy victory?" Sing, my soul, of joys to come.

I saw a beautiful being wandering up and down the earth. She touched the aged, and they became young. She touched the poor, and they became rich. I said, "Who is this beautiful being, wandering up and down the earth?" They told me that her name was Death.

What a strange thrill of joy when the palsied Christian begins to use his arm again! When the blind Christian begins to see again! When the deaf Christian begins to hear again! When the poor pilgrim puts his feet on such pavement and joins in such company and has a free seat in such a great temple! Hungry men no more to hunger; thirsty men no more to thirst; weeping men no more to weep; dying men no more to die.

Gather up all sweet words, all jubilant expressions, all rapturous exclamations: bring them to me, and I will pour them upon this stupendous theme of the soul's disenthralment!

Oh! the joy of the spirit as it shall mount up toward the throne of God, shouting *Free!* FREE! Your eye has gazed upon the garniture of earth and Heaven; but eye hath not seen it. Your ear has caught harmonies uncounted and indescribable—caught them from harp's trill, and bird's carol, and waterfall's dash, and ocean's doxology; but the ear hath not heard it.

How did those blessed ones get up into the light? What hammer knocked off their chains? What loom wove their robes of light? Who gave them wings? Ah! eternity is not long enough to tell it; seraphim have not capacity enough to realize it—the marvels of redeeming love! Let the palms wave; let the crowns glitter; let the anthems ascend; let the trees of Lebanon clap their hands—they cannot tell the half of it.

Archangel before the throne, thou failest!

Sing on, praise on, ye hosts of the glorified; and if with your sceptres you cannot reach it, and with your songs you cannot express it, then let all the myriads of the saved unite in the exclamation, "JESUS! JESUS! JESUS!"

There will be a password at the gate of Heaven. A great multitude come up and knock at the gate. The gatekeeper says, "The password." They say, "We have no password. We were great on earth, and now we come up to be great in Heaven." A voice from within answers, "I never knew you."

Another group come up to the gate of Heaven and knock. The gatekeeper says, "The password." They say, "We have no password. We did a great many noble things on earth. We endowed colleges, and took care of the poor." The voice from within says, "I never knew you."

Another group come up to the gate of Heaven and knock. The gatekeeper says, "The password." They answer, "We were wanderers from God, and deserved to die; but we heard the voice of Jesus—" "Ay! ay!" says the gatekeeper, "that is the password! Lift up your heads, ye everlasting gates, and let these people come in." They go in and surround the throne, jubilant forever!

Ah! do you wonder that the last hours of the Christian on earth are illuminated by thoughts of the coming glory?

Light in the evening. The medicines may be bitter. The pain may be sharp. The parting may be heart-rending. Yet, light in the evening. As all the stars of this night sink their anchors of pearl in lake and river and sea, so the waves of Jordan shall be illuminated with the down-flashing of the glory to come.

The dying soul looks up at the constellations. "The Lord is my light and my salvation: whom shall I fear?" "The Lamb which is in the midst of the throne shall lead them to living fountains of water, and God shall wipe away all tears from their eyes."

Close the eyes of the departed one: earth would seem tame to its enchanted vision. Fold the hands: life's work is ended. Veil the face: it has been transfigured.

Mr. Toplady, in his dying hour, said, "Light." Coming nearer the expiring moment, he exclaimed, with illuminated countenance, "Light!" In the last instant of his breathing, he lifted up his hands and cried, *"Light! LIGHT!"*

Thank God for light in the evening!

# Moving Day

*After final papers are signed . . . pack everything . . . call the mover . . . have electricity and water cut off . . . phone taken out.*

These were the instructions on a memo pad I had written two years ago when we were preparing to move from the state of Michigan to Tennessee.

I ran across the little memo pad while cleaning out a box of papers. I had almost forgotten the many, many things there are to be taken care of, especially when you are moving to another state.

Last minute things: such as waiting to the very last to call the telephone company, because you need the phone for last-minute turnings off and changing address.

A little tinge of sadness crept into my heart as I remember going back into the house that day to see if I had left anything.

Yes, we were leaving years of memories of our boys growing up in that house. The yearly birthday parties, the Christmases, the Cub Scouts.

I remembered that cold day in January when the real estate dealer handed us the key when we signed our name to final papers, and the warm spot in our hearts that day despite the *zero* cold day in January.

The little things I painted across my mind that day—the little things I just couldn't leave behind, the many days of packing, things we had accumulated over the years that we just couldn't part with.

We were leaving our family and friends behind—friends who had shared our joys and sorrows over the years.

We were leaving the church where our children had grown up, and the many, many blessing in the fellowship around God's Word.

The final change of address.

Reading over this little memo made me think of another move that we'll make one Day—a move to my Home of many mansions prepared by my Heavenly Father.

There will be no need for a final signature then. This was taken care of when as a sinner I came for salvation and my Father wrote my name in the lamb's Book of Life. My name is still there and will be there when I move to my Father's house with many mansions.

We won't have to pack clothes. My Father will give me a robe of righteousness.

We won't have to worry about the electricity being turned on before we arrive. There will be no need for light. The Lamb will be the Light.

There will be no water to be turned on before we arrive, because my Saviour has given me living water so that I will never again thirst.

There will be no address to change. Heaven will be my eternal Home.

There will be no mover to hire, because my Heavenly Father will meet me in the air to escort me to my final Home.

There will be no ticket to buy. My Saviour purchased my ticket by shedding His blood on the cross of Calvary for my sins.

There will be no tears when leaving. God will wipe away my tears.

There will be no sadness in leaving my personal things, because my Heavenly Father will supply my every need.

I don't know the moving date. One day, though, my Heavenly Father will say, "It's MOVING DAY."

BILLY SUNDAY
1862-1935

## ABOUT THE MAN:

William Ashley (Billy) Sunday was converted from pro baseball to Christ at twenty-three but carried his athletic ability into the pulpit.

Born in Ames, Iowa, he lost his father to the Civil War and lived with his grandparents until age nine when he was taken to live in an orphanage. A life of hard work paid off in athletic prowess that brought him a contract with the Chicago White Stockings in 1883. His early success in baseball was diluted by strong drink; however, in 1886, he was converted at the Pacific Garden Mission in Chicago and became actively involved in Christian work.

Sunday held some three hundred crusades in thirty-nine years. It is estimated that a hundred million heard him speak in great tabernacles, and more than a quarter million people made a profession of faith in Christ as Saviour under his preaching. His long-time associate, Dr. Homer Rodeheaver, called him "the greatest gospel preacher since the Apostle Paul."

Billy Sunday was one of the most unusual evangelists of his day. He walked, ran, or jumped across the platform as he preached, sometimes breaking chairs. His controversial style brought criticism but won the admiration of millions. He attacked public evils, particularly the liquor industry, and was considered the most influential person in bringing about the prohibition legislation after World War I.

Many long remembered his famous quote: "I'm against sin. I'll kick it as long as I've got a foot, and I'll fight it as long as I've got a fist. I'll butt it as long as I've got a head. I'll bite it as long as I've got a tooth. And when I'm old and fistless and footless and toothless, I'll gum it till I go home to Glory and it goes home to perdition!"

Those who heard him never forgot him—or his blazing, barehanded evangelism.

The evangelist died November 6, 1935, at age 72. His funeral was held in Moody Church, Chicago, and the sermon was preached by H. A. Ironside.

# VI.

# *Heaven Is a Place*

## BILLY SUNDAY

*"Let not your heart be troubled: ye believe in God, believe also in me. In my Father's house are many mansions: if it were not so, I would have told you. I go to prepare a place for you. And if I go and prepare a place for you, I will come again, and receive you unto myself; that where I am, there ye may be also. And whither I go ye know, and the way ye know. Thomas saith unto him, Lord, we know not whither thou goest; and how can we know the way? Jesus saith unto him, I am the way, the truth, and the life: no man cometh unto the Father, but by me."*—John 14:1-6.

Everybody wants to go to Heaven.

We are all curious. We want to know:

  Where Heaven is,

  How it looks,

  Who are there,

  What they wear,

  And how to get there.

Some say Heaven is a state or a condition. You are wrong. Your home is not a state or a condition; it is a place. The penitentiary is not a state or a condition; it is a place.

Jesus said: "I go to prepare a place for you . . . that where I am, there ye may be also."

The only source of information we have about Heaven is the Bible. It tells us that God's throne is in the heavens and that the earth is His footstool. And if our spiritual visions are not blinded, we believe it is true.

Enoch walked with God and was not, for God took him to Heaven. He left this earth at the behest of God and went to Heaven where God has His dwelling place.

Elijah, when his mission on earth was finished, in the providence of God, was wafted to Heaven in a chariot of fire. The former pupils went out to search for the translated prophet, but they did not find him.

But it was the privilege of Peter, James and John on the Mount of Transfiguration with Jesus to see the gates of Heaven open and two spirits jump down on the earth whom they recognized as Moses and Elijah, who so many years before had walked through Palestine and had warned the people of their sins and had slain 450 of the false prophets of Baal.

When Jesus began His public ministry, we are told the heavens opened and God stopped making worlds and said from Heaven: "This is my beloved Son. Hear ye him."

Then Stephen, with his face lit up with the glories of the Celestial Kingdom as he looked steadfastly toward Heaven, saw it open. And Jesus Himself was standing at the right hand of God, the place He had designated before His crucifixion and resurrection would be His abiding place until the time of the Gentiles should be fulfilled, when He would leave Heaven with a shout of triumph and return to this earth in the clouds of Heaven.

Among the last declarations of Jesus, in which we all find so much comfort in the hour of bereavement, is: "In my Father's house are many mansions: if it were not so, I would have told you."

When Heaven's music burst upon human ears that first Christmas morning while the shepherds guarded their flocks on the moonlit hills of Judaea, the angels sang: "On earth peace, good will toward men. For unto you is born this day in the city of David a Saviour, which is Christ the Lord."

We have ample proof that Heaven is a real place.

> **When we've been there ten thousand years,**
> **Bright shining as the sun,**
> **We've no less days to sing God's praise**
> **Than when we first begun.**

## What a Wonderful Place!

Oh, what a place Heaven is! The Tuileries of the French, the Windsor Castle of the English, the Alhambra of the Spanish, the Schonbrunn of the Austrians, the White House of the United States—these are all dungeons compared with Heaven.

There are mansions there for the redeemed—one for the martyrs with blood-red robes; one for you ransomed from sin; one for me plucked like a brand from the fire.

Look and see—who are climbing the golden stairs, who are walking the golden streets, who are looking out of the windows? Some whom we knew and loved here on earth. Yes, I know them. My father and mother, blithe and young as they were on their wedding day. Our son and our daughter, sweet as they were when they cuddled down to sleep in our arms. My brother and sister, merrier than when we romped and roamed the fields and plucked wild flowers and listened to the whip-poorwill as he sang his lonesome song away over in Sleepy Hollow on the old farm in Iowa where we were born and reared.

Cough gone, cancer gone, consumption gone, erysipelas gone, blindness gone, rheumatism gone, lameness gone, asthma gone, tears gone, groans and sighs gone, sleepless nights gone.

I think it will take some of us a long time to get used to Heaven.

Fruits without one speck upon them.

Pastures without one thistle or weed.

Orchestra without one discord.

Violin without a broken string.

Harps all in tune.

The river without a torn or overflowed bank.

The sunrise and sunset swallowed up in the Eternal Day. "For there shall be no night there."

Heaven will be free from all that curses us here.

No sin—no sorrow—no poverty—no sickness—no pain—no want—no aching heads or hearts—no war—no death. No watching the undertaker screw the coffin lid over our loved ones.

When I reach Heaven I won't stop to look for Abraham, Isaac, Jacob, Moses, Joseph, David, Daniel, Peter or Paul. I will rush past them all saying, "Where is Jesus? I want to see Jesus who saved my soul one dark, stormy night in Chicago in 1887."

If we could get a real appreciation of what Heaven is, we would all be so homesick for Heaven the Devil wouldn't have a friend left on earth.

The Bible description of Heaven is: the length and the breadth and the height of it are equal. I sat down and took 12 inches for a foot, our standard. That would make it two thousand five hundred miles long, two thousand five hundred miles wide, two thousand five hundred miles high. Made of pure gold like glass. Twelve gates, each gate made of one pearl. The foundations are of precious stones. Imagine eight thousand miles of diamonds, rubies, sapphires, emeralds, topaz, amethysts, jade, garnets!

Someone may say: "Well, that will be pleasant, if true."

Others say: "I hope it's true"; "Perhaps it's true"; "I wish it were true." IT IS TRUE!

## Heaven: Where There Is No More Death

The kiss of reunion at the gate of Heaven is as certain as the good-by kiss when you drift out with the tide.

> God holds the key
> Of all unknown,
>   And I am glad.
> If other hands should hold the key,
> Or if He trusted it to me,
>   I might be sad.

Death is a cruel enemy. He robs the mother of her baby, the wife of her husband, the parents of their children, the lover of his intended wife. He robs the nation of its President.

Death is a rude enemy. He upsets our best plans without an apology. He enters the most exclusive circles without an invitation.

Death is an international enemy. There is no nation which he does not visit. The islands of the seas where the black-skinned mothers rock their babies to sleep to the lullaby of the ocean's waves. The restless sea. The majestic mountains. All are his haunts.

Death is an untiring enemy. He continues his ghastly work spring, summer, autumn and winter. He never tires in his ceaseless rounds, gathering his spoils of human souls.

But Death is a vanquished enemy. Jesus arose from the dead and abolished Death, although we may be called upon to die.

Death to the Christian is swinging open the door through which he passes into Heaven.

"Aren't you afraid?" said the wife to a dying miner. "Afraid, lassie? Why should I be? I know Jesus, and Jesus knows me."

This house in which we live, "our body," is beginning to lean. The windows rattle. The glass is dim. The shingles are falling off.

> You will reach the river's brink,
> Some sweet day, by and by.
> You will clasp your broken link
> Some sweet day, by and by,

There's a glorious kingdom waiting
In the land beyond the sky,
Where the saints have been gathering
Year by year.

And the days are swiftly passing
That shall bring the Kingdom nigh,
For the coming of the Lord
Draweth near.

Thank God for the rainbow of hope that bends above the graves of our loved ones.

We stand on this side of the grave and mourn as they go. They stand on the other side and rejoice as they come.

On the Resurrection morning
Soul and body meet again;
No more sorrow, no more weeping,
No more pain.

Soul and body reunited
Thenceforth nothing can divide.
Waking up in Christ's own likeness;
Satisfied!

On that happy Easter morning,
All the graves their dead restore,
Father, sister, child and mother,
Meet once more.

To that brightest of all meetings
Brings us Jesus Christ, at last,
By the cross through death and judgment,
Holding fast.

The Bible indicates that angels know each other. If they have the power to recognize each other, won't we?

The Bible describes Heaven as a great home circle. It would be a queer home circle if we did not know each other.

The Bible describes death as a sleep. Well, we know each other before we go to sleep, and we know each other when we wake up. Do you imagine we will be bigger fools in Heaven than we are here on earth?

A woman lay dying. She had closed her eyes. Her sister, thinking her dead, commenced the wail of mourning. The dying woman raised her hand and said: "Hush! Hush! I am listening to the breezes waving the branches in the tree of life."

You will be through with your backbiting enemies. They will call you vile names no more. They will no longer misrepresent your good deeds.

Broken hearts will be bound up. Wounds will be healed. Sorrows ended.

The comfort of God is greater than the sorrows of men. I've thanked God a thousand times for the roses but never for the thorns, but now I have learned to thank Him for the thorns.

You will never be sick again, never be tired again, never weep again.

What's the use of fretting when we are on our way to such a coronation!

## Jesus, the Only Way to Heaven

You must know the password if you ever enter Heaven. Jesus said, "I am the way, the truth, and the life; no man cometh unto the Father, but by me."

Here comes a crowd. They cry: "Let me in. I was very useful on earth. I built churches. I endowed colleges. I was famous for my charities. I have done many wonderful things."

"I never knew you."

Another crowd shouts: "We were highly honored on earth. The world bowed very low before us. Now we have come to get our honors in Heaven."

"We never knew you."

Another crowd approaches and says: "We were sinners, wanderers from God. We have come up, not because we deserve Heaven, but because we heard of the saving power of Jesus; and we have accepted Him as our Saviour."

They all cry, "Jesus, Jesus, Thou Son of God, open to us."

They all pass through the pearly gates.

One step this side and you are paupers for eternity. One step on the other side and you are kings and queens for eternity. When I think of Heaven and my entering it, I feel awkward.

Sometimes when I have been exposed to the weather, shoes covered with mud, coat wet and soiled with mud and rain, hair disheveled, I feel I am not fit to go in and sit among the well-dressed guests.

So I feel that way about Heaven. I need to be washed in the blood of the Lamb and clothed in the robe of Christ's righteousness. I need the pardoning waves of God's mercy to roll over my soul. And, thank God, they have.

If you go first, will you come down halfway and meet me between the willow banks of earth and the palm groves of Heaven? You who have loved ones in Heaven, will you take a pledge with me to meet them when the day dawns and the shadows flee away?

Some who read this are sadly marching into the face of the setting sun. You are sitting by the window of your soul looking out toward the twilight of life's purple glow. You are listening to the music of the breaking waves of life's ebbing tide and longing for the sight of the faces and the sound of voices loved and lost a while.

But if you have accepted Jesus as your Saviour, at last you will hail the coming morning radiant and glorious when the waves of the sea will become crystal chords in the grand organ of Eternity.

A saint lay dying. She said: "My faith is being tried. The brightness of which you speak I do not have. But I have accepted Jesus as my Saviour; and if God wishes to put me to sleep in the dark, His will be done."

## Blessed Hope for the Christian!

Sorrow sometimes plays strange dirges on the heartstrings of life before they break, but the music always has a message of hope.

### Should You Go First

Should you go first, and I remain
  To walk the road alone,
I'll live in memory's garden, dear,
  With happy days we've known.
In Spring I'll watch for roses red,
  When fade the lilacs blue;
In early Fall, when brown leaves fall,
  I'll catch a breath of you.

Should you go first, and I remain
  For battles to be fought,
Each thing you've touched along the way
  Will be a hallowed spot.
I'll hear your voice, I'll see you smile,
  Though blindly I may grope;
The memory of your helping hand
  Will buoy me on with hope.

Should you go first, and I remain
  To finish with the scroll,
No length'ning shadows shall creep in
  To make this life seem droll.
We've known so much of happiness,
  We've had our cup of joy;
Ah, memory is one gift of God
  That death cannot destroy.

**Should you go first, and I remain,**
**One thing I'd have you do;**
**Walk slowly down the path of death,**
**For soon I'll follow you.**
**I'll want to know each step you take,**
**That I may walk the same;**
**For some day—down that lonely road—**
**You'll hear me call your name.**

—A. K. Rowswell.
(Rosey)

One day when the children were young, I was romping and playing with them; and I grew tired and lay down to rest. Half asleep and half awake I dreamed I journeyed to a far-off land.

It was not Persia, although the Oriental beauty and splendor were there.

It was not India, although the coral strands were there.

It was not Ceylon, although the beauty and spicy perfume of that famous island paradise were there.

It was not Italy, although the dreamy haze of the blue Italian sky beat above me.

It was not California nor Florida, although the soft flower-ladened breezes of the Pacific and the Atlantic were there.

I looked for weeds, briars, thorns and thistles, but I found none.

I saw the sun in all his meridian glory. I asked, "When will the sun set and it grow dark?" They said: "Oh, it never grows dark in this land. There is no night here. Jesus is the light."

I saw the people all clothed in holiday attire with faces wreathed in smiles and halos of glory about their heads. I asked: "When will the working men go by with calloused hands and empty dinner buckets and faces grimed with dust and toil?" They said: "Oh, we toil not, neither do we sow nor reap in this land."

I strolled out into the suburbs and the hills which would be a fit resting place for the dead to sleep. I looked for monuments, mausoleums, marble slabs, tombs and graves; but I saw none. I did see towers, spires and minarets. I asked: "Where do you bury the dead of this great city? Where are the gravediggers? Where are the hearses that haul the dead to their graves?" They said: "Oh, we never die in this land."

I asked: "Where are the hospitals where you take the sick? Where are the doctors with scalpel and trocar? Where are the nurses with panacea and opiates to ease the pain?" They said: "Oh, we are never sick. None ever die in this land."

I asked: "Where do the poor people live? Where are the homes of penury and want?" They said: "Oh, there are no poor in this land. There is no want here. None are ever hungry here."

I was puzzled.

I looked and saw a river. Its waves were breaking against golden and jewel-strewn beaches.

I saw ships with sails of pure silk, bows covered with gold, oars tipped with silver.

I looked and saw a great multitude no man could number, rushing out of jungles of roses, down banks of violets, redolent of eternal Spring, pulsing with bird song and the voices of angels.

I realized Time had ended and Eternity had dawned.

I cried: "Are all here?"

They echoed: "Yes, all here."

And tower and spire and minaret all caroled my welcome home. And we all went leaping and singing and shouting the eternal praises of God the Father, God the Son, God the Holy Spirit.

Home, home, at last!

> **Here's to you, my friends.**
> **May you live a hundred years,**
> **Just to help us**
> **Through this vale of tears.**
>
> **May I live a hundred years**
> **Short just one day,**
> **Because I don't want to be here**
> **After all my friends have gone away.**

## Threshold of Heaven

Do not ask me not to speak
About this journey I shall take.
'Tis but a step and then my eyes
Shall open to the great surprise
He has prepared. Do you recall,
At Christmastime when we were small,
Our rapture and our eagerness,
And how we always tried to guess
What gifts our mother's hands had made?
Dear memories that will not fade!
Don't you remember, half our fun
Was in anticipation!
And then at last the opened door.
A breathless pause, a rush, and there
Beneath the tree our gifts were laid,
The gifts our mother's hands had made!

So at His threshold now I pause,
And ask you not to grieve because
I go into His other room.
Surely He would have me come
With eager wonder in my eyes
To see at last what rich surprise
The loving hands of our dear Lord
Made for His own. Ear has not heard,
Eye has not see, nor can the mind
Obscurely guess what we shall find
Beyond that opened door. And so,
I pray that you will let me go,
Will loose love's last restraining bands.
A hush . . . a light . . . and lo, His hands
Have unveiled glory in a breath!
O gifts undreamed of—brought by death!

Martha Snell Nicholson

WILLIAM EDWARD BIEDERWOLF
1867-1934

# ABOUT THE MAN:

Presbyterians produced some of the most noteworthy evangelists of the late 1800's and early 1900's—and a notable among them was William E. Biederwolf.

After his conversion, he continued his education at Princeton, Erlangen and Berlin universities, and at the Sorbonne in Paris.

Biederwolf's first church was the Broadway Presbyterian Church of Logansport, Indiana, the state where he was born. Then he became a chaplain in the Spanish-American War and then entered evangelism—a ministry he was to serve for 35 years.

In conjunction with his evangelism, Dr. Biederwolf was associated with the world-renowned Winona Lake Bible Conference for 40 years.

In 1929, he became pastor at the storied Royal Poinciana Chapel in Palm Beach, Florida, a position he held until his death.

Biederwolf's ministry was mighty. Perhaps his greatest campaign was in Oil City, Pennsylvania, in the bitter winter of 1914. Thousands thronged the tabernacle. Twice it was enlarged. His messages were pungent and powerful.

His kind of preaching brought men and women from every walk in life coming in deep contrition for their sins—the mayor of the city, physicians, lawyers, and men from the factories, young people from the schools; and the whole city and county were mightily stirred in deep concern about the things of God.

He was the author of several books.

# VII.

# *Beautiful Heaven*

## WILLIAM EDWARD BIEDERWOLF

*"I go to prepare a place for you."* —John 14:2.

If you should ask me why I know there is such a place as Heaven, I would give you five reasons.

*First: Because the human soul has always longed for such a place.*

You can go as far back as history will take you and find that that is true. The Egyptians had a heaven they called Yaru. You can go to the pyramids today and find inscriptions on their hoary walls that were written 3,000 years before the feet of Jesus pressed the Galilean hills, addressed to the ferryman who was supposed to ferry the dead across the river into those happy fields.

There was an old heathen by the name of Cleombrotus who read those great arguments of Plato about Heaven, and he ran and threw himself down from a precipice that he might die and enter on that blessed life.

Now I don't believe God would plant in the soul a universal longing like that without making some provision for its realization.

If I knew I was going to be annihilated or had to go to Hell, I never would want to leave this world. I don't anyhow. I'd like to stay here a thousand years. I'm getting along fine. I think old Cleombrotus was a fool.

But when the time comes and I have to die, I want something better and bigger in every way. And if I can only know that this longing of mine is going to be satisfied, then it doesn't make so much difference when I go, whether I live a thousand years or die before the whistle blows tomorrow morning.

*Second: Because the human soul has always felt there was such a place.* When the soul gets tired of philosophy and argument it can just turn back and commune with itself. And deep within itself it hears a voice as gentle and as unmistakable as an evening zephyr which says, "It must be so." That's the instinct of Heaven that God planted in every soul.

Like the little boy flying his kite. The kite was out of sight; and when someone asked him where it was, he pointed up into the skies. They asked him how he knew it was there if he couldn't see it. He answered, "I know it is there because I can feel it tug."

And in some such way as that, I know there is a Heaven because I feel the pull of it, the tug of it in my soul.

*Third: Because the human soul needs just such a place as Heaven.* The best developments of this life are only fragmentary, and the soul needs another life in order to go on to perfection. Sir Isaac Newton had a mind that could master the profoundest truths as easily as the average man can handle his A B C's. One day someone complimented him on his vast learning. Do you remember his humble reply? He said, "I seem to be only a child picking up a few pebbles on the shore while the great ocean of truth stretches unexplored before me."

Think of the mysteries that are yet to be unraveled, the riddles yet to be solved!

Then a great many never have a chance to develop. Their intellects have been hampered by diseased bodies. Some of them have been what Tennyson calls the "forbidden builders," dying almost before they got started. Keats died when he was only 22; and Raphael, the unrivaled artist, at 37.

Others have been denied the opportunity by the force of social circumstances. What chance had Oliver Twist living with Fagin in a den of thieves? In fact, every worthy development of life, every faculty and every virtue is imperfect here. The soul needs Heaven, and Heaven alone can finish out what life must leave unfinished here.

*And then in the last place, and chiefly, I believe there is such a place as Heaven because God says there is.* The whole Bible is full of it; and to doubt it for one second is to impeach divine wisdom, divine love and God's omnipotence.

I'd rather have God's Word about anything than the opinion of all the philosophical literati and scientific dignitaries in the world when they try to make you believe that God doesn't know what He's talking about.

Some people say, "Don't talk so much about Heaven; give us something practical." But I guess if Jesus talked so much about it, we have a right to preach one sermon about it.

Jesus said, "I go to prepare a place for you." He said, "In my Father's house are many mansions." He says, "Rejoice that your names are written in heaven." It says in Hebrews, "We have no continuing city, but we seek one to come."

And so I guess these four reasons ought to be enough to persuade us that there is a Heaven.

And now you want to know something about it, and I am going to tell you. I am not going to tell you what I know about it. I could tell you a great deal that way, I suppose. In fact, I could tell you all about it, because the fellow who doesn't know is always the one who can tell the most.

Paul was caught up into Heaven, you know, and he found it impossible to express what he saw. But the man who has never been there, it's dead easy for him. He can just throw open the door and let you see the whole thing. He'll take the door clear off the hinges for you.

Now I am not going to tell you what I imagine Heaven to be. Fancy and imagination and speculation don't amount to anything here, but God has told us a great deal about Heaven, and what He has revealed is worth our while to consider.

## I. HEAVEN IS A PLACE

Jesus said, "I go to prepare a place for you." Canon Farrar wrote a book and called it *Eternal Hope*. It's long on surmise and short on logic. He says, "Heaven is to be something rather than to go somewhere."

Well, it is to *be* something; it is a condition—sure; it's a state of mind and heart, but it's more.

If Jesus went anywhere, He must have gone somewhere. He couldn't go nowhere. Where is nowhere? Heaven is a place. Of course you couldn't be in a place without being in a condition. And I am sure the condition you are in is more important than the place. And it would be better for a man to be in Hell if he could keep the proper spirit in him there, than to be in Heaven and have the mind of the Devil in him. Some of you wouldn't be fit for Heaven if you did get in.

"I go to prepare a place for you." That's what He said. "In my Father's house are many mansions." They are just as real as your home down here, and you can trust God to make good on His promise.

## II. HEAVEN IS A PREPARED PLACE

*"I go to prepare a place for you."*

(1) *It's commodious.* He has made it big enough. God is never embarrassed for the want of space. When He made the universe, He didn't use the earth and its moon as a model. You talk about size! Why, this earth is so small it's a wonder God hasn't forgotten He ever made it.

You can take an auger and bore a hole into the sun and pour 1,200,000 earths like this one into it and still have room for 4,900,000 moons to lie around the inside edge. You think that's big! But some of the fixed stars, like Alpha Centauri, for instance, are five times bigger even than the sun.

Talk about size! Do you know how big old Neptune is? She's 75 times bigger than this earth you live on. She's close to 3 billion miles away; and you can't see her unless you climb Mt. Hamilton and look through the Lick telescope, or go to Lake Geneva and point that powerful Yerkes telescope with its forty-inch diameter lens at her.

Well, if that is so, then tell me how big do you suppose that beautiful star Lyra is that is 100,000 times farther away than Neptune, and you can see it with your own naked eye.

And then talk about space! How far away is the sun? Well, if I could charter a Pennsylvania Limited and "hit her off" 60 miles an hour, it would take me 177 years to go to the sun. Figure it out, and it makes the sun 93 million miles from where you are now. Some distance, you say that is. Yes, but wait a minute and look up into the skies and tell me what you see.

There's Mercury, nearest to the sun and whizzing around her orbit at the rate of 109,000 miles an hour. You know the nearer the planets are to the sun, the faster they go. There are no speed limit signs up there and no smash-ups either. The General Traffic Manager is onto His job.

Then in the evening if you'll look out into the southwest you'll see the object most beautiful to the naked eye in all the skies. It's Venus, about 35 million miles further out. She swings around the sun once in 224 days; and when she gets on the other side, she is nearly twice as far away from the earth as the sun is.

Third in distance from the sun is the earth. She spins on her axis 19 miles a second. You're whirling that fast now; and at the same time you're speeding around the sun at the rate of 68,000 miles an hour. Thank you, good old gravitation!

Then comes Mars, 140 million miles from the sun; and it takes her 687 days to get around.

Fifth in order is old Jupiter, "giant planet" of the skies, champion of the starry world with his two big, light-brown belts of shining vapor. He's three times as big as all the rest of the planets put together. And my, how he spins! He's 1,250 times bigger than the earth but turns on his axis every 10 hours; that's 47 miles a second, or 2½ times faster than the earth. But he can't hit the track like the old earth. 30,000 miles an hour is the best he can do, and it puts him around the sun only once in 12 years.

If you lived on Jupiter and wanted to go to the sun, if you'd charter a Pennsylvania Limited and travel 50 miles an hour, it would take you *nine centuries* to get there. "Well," you say, "that's some distance." No, it isn't. Jupiter is just one of our next-door neighbors.

Yonder in the southeastern sky is old Saturn with her rings that got old Galileo going so. She is second largest of all the planets and is 790 million miles from the earth at the nearest point. It takes her 10½ years to turn on her axis and 29 years to make the trip around the sun. How fast does the shell of a 13-inch gun travel? 15 miles a minute. Well, if the modern Krupp gun could fire a projectile far enough, at that rate it would take it 111 years to drop down on the shores of that far-off, prodigious luminary.

Seventh in order is Uranus, 64 times as big as the earth and more than twice as far away as Saturn—1,800,000,000 miles. She goes on her tireless circuit around the sun, but it takes her 87 years to make the journey once.

And then way out yonder, too far for the naked eye to see, is one of the outermost planets of the solar system, old Neptune. If I'd take an airship and sail 100 miles an hour it would take me 3,000 years to get to old Neptune with her satellite. It takes her 155 years to go around the sun.

She is 2,780,000,000 miles away. You don't know how much a billion is. You can't conceive of it. If you'd count 100 a minute, it would take you 19 years to count one billion counting day and night.

"Well," you say, "it's certainly a long, long way to Neptune." Not very far. Do you know how fast light travels? 192,000 miles a second. Well, I could close this meeting promptly at ten o'clock tonight, jump on a ray of light; and in exactly one and one-quarter seconds I could say, "Hello" to the man in the moon; in four minutes I could tip my hat to those wonderful folks that you think live on Mars (but I don't), and I could jump off at Neptune before the roosters crow and get back here in time for breakfast at 6 a.m. tomorrow.

Neptune, nearly 3 billion miles away! But the nearest star you ever saw in the sky is 10,000 times farther away than that. It's Alpha Centauri, 250,000 times farther away than the sun. The light you see from Alpha Centauri is four years old. It takes it that long to get there traveling at the rate of 192,000 miles a second as all light does.

But Alpha Centauri isn't very far away. The North Star is 14 times farther.

When we get an inter-stellar aeroplane system in operation, you can make the trip to the North Star. If you paid 2½ cents a mile it would cost you only $8,950,000,000,000.00 (eight trillion nine hundred and fifty billion dollars) one way; and making 100 miles an hour, which is dead easy for an airship, it would take you 409 million years to arrive at the Union Depot.

Whew!

But that isn't far away. There are stars 500 and 800 and 1,000 times farther. It takes the light from Arcturus 200 years to get here. Find out how many seconds in 200 years and multiply by 192,000 and you'll know how far it is to Arcturus.

Talk about space! Do you know that the whole solar system—sun, moon, earth, and all the other planets—is flying straight ahead this very second through space 400 times faster than a ball shot from a cannon. Where are we going? We're heading straight for that beautiful constellation of Lyra, and every second the clock ticks off we are 10 miles nearer to that beautiful star. We've made 150 miles since I just told you! And we've been going that way—the whole solar system—since the beginning of time and we're not there yet. When will we get there? I don't know.

Who conceived all this and brought it into existence? God! God! God! It makes me so warm under the collar to hear some little, puny, pygmy, pusillanimous infidel disputing about God and finding fault with God's plan of salvation and other things that came out of the divine mind. Why, you poor fool! You're so small, compared with the rest of God's universe, that He could blow you into a gnat's eye and it would make it wink.

God has got plenty of room. Billions have died, and billions are here, and billions are still to come, and people say, "Where is God going to put them all?" He has plenty of room. Over in Revelation it says an angel took the measurement of Heaven. "And it was 12,000 furlongs; the length, height and breadth of it are equal." 12,000 furlongs. That's nearly 8 million feet and if you cube it you'll get 512,000,000,000,000,000,000 (512 quintillion) cubic feet.

Now if the world stood for 100,000 years and always had and always will have a billion people on it dying off every generation, that would only make 300 (trillion) 000,000,000,000,000 people and this would give every one of them 177,000 cubic feet or a room 56 feet each way.

And if that isn't big enough, God could send His surveying angels out and throw His boundary line around a few sextillion acres more.

There's room for the millions that have gone and for the millions and billions and trillions that are still to go. "In my Father's house are many mansions"—many rooms is what it really says. God made it commodious and there's plenty room.

(2) *It's beautiful.* God made it beautiful. The Bible doesn't go into detail, but it tells us enough to let us know that beauty in Heaven has reached it perfection.

God loves beauty or He wouldn't have put so much of it in this world.

Who painted the butterfly's wing with all those gorgeous hues and threw around the evening sun her drapery of a thousand colors?

Who put the red on the robin's breast?

From whose pastel were the colors mixed that gave the rose its blushing charm and touched the lily with its dreamy white?

Who taught the raindrop to take a ray of light from Heaven's shining orb and pencil it on the sky in one huge arch of bewildering elegance?

God did it all! He made everything beautiful, and only sin has marred it. In Heaven you'll find God's beauty at its best.

The fairest visions on earth, all of her enrapturing scenery, all her matchless music and all her sweetest fragrance, are but the faintest indication possible of the ineffable and entrancing beauty that shall greet us everywhere as we enter and dwell in that celestial city whose builder and maker is God.

John got a glimpse of it one day from his lonely island and tried to tell us about it, but the best he could do was to use a few symbols our poor little minds could understand, and he said, "The walls are of jasper, the foundations garnished with precious stones and every gate a pearl and the city is of pure gold."

"Every gate a pearl." Who doesn't go into ecstasy over the luster of a perfect pearl?

I heard one day that Bailey, Banks & Biddle of Philadelphia carried a fine selection of them; and I managed to find someone who could introduce me to the pearl connoisseur—that's what you call them, I guess, the fellow that knows all about them—and I asked to see his finest pearls. He looked me over and seemed surprised. "Oh!" I said, "I don't want to buy but I would just like to look at them."

He took me through some iron gates, and he laid on the palm of his hand one pearl about the size of a bullet. When I caught my breath I said, "How much?" And he said, "$7,000.00."

Oh, I can see it yet! I thought I was in a dream—the tint of it—the luster of it! Keep all the other precious stones but give me a pearl. I carry one with me just to look at—not like that one though. And, oh, the wonderful thought that every gate is a pearl, and one day it will swing open and admit you and me to the dazzling beauty within.

I have heard of a little girl who was blind from birth and only knew of the beauties of earth from her mother's lips. A noted surgeon worked on her eyes, and at last his operations were successful. As the last bandage dropped away she flew into her mother's arms and then to the window and the open door; and as the glories of earth rolled into her vision, she ran screaming back to her mother and said, "O Mama, why didn't you tell me it was so beautiful!" The mother wiped her tears of joy away and said, 'My precious child, I tried to tell you; but I couldn't do it."

One day when we go sweeping through those gates of pearl and catch our first vision of the enrapturing beauty all around us, I think we'll hunt up John and say, "John, why didn't you tell us it was so beautiful!" John will say, "I tried to tell you when I wrote the 21st and 23rd chapters of the last book in the Bible after I got my vision, but I couldn't do it."

This is the Heaven God has prepared for you and for the poorest of them that believe on Him. He has made it beautiful.

(3) *It's comfortable.* This old world of ours would be a mighty fine place if there weren't so many things in it that curse and blight and damn it. God might transfer His headquarters and bring His angels down if it weren't for that. But in Heaven all these things are known.

There won't be any Monday up in Heaven. It'll all be one long Sabbath.

The pass of Glencroe in Scotland is reached by a long, steep, tiresome road; but at the end is a sign, "Rest and be thankful." That's what you'll find at the end of the way that leads to Heaven.

"There remaineth therefore a rest to the people of God." There won't be any grinding toil. No blasting furnace to swelter around in steel mills and iron works. No heavy burdens to carry on tired shoulders. No sweat shops where poor widows toil in the foul air and dim light. Rising up early in the morning and wearing out your life all day long will be all over; for toil, poverty and misery are words that Heaven cannot spell.

There'll be no trouble in Heaven. The first thing you do when you are born is to cry, and the last thing you do when you die is to groan, but "Earth has no sorrow that Heaven cannot heal."

There'll be no sickness there, no suffering. When Wilberforce asked Robert Hall for his idea of Heaven, the great preacher replied, "Heaven is rest." And you know Robert Hall was a great sufferer. His poor body was racked and tortured in the ruthless grip of a vicious disease; and to his poor pain-racked body, rest, more than anything else, would be Heaven to him.

Some of us, when we suffer just a little, make such a fuss about it there's no living with us; but some people suffer all their lives through and live in a moving prison, and it must be hard, but it will all be over there.

Listen to Revelation 21:4, "And God shall wipe away all tears from their eyes; and there shall be no more death, neither sorrow, nor crying, neither shall there be any more pain."

"And there shall be no more death." No gasping for breath and failing to get it. The cheeks will never turn ashen. The eyes will never set in glassy stare. There will be no crepe to hang on the door. The undertaker will not come and screw down the coffin lid, and there will be no hearse to head the sad journey to the grave. There will be no heartbreaking moment when the coffin is lowered and the clods fall down.

But our dear ones, whom we love so much and miss so much, when they are gone will never die. What a place it must be! No wonder the inspired apostle cried, "Eye hath not seen, nor ear heard, neither have entered into the heart of man, the things which God hath prepared for them that love him" (I Cor. 2:9).

## III. HEAVEN IS A BUSY PLACE

A heaven where we didn't do anything but sit by the side of crystal seas and pearly streams and gaze forever on the eternal beauty and dazzling effulgence about us would be too ghostly. It would be too senseless and insipid. That'll do for some old monk or idle dreamer, but I wouldn't want to go there.

But there's going to be something doing in Heaven all the time.

(1) *It's a place of Intellectual Activity.* Sir Isaac Newton with his profound mind has long ago stopped picking up pebbles and has gone down to the very bottom of the unexplored ocean of truth that one time stretched out before him. Tennyson is singing loftier strains, and Herschel is busy exploring the stars of the new heavens that appeared when the old passed away. Heaven is a place of never-tiring thought. No stagnation there. And you can learn as much there in a day as you can learn here in a year.

The brainiest men know a mighty little here, but up there our faculties will all be quickened and intensified, and all the pages of knowledge will unroll before us.

Some of us have been too poor to get an education down here or too stupid, but up there God will give you one free and touch your dull mind into such intellectual acumen that you can grapple with the infinite mysteries of the universe. Mighty God, how we thank You!

(2) *It's a place of Social Activity.* "In my Father's house are many mansions" — many rooms, it says; and there'll be a reception room sure. But the reception won't be like the average one down here. Did you ever attend one?

Some of you lady folks spend more money for music and flowers and refreshments to give one afternoon or evening reception than you give in a whole year to the church to help spread the Gospel of Jesus Christ.

But up there, oh, what a reception that will be! There won't be any idle gossip about your neighbor, no sham respectability and a lot of nonsense you've got to go through down here.

I tell you, the society up there is going to be mighty select. This old town I'm preaching to wouldn't be such a bad place to live in if it weren't for some of the people you have to tolerate.

Here you have backbiters and gossipers and meddlers in other people's business. In Heaven you don't. Here you have the avaricious and the lewd and lustful. In Heaven you don't. Here you have the sneering skeptic and godless, good-for-nothing infidel. In Heaven you don't. Here you've got booze fighters and a lot of the dirty gang that sells the rotten stuff. In Heaven the odor of the dirty stuff never defiles the nostrils.

There are no gamblers there, no liars, but only the pure and noble; and we shall enjoy their society forever.

Then Christ will be there and will be the first to greet you when you come. He redeemed you, blessed be His name; and He has a right to the first embrace.

Someone was asked what he expected to do when he got to Heaven, and he said he would take one good look at Jesus for about five hundred years, and then he might look around for someone else he knew and loved on earth. It seems to me I'd never get through looking at Jesus.

And then there'll be some loved ones there. If God should call me before He does my wife, and I expect He will, after I have seen Jesus I know who I'll look for next. It'll be my dear old mother who went away with her furrowed cheeks and her silver hair. And I'll feel the touch of her blessed hand again on my head and hear her say, "My precious boy! I'm so glad to see you!" Next then will be Father. He worked alongside of Mother till they were stoop-shouldered for their children down here, and I'm so glad they'll have them all with them up there.

Yes, thank God, brothers and sisters will be there, too. Some of them are there now, and we'll have a sure enough family reunion when we all get Home.

And then one glad hour the angels will announce the coming of Wife, and after the first glad meeting I'll say, "Come on, Wife." We'll go and sit down in some bright restful spot, and what a time we will have talking it all over; and I'll say, "How is old Deacon N?"

"Been dead four years," she'll say.

"Strange he isn't here, Wife; he's had plenty of time to arrive. And tell me about Mrs. R. She was president of the Ladies' Aid Society when I left; she occupied such a prominent pew and always came in just a little late; she was always having trouble with everybody, and we never could get her church subscription out of her."

"Why, isn't she here?"

"No, I've never seen her."

"Well, what about old Jerry, the shoemaker; he's here, isn't he?"

"Oh, yes. I see him every day. He's got a mansion just around from ours. You ought to see how his face shines! He had no trouble to get in. The angels sang him a welcome."

Someone, you know, said that when we get to Heaven there will be three surprises. First, to see some people there we did not expect to see. Second, not to see some people there we did expect to see.

And third, the greatest surprise of all, to find ourselves there.

The first two are all right, but that third is not true; it would be to doubt the Word of God and to slander the sacrifice of Jesus Christ in our behalf. "I know whom I have believed, and am persuaded that he is able to keep that which I have committed unto him against that day." I would be surprised if I found myself in Hell, but I've got my Lord's word about my heavenly inheritance; and when I get to Heaven, I don't expect to be surprised to find that Jesus has kept His word. But the other two surprises will be real enough.

I don't know when I'll go. I would live longer if I would quit this terrible strain on my tired body and nerves every night. But I would rather live ten years less and amount to something for God than to loll around like some of you do and die in disgrace with nothing in Heaven to show for the time spent here.

They tell us the story of a girl who had a dream. In her dream she died and went to Heaven and an angel said, "Come on, Mary, I'll show you where you are to stay."

Along the way they came to several beautiful, shining palaces. Mary was informed that one was for her minister, one for Aunt Lizzie, the old washerwoman, and the other for old Jerry, the cobbler. Then they came to a very humble, plain-looking cottage, and the angel said, "This, Mary, is yours."

She was bitterly disappointed and said she didn't want it. But the angel said, "It's not what you want; it's what you get."

Then he told her they had done for her the very best they could. He said, "You see, Mary, it's like this; we build the mansion out of the material sent up. We took every kind word you ever spoke, every flower you ever carried to the sick, every penny you ever gave, and this is the best we could do."

When the girl woke up she found herself in tears.

"In my Father's house are many mansions," but those are the kinds of mansions some of you religious loafers are going to have if you don't pretty soon get busy for God.

There are other activities, besides intellectual and social, too numerous to mention. David hasn't hung up his harp, and the redeemed of God led by the majestic sweep of his fingers over the strings will sing a new song, and it will be, "Amen! blessing and glory and wisdom and thanksgiving and honour and power and might be unto God forever and ever, Amen!" (Rev. 7:9-12). And Heaven's Temple will be filled with music, the enchanting sweetness and power of which no mortal being can conceive.

Then I read in another place, "They serve him day and night in his temple." God put man in the first paradise and told him to "dress it and keep it"; and God expects His servants to keep busy in the second Paradise. There won't be any tramps in Heaven. Just what our employment will be nobody knows. It may be on some other planet amid His countless worlds far beyond the range of the Lick or Yerkes observatory He may have work for us to do. But whatever those radiant ministries are, our chiefest joy will be to do the will of God.

Heaven is a busy place.

## IV. HEAVEN IS AN ETERNAL PLACE

Paul says, "Here we have no continuing city, but we seek one to come." Where are Nineveh and Babylon with their dazzling glory of other days? Gone, and the wild beasts roam where once their temples stood. Where is Rome that was once called the "eternal city"? Gone! Gone!

But Heaven is a city whose builder and maker is God and whose foundations shall never crumble away. There'll be no end to its glory and beauty. And when we go in, we go in to go out no more forever. Its ages will never end.

How can I make sure of Heaven? We must not stop until we settle this. Don't make any mistake about the way in. Jesus says, "I am the way." Jesus says, "I am the door." And if you ever enter in, it will be that way and by that door, by the way of repentance and faith in the Lord Jesus Christ.

Theosophy can't save you. Christian Science can't do it. Spiritualism is no good. And Unitarianism and Universalism and Bahaiism and all the rest of them can never save you. It's not by works that any man can do. "By grace are ye saved," says Paul, "through faith."

Over in one of our eastern cities was an engineer who had been on the road for a good many years. He was one day addressing a crowd of men among whom were a good many railroad men. In closing his address he said:

> Men, I can't begin to tell you what Jesus has meant to me. Years ago on every night when I would finish my run I would pull open the whistle and let out a blast just as we came around the curve. I would look up to a small hill where stood a little white cottage,

and there would be a little old man and a little old woman standing in the doorway. I would lean out of the old cab window and
we would wave at each other. As my engine would go shooting
into a tunnel the old couple would turn and go back inside and
the little old woman would say to the little old man, "Thank God,
Father, Bennie is safe home tonight."

But at last the day came when we took Mother out and laid her
away. Then each night as I came around the curve and blew the
whistle the little old man would be at the door. I would wave to
him and he would wave to me. Then as my train shot through the
tunnel he would turn and go slowly back into the cottage and say,
"Thank God, Bennie is safe home tonight."

But by and by the time came when we carried Father out, too.
Now when I finish my run, although I pull open the whistle and
let out a blast, there are no dear ones to welcome me home. But
when my work on earth is done, when the last run has been made
and I have pulled the throttle and the whistle for the last time, as
I draw near to Heaven's gate, I know I shall see that same little
old couple waiting there for me. And as I go sweeping through the
gate I will see my dear old mother turn to my dear old father and
hear her say, "Thank God, Father, Bennie is safe home at last."

Heaven is not far away. The miles are few and short even for the
youngest of us. If for no other reason than for this one, I would give
my heart to Christ because it means a reunion, a meeting again with
the loved ones on the other side of the dark valley through which we
all must go.

"I go to prepare a place for you." God pity us if we should make
a mistake and say "No" to Jesus Christ!

# VIII.

# The Wedding in the Sky

## W. E. BIEDERWOLF

*"The marriage of the Lamb is come, and his wife hath made herself ready."*—Rev. 19:7.

Weddings are always interesting, especially to the circle of society in which the married couple registers, whether it be among the so-called select "four hundred," or among the less socially prominent. And there are marriages sometimes upon which the interested eyes of the whole world are centered. The pity of it all is that too many are married but not mated.

Some of the most magnificent, the most elaborate, the most brilliant and beautiful of earthly events have been weddings. But I am to tell you of a wedding with which, from the standpoints just mentioned and all others, anything this earth could possibly produce is utterly unworthy to be compared; a million times more so than is a charcoal sketch worthy to be compared with the blazing beauty of a golden sunset.

This earth has seen weddings where the groom was fabulously rich; weddings where he has been counted as one of the most scholarly of men; and again where he has been a man of tremendous power and influence. But his riches and his wisdom and his power were as nothing compared with those of the Groom of this Wedding in the Sky.

Weddings have taken place where the bride's trousseau has been described in the most glowing and extravagant language. But the wedding garments worn by the Bride of this marriage in the sky so far outshine anything that earth's most magnificent marriages have ever known that no words can be found in any language to adequately express their beauty and their glory.

Royal weddings have taken place in palaces of marble and upon thrones of gold, weddings so magnificent and brilliant that they beggar description. But before this wedding in the sky they all fade away as the pale light of a tallowdip fades away before the blazing light of the noonday sun.

And now, doubtless many of you are saying within yourselves, *I would know more about this extraordinary event which you call the "Wedding in the Sky"; who the groom is; who the bride is; when, where, and why does it take place? and who are the invited guests?*

## Who Is the Groom?

The Groom? As well expect to paint a rainbow with a lead pencil as to expect human language to adequately express for us all that He is. All comparison, all metaphor, all illustration, all rhetoric do but skirt the margin of the glory of this illustrious Person of whom it is said in Holy Writ, "His name shall be called Wonderful." It is none other than the blessed Lord Himself, "King of kings and Lord of lords."

You tell me that he was born among cattle in a lantern-lit barn in Bethlehem. Yes, but before the world was made, His dwellingplace was resplendent with light from the throne of the Eternal God.

You tell me His royal robes were but the garments of a common Nazarene. Yes, but Solomon in all his glory was not arrayed like Jesus on the Mount of Transfiguration when he chose to let the splendor of His celestial attire shine through.

You tell me that His palace was but a carpenter's cottage and that sometimes He had not where to lay His head. Yes, but why should He care? He was a voluntary exile from the mansions of the highest heavens.

You tell me that His court attendants were twelve ignorant fishermen and that His state chariot was but a borrowed ass. Yes, but angels were at His command, and the wind and the waves obeyed His will; and if a borrowed colt was His royal carriage, when the time arrived for returning to His Father and His God, "the clouds," as another has said, "lent the chariot and the obsequious air bore Him up in its reverent hands."

The Groom, in our text, is called "the Lamb." This is John's special name for his Lord. He learned it, doubtless, from hearing John the Baptist cry at the Jordan, "Behold the Lamb of God that taketh away the sin of the world!" In the Book of Revelation he uses this name over and over again. "The marriage of the Lamb is come."

As the Lamb He was the one everlasting sacrifice for sin; and John wishes us above all else to remember that as the sacrifice for sin the Lord appears in His glory when He comes to take unto Himself His Bride, His first and only love.

## Who Is the Bride?

Who is the Bride? She is none other than the church; not the church visible, not church members but the church invisible and triumphant—a composite bride, if you please, made up of all the redeemed, all of those "who have washed their robes and made them white in the blood of the Lamb."

"And his wife hath made herself ready." Talk about brides' apparel and wedding trousseaus! What is this we read about the bride at the Wedding in the Sky? "And to her it was granted that she should be arrayed in fine linen, clean and white; for the fine linen is the righteousness of the saints."

The nuptial ornaments of this glorious bride she did not purchase by any price of her own. It is all of grace. "And it was given unto her," is the way the American Standard puts it. She received them all as the gift and grant of her blessed Lord.

And thus "made ready," the Bride now enters with the Bridegroom into the palace of the Great King, where the marriage feast is spread. And there is music, festivity, and joy unspeakable. There is no cloud upon any countenance, no burden upon any soul, no sorrow in any heart, for former things are passed away; and He that sitteth upon the throne shall say, "Behold I make all things new." What other is this Wedding in the Sky than the inaugural ceremony, the introductory scene to that inheritance incorruptible, undefiled, and that fadeth not away, reserved in Heaven for all who are privileged to be there. No wonder the angel commissioned John again to write, saying, "Write, Blessed are they which are bidden to the marriage supper of the Lamb."

## Where and When Is This Wedding?

Where is the wedding to take place? That question has already been answered. It is, of course, in Glory. We are told in the Epistle to the Thessalonians that "we shall be caught up together . . . to meet the Lord in the air."

Says Paul in I Corinthians, "Behold, I show you a mystery. We shall not all sleep"—that is, we shall not all experience physical death—"but we shall all be changed"; and then in I Thessalonians he has this to say: "For this we say unto you by the word of the Lord, that we who are alive and remain unto the coming of the Lord shall in no wise precede them that have fallen asleep. For the Lord himself shall descend from heaven with a shout, with the trump of God; and the dead in Christ shall rise first. Then we who are alive and remain shall together with them be caught up in the clouds to meet the Lord in the air."

In the air, in the sky, in that "beautiful land where . . . angels sing . . ." the wedding of the Lamb and His bride and the marriage supper are to be consummated.

When will this wedding take place? At the Second Coming of Christ. Just when, of course, is not given us to know. "Of that day and hour knoweth no man, no, not the angels which are in heaven, neither the Son, but the Father." "It is not for you to know," He said to the inquiring disciples, "the times and seasons which the Father hath put in his own power."

The Father is engaged now in taking out of the nations, out of the Jews and Gentiles, "a people for his name." This body of believers is to constitute the church, the body and the bride of Christ.

Christ is not coming for His bride until that body is complete. No one knows when it will be, but Bible chronology and current signs seem to indicate that this glorious coming cannot be very far away. The next soul converted, the next individual to yield himself to Christ, may complete the necessary number, and then "look up, for your redemption draweth nigh."

There are nearly four hundred references in the New Testament alone to the Second Coming of Christ. It is mentioned throughout the Word of God more frequently and more expressly than any other one single truth. Surely this is enough to establish its importance, and any one who can read the Bible without seeing the clear and indisputable evidence of this truth certainly needs to read it again.

## All Invited

Who are the invited guests? In a sense there are to be no guests. "Whosoever will may come." The invitation to be there goes out everywhere and to everybody. The pity of it is that so many begin to make excuse and say, "I cannot come." But here is a blessed fact, namely, that everyone who accepts the invitation is made to be, not a guest but a part of the bride herself. "Blessed are they which are invited to the marriage supper of the Lamb."

What a glorious, satisfying truth is this Second Coming of the Lord with its wedding in the sky and the marriage supper that follows immediately after!

"The marriage of the Lamb has come, and his wife hath made herself ready."

There is one question yet—

## Will You Be there?

It is Christ alone, and faith in Him, crucified, resurrected, exalted to the right hand of God, and coming again to take home His Bride—it is this Christ who is the Saviour of the world, my Saviour and your Saviour, if you will have it so.

*"Neither is there salvation in any other; for there is none other name under heaven, given among men, whereby we must be saved."*

The invitation to "the marriage of the Lamb" has gone out. Have you accepted it? Will you accept it now?

## *Afterwards*

Light after darkness, gain after loss,
Strength after weakness, crown after cross;
Sweet after bitter, hope after fears,
Home after wandering, praise after tears.

Sheaves after sowing, sun after rain,
Sight after mystery, peace after pain;
Joy after sorrow, calm after blast,
Rest after weariness, sweet rest at last.

Near after distant, gleam after gloom,
Love after loneliness, life after tomb;
After long agony, rapture of bliss—
Right was the pathway leading to this.

Frances R. Havergal

JOHN WILBUR CHAPMAN
1859-1918

# ABOUT THE MAN:

Though J. Wilbur Chapman was not converted until years later, at the age of four he was often seen standing on his chair for a pulpit, acting out the role of preacher. A Presbyterian, he had great success in four pastorates, but is best remembered as a powerful evangelist. Greatly influenced for Christ as a young man by a godly mother and a spiritual father, he was led to accept Christ by his Sunday school teacher and later found absolute assurance that he was a child of God through the personal counseling of Dwight L. Moody.

Why was he such a success as a pastor and leader? "His unusual power with men, his never-failing friendliness, his positive and comprehensive preaching, his extraordinary genius for organization, and the unprecedented results of his manifold labors," are the reasons given by his biographer, Mr. Ford Ottman. Mr. Ottman reports, "He made fluent use of an adequate vocabulary, and it was said his full, round and firm voice, when rising to a climax, developed a depth and power comparable to thunder at a distance; yet it had a musical tenderness, a pathos almost like tears, a throb, a tremolo-stop, as in the grand organ, perfectly adapted to the wonderful expression of God's symphony, of God's love and grace and sufficiency." Through his teaching, preaching, and greatly used Bible conferences, he influenced thousands of Christians to have a deeper, more effective devotion to Christ and the Bible. He won many thousands to the Lord in his evangelistic meetings.

Though he had an unusual sense of humor, he seldom joked; yet he trained an excitable, vehement seeker of souls to carry on after he was gone—a young baseball player named Billy Sunday. No two men were ever more different in their methods; no two ever agreed more completely on their message.

# IX.

# *"And the Twelve Gates Were Twelve Pearls"—Rev. 21:12*

### J. WILBUR CHAPMAN

When Lafayette last visited this country, the people gave him a royal reception. A fleet of vessels went out to meet him; the band played, "Hail to the Chief," and the national music of France; and it is told that he was unmoved.

As he came ashore, land and water trembled with the power of artillery. Old soldiers saluted him as they shouted his welcome; yet he was still unmoved. With waving banners and under triumphal arches, he was taken to Castle Garden, where most of the great men of the nation were gathered together to give him greeting; yet he was still not moved. But when he had taken his seat in the great amphitheater, and when the curtain was lifted, he saw before him a perfect representation of the place in France where he was born and brought up; and when he saw the old home so filled with the tender memories, the home where his father and mother had lived and died, it is said that the great man was touched and bowing his face in his hands, wept like a child.

If I could only draw aside the veil which separates the seen from the unseen so that you could behold that city which hath foundations, there would be no need for me to preach, for in the very thought of Heaven you would be almost overwhelmed.

I have read descriptions of cities both in ancient and modern times, but never such a description as this: adorned like a bride for her husband; a city in which there is neither sickness nor sorrow, death nor crying; a city of walls and gates; on the east three gates, on the west three gates, on the south three gates, on the north three gates; and the walls had twelve foundations, and in them the names of the twelve apostles of the Lamb.

The angel that made the revelation had a golden rod in his hand with which he was measuring the city, and found that the length was equal to the breadth, and that the wall was 144 cubits; that the building of the wall was of jasper; that the city was pure gold, and that the twelve gates were twelve pearls. It is said that they were wide open by day— there is no night there; and in that city there was no need of the sun, for the glory of the Lord did lighten it, and the Lamb was the light thereof.

It comes to me like an inspiration that one day I shall enter that City. Can you say it? Your children are going in; your parents are going in; your husband is going in; your wife is going in; are you going in? It is a great joy to know that the things that bring us the representations of Heaven are so substantial.

Some people tell us that Heaven is *a state,* not *a place.* What then did Christ mean when He said, "I go to prepare *a place* for you," and what again when He said, "In my Father's house are many mansions"? What is the doctrine of the resurrection? Is it that only the spirits of men are raised? This is not our teaching. There must be some place for the resurrected body. When Christ went out with His apostles to Bethany and a cloud received Him out of their sight, He arose bodily from their presence. It is certain, absolutely certain, that Heaven is a place.

Perhaps some may question, at first, the meaning of the text; and yet I am very sure if we only had the mind of the Spirit, we would find in it much of beauty, sweetness and power.

When the army of Galerius sacked the camp and routed the Persians, one of the soldiers found a bag of shining leather filled with pearls. He preserved the bag because of its brightness and threw away the jewels, ignorant of their almost priceless value. In many cases, passages of Scripture are treated in the same way. There is something for us all in the fact that the twelve gates were twelve pearls.

## What Is Heaven?

It is *a place of overpowering brightness.* Everything that ever came from thence tells us so. Chariots so bright that the only thing to which they could be likened was fire. Angels with faces shining so that men must veil their eyes before them. Moses and Elias so surrounded with glory that the three disciples were overcome with the vision on the Mount of Transfiguration.

The walls are like a great jewel, the streets of pure gold, and every single gate a pearl. You know the brightness of one little gem as it sparkles on your finger; but, oh, the wonderful thought that every gate is a pearl; and the day will come when we may go sweeping through the gates if we will! God has done everything that He could do, and our entering in now rests upon ourselves. But the brightness of Heaven, aside from the presence of Christ, is not due to the gates, nor to the walls, nor to the streets, but to the presence of those who have been redeemed.

I have been told that the deeper the water, the larger the pearl. Whether that be true or not, I cannot tell; but I know that from the greatest depths God sometimes takes His brightest jewels. It is no cause for discouragement if you have been a great sinner. Paul was a persecutor, Bunyan a blasphemer, Newton a libertine, yet they shine today as the jewels of Christ.

Geologists tell us that the diamond is only crystallized carbon, charcoal glorified. This Book tells us something better than that, that "though your sins be as scarlet, they shall be as white as snow; though they be red like crimson, they shall be as wool."

Heaven is *a place of unutterable sweetness*. Can you imagine the number of little children there? Can anyone describe the sweetness of a child's song? And when you remember that your own little one may be there! What wonderful singing it is as their lips are touched by the finger of Christ, and their hearts are thrilled with His presence.

> **Oh, the joys that are there mortal eye hath not seen,**
> **Oh, the songs they sing there with hosannas between,**
> **Oh, the thrice blessed song of the Lamb and of Moses,**
> **Oh, the white tents of peace where the rapt soul reposes,**
> **Oh, the waters so still and the pastures so green,**
> **There, there they sing songs with hosannas between!**

The boy who was blind makes the best expression of Heaven to me. The doctor had cut away the obstruction from his eyes, and the bandages placed there were removed one by one until after a little they had been all taken off. When he opened his eyes in silent wonder as if a new world had been opened to him, he beheld his mother, and yet he did not know that it was she. Finally he heard her familiar voice asking him, "My son, can you see?" He sprang into her arms, exclaiming, "O Mother, is this Heaven?"

That is the best definition. Heaven is seeing eye to eye, knowing even as we are known. If there is one word which better than another will describe Heaven to me, it is an *explanation*.

> **"What is Heaven?" I asked a little child,**
> **"All joy"; and in her innocence she smiled.**

I asked the aged, with her care oppressed
All suffering o'er, "Oh, Heaven at last is rest."

I asked the artist who adored his art—
"Heaven is all beauty," spoke his raptured heart.

I asked the poet with his soul of fire,
"'Tis glory," and he struck his lyre.

I asked the Christian waiting his release,
A halo 'round him, low he answered, "Peace."

So all may look with hopeful eyes above,
'Tis beauty, glory, joy, rest, peace and love.

## A City of Gates

There is something significant in the fact that *Heaven is a city of gates.* The idea must be that there is some special way to get in. We cannot live just as we please and at the last enter Heaven; we might if it were not enclosed. The Bible tells us that we may come in from the north, the south, the east and west; but we are obliged to pass through the gates, and it is not always easy. "Straight is the gate and narrow is the way"; one might be liable to miss it. "Strive to enter in," says the Bible; so one must be very earnest. Christ said, "I am the way, the truth, and the life"; "I am the door"; and again, "No man cometh unto the Father, but by me."

Some people think that God is so merciful that after awhile they may stand in His presence; but He is just as well as merciful, and He has provided the way by which everyone must enter Heaven. It is through the gate. Reformation will not do; morality cannot answer; it is giving up yourself to Him, putting your hand in His and trusting Him to lead you all the journey of life, until you pass through the gates.

A child dying said to his father, "I wouldn't be afraid to go if Mamma would go with me." "But," he said, "little one, she can't go." Then the child said, "I want you to go," and he said, "My darling, I can't go." Then when the child had prayed to Him who had promised to walk through the valley of the shadow, after a little while he said, "I am not afraid now, for Christ has said that He will be with me, and He will."

Lift up your heads, O, ye gates, lift them up, for the time is coming when with Jesus we shall pass through!

## Gates of Pearl

I am sure that there is some meaning in the fact that *the gates are* of pearl. Do you know the history of pearls? Humanly speaking, it is a history of suffering. When discovered, it is at the risk of the pearl fisher's life. It is said that pearls are formed by the intrusion of some foreign substance between the mantel of the mollusk and its shell. This is a source of irritation, suffering and pain; and a substance is thrown around about that which is intruded to prevent suffering; and thus the pearl is formed.

Do you begin to see the significance of the fact that the gates are of pearl and not of gold? There was a time when there was no entrance into Heaven for us; sin had closed it; man had grievously sinned; he had broken every law of God, and there was no hope for him at all. Then it was that the Babe was cradled in the manger, became a youth, grew to manhood, endured thirty-three years of suffering, culminating in the agony upon Calvary, when in the tremendous tension His heart broke. Then it was He died, the Just for the unjust, the Innocent for the guilty; then it was that He arose from the dead, went out into Bethany, ascended into Heaven to swing wide open the gates. And thus it is they are open today; and one never hears of the gates of pearl but he must realize in some measure what salvation cost, not so much to you and to me, but to Him—humiliation, sorrow, suffering, death; and do you realize that everyone who refuses allegiance to Him is arrayed against Him, for He said, "You are either for Me or against Me; there is no middle ground"?

## Twelve Gates

How full the Word of God is! In its teaching, beauty and sweetness come from it with every touch. It is a rock; you cannot touch it but the water of life will come forth; it is a flower; you cannot come near it without being blessed by its fragrance.

There is something to me even in the number of Heaven's gates. The twelve gates were twelve pearls, three on every side; and the city lieth foursquare. Is this not an indication that *God has made abundant provision for our entrance into the city above?* It is man who has narrowed down the way. The Bible invitation is, "Whosoever will, let him come." The provision is abundant. No one can stand at the judgment and say anything but this, "Lord, I might have entered, but I would not." Twelve gates, and if you are not in it, it is your fault alone. God has done all that He could do. The Trinity has been exhausted, almost, on a sinful world; and He will do no more; it is for us ourselves to choose to enter in; it is very easy to be saved.

In one of the schools of a great city, by the falling of a transom a cry of fire was started. The children were panic-stricken and the teachers as well. In rushing from the building many were injured; some were killed. When it was found that the alarm was false, returning to her room, one of the teachers found sitting at her desk a young girl who had not stirred. When asked the reason for her braveness, she said, "My father is a fireman, and he told me if ever there was an alarm of fire in the building just to sit still where I was, and he would save me. My father is a fireman, and he knows, and I just trusted him." That confidence in Jesus Christ would bring salvation.

Said a man in Glasgow to a distinguished evangelist, "I am very anxious to be saved; what must I do?" The evangelist quoted many passages of Scripture to him, among them John 3:16: "For God so loved the world, that he gave his only begotten Son, that whosoever believeth in him": and when he had gone this far the man stopped him, saying, "But I do believe." Then the evangelist quoted chapter 6 of John and verse 47, Christ's own words: "Verily, verily, I say unto you, He that believeth on me hath everlasting life." The man saw it in a moment and cried out rejoicing, "I have got it! I have got it!"

That kind of acceptance of God brings everlasting life. Twelve gates, and every gate a pearl, and every gate exactly alike, so after all there is only one way.

## The Gates Are Open

I am so glad that *the gates are open today*. We read that they shall not be shut at all by day; and as there is no night there, the conclusion is that they are open constantly. They are open now. Some have been going in since we have been speaking; at every tick of the clock a soul speeds away.

I wish that I might go as did Alexander Cruden, seventy years of age, giving to the world his concordance, dying in want because he had given so freely to others. Going into his room they found him kneeling, his face buried in the Bible, his white hair falling down upon the chair, his spirit gone, the very angels filling the room where he had been.

I wish that I might go as did David Livingstone. They looked into his tent door and said one to another, "Keep silence; the great leader is in prayer," for he was on his knees. After a little while they came back, and he seemed to be still praying; then half an hour later again, and when they touched him they found that Livingstone was dead. The chariots of God had halted while he prayed, and Livingstone, entering in, was caught up into the skies. Oh, the joy of such an entrance into Heaven!

Dr. Pierre, returning to France from India after a long journey, said that his men, when they came in sight of their native land, were unfitted for duty. Some of them wistfully gazed upon the land they loved. Some of them shouted; some prayed; some fainted. It is said that when they came near enough to recognize their friends on shore that every man left his post of duty, and it was necessary for help to come from off the land before the vessel could be anchored in the harbor.

Oh! the joy of thus entering Heaven! Welcome from the gates, welcome from our friends long gone, welcome from every angel in the skies. The joy, the joy of one day sweeping through the gates!

## Heaven

Since o'er Thy footstool, here below,
   Such radiant gems are strewn,
O! what magnificence must glow,
   My God, about Thy throne!
So brilliant here those drops of light—
There the full ocean rolls, how bright!

If night's blue curtain of the sky,
   With thousand stars enwrought,
Hung like a royal canopy,
   With glittering diamonds fraught—
Be, Lord, Thy temple's outer veil,
What splendor at the shrine must dwell.

The dazzling sun at noontide hour,
   Forth from his flaming vase,
Flinging o'er earth the golden shower,
   Till vale and mountain blaze—
But shows, O Lord! one beam of Thine:
What, then, the day where Thou dost shine?

Ah! how shall these dim eyes endure
   That noon of living rays?
Or how my spirit, so impure,
   Upon Thy glory gaze!
Anoint, O Lord, anoint my sight,
And robe me for that world of light.

                                        W. A. Muhlenberg

LEE ROBERSON
1909-

## ABOUT THE MAN:

When one considers the far-reaching ministries of the Highland Park Baptist Church and pauses to reflect upon its total outreach, he has cause to believe that it is close to the New Testament pattern.

In the more than forty-one years—from 1942 when Roberson first came to Highland Park until his retirement in April 1983—the ministry expanded to include Camp Joy, reaching some 3,000 children annually; World Wide Faith Missions, contributing to the support of over 350 missionaries; 50 branch churches in the greater Chattanooga area; Union Gospel Mission, which feeds and sleeps an average of 50 transient men daily; a Sunday school bus ministry, which covers 45 bus routes; a deaf ministry; "Gospel Dynamite," a live broadcast held daily over 2 radio stations, now in its 44th year; a church paper, THE EVANGELIST, being mailed free twice monthly to over 73,000 readers; and Tennessee Temple University, Temple Baptist Theological Seminary, and Tennessee Temple Academy.

He is an author of many books.

Preaching to thousands, training preachers, supporting the mission cause, Dr. John R. Rice called him the Spurgeon of our generation.

# X.

# *Heaven Is Looking On*

## LEE ROBERSON

*"Wherefore seeing we also are compassed about with so great a cloud of witnesses, let us lay aside every weight, and the sin which doth so easily beset us, and let us run with patience the race that is set before us, Looking unto Jesus the author and finisher of our faith; who for the joy that was set before him endured the cross, despising the shame, and is set down at the right hand of the throne of God."*—Heb. 12:1,2.

As we read these verses, our imaginations paint for us a mighty picture of the ancient Roman amphitheatre. Rows and rows of seats in ascending stairs surround the arena. In that day when gladiators fought the wild beasts, the cheering thousands would fill every seat. Into the arena would come men selected for their bravery. At a given signal, doors under the stand were opened; and out would dash hungry and ferocious beasts. It was then the business of the gladiator to kill or be killed. The crowds would cheer the brave and hiss the coward.

Now Paul tells us that the Christian fights in such an arena. He is surrounded by a great throng of witnesses. Against him come the tigers and lions of sin. Every Christian is drawn into the battle. But he does not fight alone, for a great crowd of witnesses looks down to encourage, inspire and spur him on.

Let us consider our text. Let us gather from this study the elements of faith and courage to help us to victorious living.

## I. THE WATCHED

*"Wherefore seeing we also are compassed about . . . ."*

"We" refers to all living children of God. We are being watched. We—poor sinners, saved by grace. Even though we have nothing whereof we can boast, we must recognize that we are being watched. By birth we become the recipients of Adam's nature. We were sinners, dead in trespasses and sin. By the new birth we became the recipients of Christ's nature. We are now the children of the living God. Still we are only sinners saved by grace.

> **Naught have I gotten, but what I received,**
> **Grace hath bestowed it since I have believed;**
> **Boasting excluded, pride I abase,**
> **I'm only a sinner, saved by grace.**
>
> **Once I was foolish, and sin ruled my heart,**
> **Causing my footsteps from God to depart;**
> **Jesus hath found me, happy my case,**
> **I now am a sinner, saved by grace.**

We are beset by Satan on every hand. Think not for a moment that salvation makes one immune from the tempter. Being saved often causes Satan to redouble his efforts against you. Peter tells us:

*"Be sober, be vigilant; because your adversary the devil, as a roaring lion, walketh about, seeking whom he may devour: Whom resist stedfast in the faith, knowing that the same afflictions are accomplished in your brethren that are in the world."*—I Pet. 5:8,9.

The Devil is sending all his forces against a Christian. You cannot pray unless you battle Satan. You will not be able to read your Bible unless you war against the evil one. You will not engage in soul winning unless you confront and overcome his obstacles. You cannot even go to church without being beset by this roaring lion.

The Devil is on every hand. He fights viciously and ferociously. He abides by no rules. He is trying to kill your influence and destroy your effectiveness.

We—the watched ones—are encircled by an unfriendly world. A few times in my life the Devil has deceived me into believing that this world is my friend. When I received such an idea, I was willing to compromise with the world and worldly interests. But let us not forget for a single moment that this world is against the Christian. It despises God and the Christian way of life. Do not be ensnared by the world's tricks. Cut yourself loose from it. Avoid all doubtful things as you would avoid a room full of rattlesnakes.

Poor sinners, saved by grace, beset by Satan, and encircled by an unfriendly world, are being watched. Paul said, "We are made a spectacle unto the world, and to angels and to men."

## II. THE WATCHERS

*"Wherefore seeing we also are compassed about with so great a cloud of witnesses . . . ."*

We can easily see that this Scripture refers to Hebrews 11. This chapter lists heroes of faith. By faith they were saved; by faith they conquered their enemies; by faith they obtained the victory. These now watch as we battle sin and Satan.

The Christian is in the arena. The battle is on. The stands are full of witnesses.

In one portion of the stands we find an assembly of angels. They are striving to give us their friendly encouragement as we battle the wild beasts of sin. As we look we can recognize many of the angels mentioned in the Bible.

There is the one whom God placed at the entrance of the Garden of Eden after Adam and Eve lost the Garden through sin.

There is the angel who prepared a meal for Elijah when he got under the juniper tree. Twice the angel of the Lord touched him and said, "Arise, and eat."

We can see now the angel who appeared unto Joseph in a dream and told him about the Child Mary was to bear. The angel even gave Joseph the name of the Holy Child—"And thou shalt call his name Jesus, for he shall save his people from their sins."

There is also the angel who came to Mary and announced to her the great thing which was to happen.

We also see the angel of the Lord who announced to the shepherds the birth of Jesus.

Still again, in this assembly of angels, we see the one who appeared unto Jesus from Heaven when He was agonizing in the garden.

We see, too, the angels who announced the resurrection of Jesus to the women on the first day of the week. They are clad in their shining garments, even as on the day they frightened the sorrowing women.

We see, too, the angels who said at the ascension of Jesus, "Ye men of Galilee, why stand ye gazing up into heaven? this same Jesus, which is taken up from you into heaven, shall so come in like manner as ye have seen him go into heaven" (Acts 1:11).

Look again into the stands and you will see the angel of the Lord who delivered Peter when Herod cast him into prison.

Yes, the Bible is full of the account of ministering angels. In the great crowd of witnesses are these holy ones.

Second, we find in the stands a glorious assembly of prophets and apostles. We see Elijah and Elisha, Ezra and Nehemiah, Isaiah and Jeremiah. There are Daniel and Jonah, and we must not forget the patriarchs and great men. We can name only a few: Noah, Abraham, Isaac, Jacob, Joseph, Moses and King David.

Near the patriarchs and prophets we find the apostles. Here James and John are still together. Matthew, the tax-collector who left all to follow Jesus, is present. There is Thomas who had his doubts settled when he viewed the body of the resurrected Christ. Along with the apostles is Paul who met Jesus on the Damascus road. Paul is shouting to us, "Thanks be unto God which giveth us the victory through our Lord Jesus Christ!"

Let your eyes move around to another portion of the gallery, to the great host of Christian martyrs. We see the faces of men and women who were hunted down by the forces of evil and burned at the stake. Here are those who were cast into Roman arenas and torn to bits by ferocious, wild beasts. Here are Christians who were soaked in oil by Nero and ignited so that the king's garden might be illumined. Yes, we see the men of the Plebean Legion, that legion which died to a man rather than deny the Lord Jesus. There is John Huss, burned at the stake because of his bold preaching of the Gospel.

The gallery also has its crowd of great witnesses of more recent years—Martin Luther and John Knox; John and Charles Wesley; George Whitefield and Charles Finney; D. L. Moody and Charles Haddon Spurgeon; David Livingstone and David Brainerd; Adoniram Judson and William Carey. All send their strong, encouraging shouts unto us. They are watching us today.

Listen a moment. From another part of the stands we hear sweet singing. Yes, here we have assembled those singers and composers of sacred songs of the ages. David, the sweet singer of Israel, has moved over to this crowd to lend his voice and his talent for praising God.

Charles Wesley, the brother of John, begins a song of his own composition,

**Oh, for a thousand tongues to sing,**
**My great Redeemer's praise;**
**The glories of my God and King,**
**The triumphs of His grace.**

> He breaks the power of cancelled sin,
> He sets the prisoner free;
> His blood can make the foulest clean;
> His blood availed for me.

Here now the voice of John Newton:

> How sweet the name of Jesus sounds
> In a believer's ear.
> It soothes his sorrows, heals his wounds,
> And drives away his fear.

We must not forget that Isaac Watts is in this assembly of singers. It was he who wrote,

> When I survey the wondrous cross,
> On which the Prince of Glory died;
> My richest gain I count but loss,
> And pour contempt on all my pride.

He also gave us:

> Alas, and did my Saviour bleed,
> And did my sovereign die;
> Would He devote that sacred head,
> For such a worm as I?

And then we find also the more recent writers of gospel songs who now abide in Heaven's Glory—Fanny Crosby who gave to the world such noble songs as "Jesus, Keep Me Near the Cross"; "Blessed Assurance, Jesus Is Mine"; "Safe in the Arms of Jesus"; and thousands of others.

We have not yet finished. The gallery is still full of witnesses we have not yet named. The loved ones who fought to the end and finished the course now cheer us from the stands of Glory. Your mother and your father who died in Christ are watching you. Mothers and dads, your children who have gone on are now observing your battle down here below.

Yes, there are many watchers. We are encircled by so great a cloud of witnesses.

### III. OUR THREEFOLD RESPONSE TO THEIR WATCHING EYES

Why do the faithful ones mentioned in Hebrews 11 watch us? Is it to criticize? Certainly not. They have but one reason, and that is to encourage and cheer us on to victory.

And now, notice our text which tells us what to do in order to run a successful race and wage a successful battle.

1. Let us lay aside every weight and every sin. Nine out of ten Christians fail to be victorious because of the weights and sin of the world. Some of you are carrying sinful weights and worldly burdens. You have formed entangling alliances with the enemy. You belong to organizations which are a constant hindrance to your best spiritual interests. You need to take the sharp knife of separation and cut yourself loose from all of the Devil's entanglements. The watchers in the gallery of Heaven will never see a victorious life on your part if you do not lay aside every weight and sin. Face the issue squarely. What is it that is so hindering you? Be honest with God, and have the courage to drop out of every organization or situation.

2. Let us run with patience the race that is set before us. The Christian life is not resting—it is racing. We are not campers—we are journeying on. We are not simply to sing, "Oh, land of rest, for thee I sigh," but we are to complete the song—"We'll work till Jesus comes." All Christians are participants in this race, but how poorly do many of them run!

Begin now to seek a place of service. Commit yourself to a life of activity for Christ. This is surely the will of God and the way to happiness.

3. Let us look unto Jesus, "the author and finisher of our faith." Every eye in Heaven is fixed on the precious Lamb of God. The watchers in the gallery, ever looking to Him, encourage us to do likewise.

Christ is our strength. In vain do we look to the things of this world to help us in the race of life. Instead of friends, we find enemies of righteousness. The arena of life is full of destructive foes. But there is One who can help us, even Christ. When we are weak, He is strong. If we will but look unto Him, we can be overcomers. He pours His power into us.

Christ is our inspiration. There are times when discouragement lays hold upon us. Some of you men have fought temptations until you are weary of fighting. You become discouraged and almost succumb to the tempter. But if you will look to Jesus, He will inspire you to keep on fighting and never lose heart.

Look unto Jesus now, dear friend. He knows your need and will surely come to your aid. He does not force Himself upon anyone. Your coming to Him must be voluntary. His strength and inspiring presence will not be forced upon you; but the very minute you recognize your need and look unto Him, He will help you.

Impetuous Simon Peter desired to walk upon the water. As long as he looked unto Jesus, he stayed on top; but when he saw the winds and the waves dashing high, he began to sink. Then he cried, "Lord, save me."

Christ might well have turned His back upon Peter. He could have said, "Simon Peter, it was your own request to walk upon the water. If you refuse to look unto Me, then I will let you sink." But our Christ is ever ready to hear the cry of needy ones. When in sincerity we look to Him and cry for help, He is ready to give it.

Yes, Christ is our inspiration in sorrow, in heartache, in failure, in times of discouragement. If we but look unto Him, He will help us.

There is never any disappointment in looking to Jesus. People and things may disappoint us, but Christ is sufficient for every need. He satisfies every hungering heart.

Not only is He a giver of strength and inspiration, but He is our Intercessor. Our text tells us to look unto Jesus who endured the cross, despised the shame, and is set down at the right hand of the throne of God. Christ is interceding for you and me right now. Furthermore, His intercession is always successful.

Quite often a lawyer intercedes for a person before the courts, but fails to release him. This is not true of our Christ. He is the successful Intercessor. Our souls are safe and secure in His keeping, for He successfully makes intercession for us.

God help us to lay aside the sin and weights of life. God help us to run the race with patience. God help us to look unto Jesus. Let this be our threefold response to the watchful eyes of God and Christ, and to the cloud of witnesses surrounding the arena of life.

What is the shout of every onlooker in Heaven? "Be thou faithful unto death." God is saying it. Christ is saying it. The patriarchs and prophets plead for it. The kings and great men who died in Christ call for it. The martyrs beseech you. The great world of Christians implore you. Your mother and father and loved ones and friends who are now in God's presence beg you to be faithful unto death.

## Full Satisfaction

Not here! not here! Not where the sparkling waters
    Fade into mocking sands as we draw near,
Where in the wilderness each footstep falters—
    "I shall be satisfied!"—but oh, not here!

Not here—where all the dreams of bliss deceive us,
    Where the worn spirit never gains its goal,
Where, haunted ever by the thoughts that grieve us,
    Across us floods of bitter memory roll.

There is a land where every pulse is thrilling
    With rapture earth's sojourners may not know,
Where Heaven's repose the weary heart is stilling,
    And peacefully life's time-tossed currents flow.

Far out of sight, while sorrows still enfold us,
    Lies the fair country where our hearts abide,
And of its bliss is nought more wondrous told us
    Than these few words, "I shall be satisfied."

"I shall be satisfied!" The spirit's yearning
    For sweet companionship with kindred minds—
The silent love that here meets no returning—
    The inspiration which no language finds.

Shall they be satisfied? The soul's vague longing—
    The aching void which nothing earthly fills?
Oh, what desires upoin my heart are thronging,
    As I look upward to the heavenly hills!

Thither my weak and weary steps are tending—
    Saviour and Lord! with Thy frail child abide!
Guide me toward Home, where, all my wanderings ending,
    I shall see Thee, "and shall be satisfied!"

                                        Anonymous

# XI.

# Will We Know Each Other in Heaven?

## LEE ROBERSON

*"But now he is dead, wherefore should I fast? can I bring him back again? I shall go to him, but he shall not return to me."* —II Sam. 12:23.

In Greenwood Cemetery, on the edge of our city, is our baby's grave. On the grave is a marker, and on the marker this verse—II Samuel 12:23. It tells me that we shall see our loved ones in Heaven and know them.

The story of David does not have to be repeated in detail at this time. A son was born to Bath-sheba and to him. Because of David's sin in taking Uriah's wife, Nathan prophesied the death of the child.

The child became ill. David prayed to God and fasted. He lay upon the earth in humility. The elders went to him to raise him up from the ground, but he refused. He also refused all food.

This continued for seven days. On the seventh day the child died. The servants were afraid to bring the message to the king. They reasoned that if he took the illness of the child so hard, how would he take the death of the child?

David heard the whispers of his servants. He knew they were talking about his son. He asked, "Is the child dead?" And they answered, "He is dead."

When David received this news, he did that which seemed strange to his servants. He arose from the earth, washed himself, changed his clothing, and came into the house of the Lord and worshiped. After worshiping Him, he went to his own house and asked that they set food before him.

His servants were amazed. They said, "What thing is this that thou hast done? thou didst fast and weep for the child, while it was alive; but when the child was dead, thou didst rise and eat bread."

David's answer is one that we should study carefully:

*"While the child was yet alive, I fasted and wept: for I said, Who can tell whether God will be gracious to me, that the child may live? But now he is dead, wherefore should I fast? can I bring him back again? I shall go to him, but he shall not return to me."*

In these words David gave his assurance of life after death and that in the future life he would recognize his son.

The scene on the Mount of Transfiguration also tells us that there is recognition beyond this life. Jesus went to the mount and took with Him three disciples. He was transfigured before them, and there appeared unto them Moses and Elijah talking with Him. Moses represented the law; Elijah, the prophets. Elijah, you remember, was taken up in a chariot of fire. He was translated. He did not die. Moses died upon Nebo and was buried, but his body was never found. These two came down to talk with Jesus.

We will notice that the disciples recognized Moses and Elijah. They had not known them upon the earth, but they knew them now. This indicates to us a glorious prospect of Heaven, that we will know not only the ones we know now face to face, but our knowledge will be so great that we will know others who have lived before us. Yes, we shall know each other in Heaven.

In Luke 16 we have the story of the rich man and Lazarus. It deals with Hell, but it teaches also recognition beyond the grave. The rich man knew the beggar who was laid daily at his gate. When death came to both, he still knew him and saw him in the bosom of Abraham. The story assures us of recognition beyond the grave.

The Apostle Paul surely indicates recognition beyond the grave when he wrote to the people in Thessalonica,

*"For what is our hope, or joy, or crown of rejoicing? Are not even ye in the presence of our Lord Jesus Christ at his coming? For ye are our glory and joy."*—I Thess. 2:19,20.

Doubtless other portions of the Word will establish the fact of recognition beyond the grave, but I believe that these are sufficient.

Why should we discuss this subject? The answer: So that Heaven might become to us more real and precious. Even though we try in every way to describe Heaven, we fail. It is more beautiful than our best description.

The story is told of a little blind girl who only knew the beauties of this earth from the lips of her mother. It is said that a noted surgeon worked upon her eyes. At last his operations were successful. As the last bandage dropped away, and the little girl could see, she flew into her mother's arms, then to the window and to the door. As the glories of the earth rolled into her vision, she ran screaming back to her mother, "O Mamma! Why didn't you tell me it was so beautiful?"

The mother, wiping away tears of joy, said, "My child, I tried to tell you, but I couldn't."

One day when we come into Heaven, we will be asking, "Why didn't someone tell us that it was so beautiful?" All of the writers of the Scripture will say, "We tried to tell you, but it was impossible." Yes, it is hard to talk about Heaven. It is so big, so beautiful that it goes beyond the best description that our words can form or fashion.

But allow me to say a few things about it.

## Heaven Is Real

Yes, Heaven is a real place, just as real as any country or city. Christ said, "I go to prepare a place for you." If Christ said He went to a place, then it is sure that He went to a definite place.

Heaven is a prepared place. Jesus said so, and that establishes the complete truth of it. Heavenly mansions are being made ready for us by the Lord Jesus.

## Heaven Is a Home

Home brings to our hearts the sweetest and tenderest memories and thoughts.

Heaven is our home. Hell is not. Hell is the prison of the damned. Eternal Hell has no marks of home. It is a place of suffering forever and ever.

But where is our home? Is it here upon this earth? No, the Word of God describes us as pilgrims just passing through on our way to the Home prepared for us by the Lord Jesus.

As we think of our Heavenly Home, perhaps we should give consideration to the question, "Will the circle be unbroken?" A broken and divided home is a tragedy here in this life, but it is infinitely more a tragedy in Heaven. The tragedy is that some member of your family might not make the Heavenly Home. I am not endeavoring to reconcile for your minds the thought that a broken circle in Heaven would bring sorrow. I am going to leave all of that in the hands of God. But I do want to know, is your family complete in Jesus? Are your loved ones saved and ready for Heaven?

So many never have a home upon this earth. Such an one was our Lord Jesus, who had not where to lay His head. But, friend, put your faith in Christ, and Heaven will be your Home.

## Heaven Is Love

John endeavors to give us a description of Heaven in the last chapters of the Revelation. He speaks of the size of the City of God, the gates of the city, the pearls, the jewels, the golden streets. But someone has said in the entire list one gem is not mentioned—the gem of love.

Heaven is love. All hatred, animosity, jealousy and strife will be done away. Heaven will bring us together with our loved ones, and love will flow like a river.

Dr. T. DeWitt Talmage was once asked by a woman who had just buried a Christian daughter, "Dr. Talmage, do you really think that I shall ever again look into her face and recognize her?" He answered, "What do you think of Heaven? Is Heaven a subtraction, or is it an addition? Are we to be bigger fools in Heaven than we are on earth? Do you think we will know less in Heaven than we know here? All that is beautiful will be magnified in the growing beauty of the years. But she will be yours—in memory and in knowledge."

Heaven is an addition, not a subtraction. The love that we have sustained one for the other here will remain in Heaven, only increased and purified by the power of God.

## Heaven Is Jesus

The question is often asked, "Where is Heaven?" One of the simplest answers to give is this: Heaven is where Christ is. This answer is not foolish because the Word tells us that when we are absent from the body we are present with the Lord. Wherever Heaven might be located in God's universe, of this we can be sure—it is where our Lord is.

I wonder if the realization of seeing Christ face to face ever really grips very many people. As you sing of the Lord, as you hear His name preached and mentioned again and again, are you conscious that one day you are going to see Him? That is, if you are a child of God, you are going to see the Christ who was nailed to a cross for you. The prints will still be in His hands and feet; the scars will be seen upon His brow. We should sing with a new fervor every day,

**Jesus, Jesus, Jesus,**
**Sweetest name I know,**
**Fills my every longing,**
**Keeps me singing as I go.**

## Heaven Is Eternal

Any home that we build here will rot and decay. Its age is limited. But Heaven is eternal.

Most of you have read of the unusual house in the Santa Clara Valley in California which stands in the midst of a great orchard and is said to be the largest house in the world. It was built or started in the 1890's by a Mrs. Winchester. At first it was only a pleasing country home of ordinary dimensions, but through the years it was altered, changed and added to until it covered a space of fourteen acres. Adding apartment after apartment, room after room, the owner became obsessed with the idea of building statelier mansions. Today the house is a curious and amazing labyrinth of winding stairways, intricate passages, and hundreds of windows. If one were left in an inside room, he would have difficulty finding his way out.

It is said that as the owner worked upon the house, she became obsessed with the idea that the longer she built and added, the longer she would live. But at last death found its way through the strange rooms and strange stairways, to the single room where the owner lay. She left her house. No longer can she add to or enjoy it.

So it is with everything upon this earth. Whether it is a mansion on a hill or a shanty in the slums, the home is only temporary. But Heaven is our eternal abiding place.

What happens to the cities of the world? They are built and destroyed. Nineveh and Babylon are gone; some cities in Asia and Egypt are destroyed, but Heaven is a city whose Builder and Maker is God and its foundations shall never crumble.

Can we put it all together in one sentence? Perhaps so. Heaven is a real place, the saints' home, where love and Christ abide, which the eternal ages shall never change.

It is an old story, repeated many times by Dr. Biederwolf, but a good illustration of Heaven, home, and our loved ones.

Over in one of our eastern cities was an engineer who had been on the road for a good many years. He was one day addressing a crowd of men, among whom were a good many railroad men. In closing his address, he said,

> Men, I can't begin to tell you what Jesus has meant to me. Years ago, every night when I would finish my run, I would pull the whistle and let out a blast just as we came around a curve, then I would look up to a small hill where stood a little white cottage. An old man and an old woman would be standing in the doorway. I would lean out of the cab window and we would wave at each other. And as my engine would shoot into a tunnel, the couple would turn and go back inside, and she would say to him, "Thank God, Bennie is safe home tonight!"
>
> But at last the day came when we took and laid Mother away. Then each night as I came around the curve and blew the whistle, the little old man would be at the door. I would wave to him and he would wave to me. Then as my train shot through the tunnel, he would turn and go slowly into the cottage saying, "Thank God, Bennie is safe home tonight!"
>
> But, by and by, the time came when we carried Father out, too. Now, when I finish my run, although I pull the whistle and let out a blast, there are no dear ones to welcome me home. But when my work on earth is done, when the last run has been made and I have pulled the throttle and the whistle for the last time, as I draw near to Heaven's gate, I know I shall see that same little old couple waiting there for me. And as I go sweeping through the gate, I will see my dear old mother turn to my dear old father and hear her say, "Thank God, Bennie is safe home at last!"

Heaven is a place of reunion. Are you ready to meet God? Do you know the way to Heaven? Is there someone waiting for you on the other side? Then receive Christ as your Saviour now. He is "the way, the truth, and the life; no man cometh unto the Father but by him."

(From the book, DEATH . . . AND AFTER? by Dr. Lee Roberson.)

JOHN R. RICE
1895-1980

# ABOUT THE MAN:

Preacher . . . evangelist . . . revivalist . . .editor . . .counsellor to thousands . . .friend to millions—that was Dr. John R. Rice, whose accomplishments were nothing short of miraculous. Known as "America's Dean of Evangelists," Dr. Rice made a mighty impact upon the nation's religious life for some sixty years, in great citywide campaigns and in Sword of the Lord Conferences.

At age nine, after hearing a sermon on "The Prodigal Son," John went forward to claim Christ as Saviour. In 1916, with only $9.25 in his pocket, he rode off on his cowpony toward Decatur Baptist College. He was now on the road to becoming a world-renowned evangelist, although he was then totally unaware of God's will for his life.

There was many a twist and turn before Rice rode through the open door into full-time preaching—the army, marriage, graduate work, more seminary, assistant pastor, pastor—then FINALLY, where God planned to use him most—in full-time evangelism.

Dr. Rice and his ministry were always colorful (born in Cooke County, in Texas, December 11, 1895, and often called "Will Rogers of the Pulpit" because of their likeness and mannerisms)—and controversial. CONTROVERSIAL—and correctly so—because of his intense stand against modernism and infidelity and his fight for the Fundamentals.

Dr. Rice lived and died a man of convictions—intense convictions. But, like many other strong fighters for the Faith, Rice was also marked with a sincere spirit of compassion. Those who knew him best knew a man who loved them. In preaching, in prayer, and in personal life, Rice wept over sinners and with saints. But there is more . . .

Less than seventy-one hours before the dawning of 1981, one of the most prolific pens in all Christendom was stilled. Dr. John R. Rice left behind a legacy in writing of more than 200 titles, with a combined circulation of over 61 million copies. And through October of 1981, a total of 24,058 precious souls reported trusting Christ through his ministries, not counting those saved in his crusades nor in foreign countries where his literature has been translated.

And who but God knows the influence of THE SWORD OF THE LORD magazine which he started and edited for forty-six years!

And while "Twentieth Century's Mightiest Pen"—and man—has been stilled, thank God, the fruit remains! Though dead, he continues to speak.

## XII.

# Heavenly Rest for the People of God

JOHN R. RICE

*"There remaineth therefore a rest to the people of God."* —Heb. 4:9.

"Rest" —heavenly rest—is mentioned nine times in the first verses of Hebrews 4. See what blessed promises are given concerning the heavenly rest of a Christian.

*Let us therefore fear, lest, a promise being left us of entering into his rest, any of you should seem to come short of it.*

*For unto us was the gospel preached, as well as unto them: but the word preached did not profit them, not being mixed with faith in them that heard it.*

*For we which have believed do enter into rest, as he said, As I have sworn in my wrath, if they shall enter into my rest: although the works were finished from the foundation of the world.*

*For he spake in a certain place of the seventh day on this wise, And God did rest the seventh day from all his works.*

*And in this place again, If they shall enter into my rest.*

*Seeing therefore it remaineth that some must enter therein, and they to whom it was first preached entered not in because of unbelief:*

*Again, he limiteth a certain day, saying in David, To day, after so long a time; as it is said, To day if ye will hear his voice, harden not your hearts.*

*For if Jesus had given them rest, then would he not afterward have spoken of another day.*

*There remaineth therefore a rest to the people of God.*

*For he that is entered into his rest, he also hath ceased from his own works, as God did from his.*

*Let us labour therefore to enter into that rest, lest any man fall after the same example of unbelief.*

*For the word of God is quick, and powerful, and sharper than any twoedged sword, piercing even to the dividing asunder of soul and spirit, and of the joints and marrow, and is a discerner of the thoughts and intents of the heart.*

*Neither is there any creature that is not manifest in his sight: but all things are naked and opened unto the eyes of him with whom we have to do.*

*Seeing then that we have a great high priest, that is passed into the heavens, Jesus the Son of God, let us hold fast our profession.*

*For we have not an high priest which cannot be touched with the feeling of our infirmities; but was in all points tempted like as we are, yet without sin.*

*Let us therefore come boldly unto the throne of grace, that we may obtain mercy, and find grace to help in time of need.*

In the preceding chapter, solemn warning is given from the Holy Ghost.

*"To day if ye will hear his voice, Harden not your hearts, as in the provocation, in the day of temptation in the wilderness . . . . Wherefore I was grieved with that generation, and said, They do alway err in their heart; and they have not known my ways. So I sware in my wrath, They shall not enter into my rest."—vss. 7-11.*

What happened to the children of Israel in the wilderness is a solemn warning to us, for "these things happened unto them for ensamples: and they are written for our admonition, upon whom the ends of the world are come" (I Cor. 10:11). Israelites coming out of Egypt picture new converts saying goodby to the old wicked world. The passover lamb, with its blood on the door, pictured salvation. Crossing the Red Sea and hemmed in by waters and covered completely by clouds, which made a living grave, pictured baptism.

The trials and troubles of their wilderness pilgrimage pictured the things that beset a Christian in his journey toward Heaven.

Canaan, the land flowing with milk and honey, the land of the grapes of Eshcol, the roses of Sharon, the cedars of Lebanon, a goodly land, was a symbol of Heaven.

Our fathers thought of Heaven in these terms:

**O land of rest, for thee I sigh;**
**When will the moment come**
**When I shall lay my armor by,**
**And dwell in peace at home?**

How sad that many fail to enter in by hardening their hearts in unbelief. We are warned, "Take heed, brethren, lest there be in any of you an evil heart of unbelief, in departing from the living God," and then Hebrews 3:18 and 19 says:

*"And to whom sware he that they should not enter into his rest, but to them that believed not? So we see that they could not enter in because of unbelief."*

People miss Heaven by unbelief just like the Jews missed Canaan and wandered forty years in the wilderness until their carcasses fell and their bones bleached outside the land of promise. So our chapter begins with exhortation that we ought fearfully and earnestly to make sure of our salvation so we can "enter into his rest."

The seventh-day Sabbath of the Jews was clearly a type of the eternal rest of a Christian. Under ceremonial law Jews were commanded to work six days. Six is man's number, the highest and best that man can do. The number of the Antichrist will be 666 (Rev. 13:18). The great image built by Nebuchadnezzar of Babylon was six cubits wide and sixty cubits high (Dan. 3:1). If a man lives perfectly all his life he has earned his Heaven.

Before one tries to keep the Jewish Sabbath on Saturday, let him remember that the legal, ceremonial Sabbath pictures salvation by works. Those who never sinned would deserve Heaven, but we know, like Peter, that "neither our fathers nor we were able to bear" such a law (Acts 15:10). And the weakness of sinful flesh made the law a failure.

We will never enter into a heavenly Sabbath of rest if first we must obey the commandment all our life, "Six days shalt thou labour, and do ALL thy work." For this reason New Testament Christians are commanded not to be judged by the ceremonial Sabbath which was nailed to the cross of Christ with the other ceremonial laws (Col. 2:14-17). Instead of the Sabbath under law we now have the Lord's day, an entirely different day which we observe voluntarily and not by commandment. We have sweet rest on the first day of the week before we do any work at all, and this pictures salvation by grace. Saved without works, we then try to please God because we are already saved.

Verse 4 mentions the rest of God on the seventh day after He had finished creation (Gen. 2:2). And verse 5 says some can enter into this rest of God while others miss it. God's rest, then, after making the heavens and the earth, is a type of the salvation which He offers to His creatures.

Have you, dear reader, entered into the sweet rest of God?

Let us see the wealth of meaning here. When God made man in His own image, He formed him out of the dust of the earth and breathed into his nostrils the breath of life so that man became a living soul. So Adam is called, in a peculiar sense, "the son of God" (Luke 3:38). He was created perfect and holy. God saw that all He had made was good, so He rested, content in His finished work.

But in the salvation of a soul, God makes a new creation. The Spirit of God breathes on a soul; and the soul is born again, made a new creature in Christ. He becomes a partaker of the divine nature.

That is as much a miracle as when God breathed into Adam's nostrils, and he became a living soul. The conversion and regeneration of a sinner, making him from a child of wrath into a child of God, is a creative act of God's grace. It is all of grace and none of works. "For by grace are ye saved through faith; and that not of yourselves: it is the gift of God: Not of works, lest any man should boast" (Eph. 2:8,9). God wrought the first mighty creation, then rested.

On the cross, Jesus paid the infinite, terrible price for man's redemption to make possible a new creation of sinners; then He cried, "It is finished." Later He ascended to Heaven and sat down at the right hand of God, having completed all the work necessary for the redemption of the whole world!

The Father rested after the physical creation and after making man in His own image. The Son, then, rests on the right hand of the Father, having finished His work of redemption which makes possible new creatures in Christ out of *every* poor sinner who trusts Him. Those of us who trust in Him enter into the sweet rest of God!

### The Rest That Remaineth

"There remaineth therefore a rest to the people of God." Rest! How sweet it is to the tired and weary! It is rest that Jesus promised to those who are weary and heavy laden—"Come unto me, all ye that labour and are heavy laden, and I will give you rest," and, "Ye shall find rest unto your souls."

I stand many times beside a coffin and speak what words of comfort

I can and urge those left to be ready to meet this beloved one. Through these years many is the time I have seen a simple silver plate on the coffin with these words, AT REST. How true for the Christian! It is written,

*"And I heard a voice from heaven saying unto me, Write, Blessed are the dead which die in the Lord from henceforth: Yea, saith the Spirit, that they may rest from their labours; and their works do follow them."* —Rev. 14:13.

REST! That is the blessed state of those who die in the Lord.

My mother was part of the generation that knew what toil was, such as very few modern women know. She did the family wash most of her life on a rub-board. Her water was carried from the well or spring. She sewed for the family with the treadle sewing machine. She prepared her own lard, made her own soap, dried and preserved her own fruit. I can only remember a few weeks when she ever lived in a home with running water or had an electric light. Proudly my father made the washing machine that she was to work arduously by hand.

She had five babies and how she loved each one! But some way life was too hard, so laying down her tired head, she joyfully had us promise to meet her in Heaven, then went to be with Jesus.

My heart exults as I think of Mother in the Father's house of many mansions resting from her labors. And her works do follow her! She prayed that her son would be a preacher; yea, I verily believe she had a bargain with God; and I, all unsuspecting, am an unworthy party to a holy covenant entered into by both God and Mother. "Yea, saith the Spirit, that they may rest from their labours; and their works do follow them." Praise God, there remaineth a rest for the people of God!

Hearts are tired everywhere—tired of work, tired of worry, tired of fear, tired of pain, tired of poverty, tired of disappointment. It is refreshing that God calls the death of a Christian "sleep," knowing that even our poor, worn-out, decaying bodies will rise from the grave at the Saviour's coming not only refreshed but glorified, new like that of Jesus. But while the body lies down for its sleep, the soul joyfully enters into God's rest. Joyous, conscious, alert, thrilling but peaceful rest!

The other day as I closed a funeral service someone sang Sarah Doudney's song:

**Sleep on, beloved, sleep on and take thy rest;**
**Lay down thy head upon thy Saviour's breast;**

**We love thee well, but Jesus loves thee best –**
**Good night! Good Night! Good night!**

Happy, conscious, entering into the joy of the Lord, those who sleep in Jesus rest from their labors.

Dr. George W. Truett told how he visited a poor widow in Dallas years ago. Her face was sad and her fingers pinpricked. This seamstress was earning a pitiful living for herself and fatherless children. The talk turned to Heaven, and Dr. Truett said, "My sister, what does Heaven mean to you?"

The tears started to her eyes as she laid down her worn fingers in her lap and said, "Pastor, Heaven means rest! I won't have to work in Heaven."

*"There remaineth therefore a rest to the people of God"!*

The aged Apostle Paul toiled on long after he would rather have gone to Heaven. He had written, "To die is gain" (Phil. 1:21). He was in a strait betwixt two things, whether to depart and be with Christ which was far better, he said, or to remain for the benefit of others (Phil. 1:23,24).

He toiled on. There were scars on his body from the stoning at Lystra. There must have been the long seamy marks of claws where he fought the lions at Ephesus. Perhaps his joints were stiffened and pained by the twinges gotten from his shipwreck and exposure. Surely his aged eyes were nearly blind and had been for years. Finally God whispered to him so Paul could triumphantly write:

*"For I am now ready to be offered, and the time of my departure is at hand. I have fought a good fight, I have finished my course, I have kept the faith: Henceforth there is laid up for me a crown of righteousness, which the Lord, the righteous judge, shall give me at that day: and not to me only, but unto all them also that love his appearing."* —II Tim. 4:6-8.

And through it all, there is no sadness in Paul's goodby but rather grand relief, the sweetest anticipation! Paul looked forward to the encircling arms of Christ and His happy words, "Well done, thou good and faithful servant: thou hast been faithful over a few things, I will make thee ruler over many things: enter thou into the joy of thy lord" (Matt. 25:21), then rest, sweet REST. No wonder he could say, "If in this life only we have hope in Christ, we are of all men most miserable." Paul looked forward to the rest that remains to the people of God.

How sweet the toil if there is rest to follow! How can I ever forget some of the scenes that impress themselves on youth's memory. The tired, sweat-whitened teams came in from the field in utter weariness; but who does not remember that joyful rolling in the dirt; deep, long, satisfying drinks at the trough; then the eager scramble for their feed! How good it felt to be home at night in our plain little house with such simple comforts and rest!

I can remember well how, after riding after cattle or horses eight, ten or twelve hours in West Texas, I would urge my weary beast along until we headed toward home. Then his ears would pick up; his fox-trot would quicken; and the nearer home we came, the more eager was his pace!

Rest! How sweet it is! Thank God, the toils of the ministry—and they are not easy—will be laid aside, for "there remaineth therefore a rest to the people of God."

As they draw near the borderline, many saints seem to quicken their pace. Their tired faces become glad, and happy anticipation becomes theirs as they draw near the rest! Many have told me, "I am just waiting for my summons; I am ready to go," or "I'll be so glad when Jesus comes and I can see my loved ones again."

We sing a little chorus:

> **I'll be so glad when day is done;**
> **I'll be so glad when victory's won.**
> **There'll be no sorrow**
> **In God's tomorrow;**
> **I'll be so glad when Jesus comes.**

I keep thinking of the gladness in my mother's face before she went to be with God. How happy she was! She asked my cousin, "Georgia, will you play and sing for me?" Cousin Georgia answered, "What shall I sing, Aunt Sadie?" She answered back, "Sing

> **How firm a foundation, ye saints of the Lord,**
> **Is laid for your faith in His excellent Word!**
> **What more can He say than to you He hath said,**
> **To you, who for refuge to Jesus have fled?"**

Cousin Georgia played and, brokenly, tried to sing it. And on that firm foundation Mother happily approached her "promised land," saying, "I can see Jesus and my baby now," as she fell asleep.

Let us rejoice that God has prepared for us a rest in a mansion in the Father's house. We will lay down all toil and sorrow, will say our last goodby forever to sin, death and the curse of our mortality!

## Resting Our Way to Heaven

However, verse 10 of chapter 4 tells us that we can enter into this blessed rest of God here and now. God has a rest that remains for us, waits for us, but, blessed thought that we can partly enter into that rest now. This verse says, "For he that is entered into his rest, he also hath ceased from his own works, as God did from his."

The Christian "is entered into his rest." The child of God can rest now, spiritually, just like God rested from His labor on the seventh day when He finished the creation. I have not finished my work, but salvation is finished for me, and I can enter into that sweet rest.

It is this rest that the Saviour promises in Matthew 11:28-30:

*"Come unto me, all ye that labour and are heavy laden, and I will give you rest. Take my yoke upon you, and learn of me; for I am meek and lowly in heart: and ye shall find rest unto your souls. For my yoke is easy, and my burden is light."*

Soul rest, sweet heart rest, can be yours today, troubled, weary, sin-sick sinner. And you, dear Christian, if you have not completely entered this rest promised while yet on earth, I want to help you to "let go and let God."

How shall I enter into this rest? The way is plain. If I am to rest like God did after creation, if I am to enter now a sweet Sabbath of heart, then I must cease *from my own works* and depend upon the finished work of Christ, "For he that is entered into his rest, he also hath ceased from his own works, as God did from his." Jesus finished His work, then we are told:

*"But this man, after he had offered one sacrifice for sins for ever, sat down on the right hand of God; From henceforth expecting till his enemies be made his footstool. For by one offering he hath perfected for ever them that are sanctified."*—Heb. 10:12-14.

Jesus sat down at the right hand of God. By one sacrifice He has finished His work. Now He confidently rests in the assurance that the Father is satisfied with the work which He has done. He rests in sweet assurance, confidently expecting the kingdom which His Father will give Him on this earth at the complete triumph over Satan.

And when He finished His own work, He finished ours! Jesus has my salvation in charge. The Father committed it to Him, and I commit it to Him. If Jesus has sat down, then I may safely sit down and rest. Yea, I have sat down and am now resting my way to Heaven. I am going to Heaven sitting down!

Let others, if they will, make their boast, "I am determined to go through with Jesus." I am not getting to Heaven by determination, nor by the works I do or plan to do. I am going to Heaven because I have "ceased from my own works" as God did from His. About salvation, I have simply taken hands off. I have no more to do with it. Jesus did it and sat down; and I, too, have sat down, and in my heart I have entered into rest.

Others talk about expecting to get there if they hold out faithful, but I am depending on no such frail and slender hope. Rather,

> My hope is built on nothing less
> Than Jesus' blood and righteousness;
> I dare not trust the sweetest frame,
> But wholly lean on Jesus' name.
>
> On Christ, the solid Rock, I stand;
> All other ground is sinking sand,
> All other ground is sinking sand.
>
> His oath, His covenant, His blood,
> Support me in the whelming flood;
> When all around my soul gives way,
> He then is all my hope and stay.

Dear reader, if you have not entered into sweet rest about your soul's salvation, there is but one way. The only way to enter into rest is to cease from your own works. That means, do not depend upon them. You will never have peace in your good works. You will never have peace in resolutions, reformation, or in anything else that you have done or can do.

A Christian should want to work out his salvation to others, to let his light shine so that others may glorify his Father which is in Heaven; but as far as his soul's salvation is concerned, he should sit down, once for all, on the finished work of Christ and there rest. "For he that hath entered into rest hath ceased from his own works as God did from his."

Rest, sweet rest, is found in Jesus alone. His work satisfies the Father as the basis for our salvation, and it ought to satisfy us. If Jesus Himself could say on the cross, "It is finished," then sit down at the right hand of the Father when He ascended on High, you and I, too, may safely sit down, and so ceasing from our own works, with no dependence in the world upon them, enter into the rest of God.

### "Let Us Hasten Therefore to Enter Into That Rest"

Since there is sweet rest for those who simply sit down on the finished work of Christ, then, dear reader, I beg of you to enter into that rest at once. Verse 11 says, "Let us labour therefore to enter into that rest, lest any man fall after the same example of unbelief."

The American Standard Version has, "Let us give diligence," instead of, "Let us labour," as the King James Version has it. A much clearer translation is, "Let us hasten therefore to enter into that rest." The Greek word is often translated "hasten" making the meaning clearer. We are not to labor for rest, but to hasten into the rest which is free.

The Jews in the wilderness missed their opportunity, and, because of unbelief, did not enter into the rest of the promised land. When they saw the wrath of God at Kadesh-Barnea, then belatedly they said, "We will go"; but it was then too late. They were condemned to wander in the wilderness until their carcasses would fall, and only their children could enter into the sweet rest which could have been theirs.

Many a man intends to be saved, but he intends to be saved tomorrow, and tomorrow never comes. He intends to be saved sometime; but his heart gets no more tender with waiting, his mind no clearer, his will grows no firmer. The contrary is true. His heart and mind and will harden against God, and so he is never saved. Therefore the Scripture says, "Let us hasten therefore to enter into that rest." Today, look to Jesus, trust in Him and be saved at once. Let Heaven come into your heart.

God clearly sees the innermost recesses of your soul. Sins are not hidden from His sight. The Word of God is sharper than any two-edged sword and "is a discerner of the thoughts and intents of the heart." God knows all about you. Excuses will not do. Nothing is hidden from Him. Only the wickedness of an unregenerate, Christ-rejecting, sin-enslaved heart would cause one to postpone salvation. He knows. Verse 13 says, "Neither is there any creature that is not manifest in his sight: but all things are naked and opened unto the eyes of him with whom we have to do."

Make haste, dear brother; turn from your sins to trust in Jesus. Cease from your own works and enter into sweet rest.

### Hold Fast Your Profession

One's courage must often fail if he rests in his own work. How often every Christian feels condemned for his weakness. Surely any Christian with clear spiritual insight must see that he has nothing to boast of, nothing to depend on in his own life and works. But since it is all in Jesus Christ, in His work, His sacrifice, His unfailing love, His unquestioned righteousness, then safely we may rest. "Seeing then that we have a great high priest, that is passed into the heavens, Jesus the Son of God, let us hold fast our profession" (vs. 14).

Here is my boast and I will maintain it: My sins are forgiven. I have entered into rest by ceasing from my own works. I will hold fast my profession. I have a great High Priest who has entered into the heavens. He sits at the right hand of God. "He ever liveth to make intercession" for us according to the will of God. "If any man sin we have an advocate with the Father, Jesus Christ the righteous." "He is our peace who hath made both one, and hath broken down the middle wall of partition between us, having abolished in his flesh the enmity."

Through Christ I am reconciled to God and have entered into peace. Therein I rejoice, yea, and will rejoice; and to every reader, I urge, hold fast your profession. Let your dependence be on Christ alone and in His finished work.

Our infirmities, our weakness, our sins are many. The consciousness of our guilt grieves our hearts. But for the amazing grace of God manifested in Jesus Christ, there would be for us only utter despair. But He knows, and verses 15 and 16 say:

*"For we have not an high priest which cannot be touched with the feeling of our infirmities; but was in all points tempted like as we are, yet without sin. Let us therefore come boldly unto the throne of grace, that we may obtain mercy, and find grace to help in time of need."*

Jesus feels and is touched by feeling the weight of our infirmities since He was tempted in all points like as we are, yet without sin. No one else ever loved sinners like Jesus, and no one else ever understood them as well. The compassionate heart of the Saviour knows all our sins.

He knew the broken heart of David and inspired him to write the fifty-first Psalm. He knew when Peter turned away and wept bitterly after denying his Lord. He knew the weakness of Samson on the lap of Delilah, and yet again heard his prayer.

He can be touched with the feeling of our infirmities. In this sweet thought there is infinite peace and rest, and in this a Christian can find boldness—boldness to pray, boldness to rest unafraid on the promises of God.

Whoever needs such a Saviour, let him come boldly. Whoever has such a Saviour and needs anything else, let him come boldly. At His throne of grace we may obtain mercy for every sin and grace to help in every time of need.

ADONIRAM JUDSON GORDON
1836-1895

# ABOUT THE MAN:

Adoniram Judson Gordon was born in New Hampshire in 1836 to devout Christian parents. At about age fifteen he was saved. One year later he expressed his desire to prepare for the ministry.

In 1856 he attended Brown University, and in 1860 entered Newton Theological Seminary. Upon graduation in 1863 he accepted a pastorate at Jamaica Plain, near Boston. After six very successful years there, he went to pastor Clarendon Street Baptist Church in Boston, which was in a very sluggish spiritual condition.

In 1877 Moody and Sankey reached Boston. Moody's Tabernacle stood across the street from Clarendon Street Church. When Moody, as Henry Drummond said, "laid one hand on America and one on Britain, and moved them toward God," he more than moved Gordon and his church.

Dr. Gordon remained there for more than a quarter of a century, seeing the church completely transformed into one of the most spiritual and aggressive in America.

Dr. Gordon's Spirit-filled life and deeply spiritual books have had a powerful influence throughout the land. He was a prominent leader and speaker at D. L. Moody's Northfield Conventions.

In his book, *Ministry of the Spirit,* Dr. Gordon presents the work of the Holy Spirit in a threefold aspect: Sealing, Filling, Anointing. He was also a firm believer in the premillennial coming of Christ.

On the morning of February 2, 1895, Dr. Gordon, with "victory" as the last clearly audible word on his lips, fell asleep in Jesus.

# XIII.

# The "No Mores" of Revelation

## A. J. GORDON

You will observe how the happiness of our glorified state is described entirely by negative terms—no curse, no pain, no death, etc. Thus God tells us what the eternal glory shall **not** be, rather than what it shall be. Does not the photographer use a negative with which to take your picture? The principle is precisely the same. The negatives are used in order to show us the positive. We know what suffering and pain and death are: show us their opposites and we shall have the best possible idea of the perfect state. These negatives are given us in seven terms:

1. No more sea (Rev. 21:1).
2. No more sorrow (Rev. 21:4).
3. No more crying (Rev. 21:4).
4. No more pain (Rev. 21:4).
5. No more curse (Rev. 22:3).
6. No more night (Rev. 22:5).
7. No more death (Rev. 21:4).

**No more sea!** How did Christ describe the present disturbed and troubled state of things in His sermon on the last things? He speaks of wars and persecutions and distress, and then adds: "**The sea and the waves roaring;** men's hearts failing them for fear, and for looking after those things which are coming on the earth." Twice our Lord came to His disciples on the sea: once He calmed the waves and once He calmed their hearts. The latter is what He does now. He gives to His people peace *in* conflict, but not yet peace *from* conflict. "In the world ye shall have tribulation," He says, "but in me ye shall have peace."

During this whole present order of things there will be tumult and disorder and strife. "The wicked are like the troubled sea, when it cannot rest, whose waters cast up mire and dirt." In the midst of all this storm and upheaval it is possible for us so to sink into Christ, that we have calmness and quietness of spirit, so that "the peace of God, which passeth all understanding, shall keep [our] hearts and minds through Christ Jesus." Christ calms the heart now, but only when He comes in glory will He calm the sea. Then stretching His nail-pierced hands over the great deeps of the world's sorrows He will say, "Peace, be still," and all the waves will be hushed into silence: all turbulence silenced, all strife ended, and only that peace which is like a river, flowing forth from the City of God, to all earth's weary nations.

**No more sorrow!** We take no melancholy view of things but we believe that a perfectly candid estimate compels the conviction that the sum of human misery in this world vastly outweighs the sum of human happiness. Job gave in a few words the inspired estimate of human life: "Man that is born of a woman is of few days, and full of trouble." Those whose outward lot is most fortunate confess that they are haunted by a strange melancholy at times, a kind of homesickness as though somehow they had wandered away from their father's house.

How the Psalmist expresses this: "O that I had wings like a dove! for then would I fly away, and be at rest"; but as the dove sent forth from Noah's ark found no rest for the soles of its feet, so with the restless human spirit. It may change the scene, but it escapes not the sorrow. There is no place where it can build its nest, where storm cannot reach and the tempest shake. "Who are these that fly as a cloud, and as the doves to their windows?" asks the prophet. It is the Homegoing of God's saved. The windows of the New Jerusalem are at last open: man's long lost home in Paradise is restored to him. He hears a word uttered that was never spoken since Adam was thrust forth from Paradise, **"There shall be no more sorrow."**

**No more crying!** Tears are the outward emblem of sorrow, and now God has wiped away all tears from the eyes of them that mourn. And there shall be "no more crying." Do you know of any promise anywhere like that? We hear people talk about the blessed release of death; but the death that gives you release opens a fountain of sorrow in the hearts of those whom you leave behind that years cannot close; so that triumph for the departing means fresh tears for those who remain behind. "Put thou my tears into thy bottle," prays David. We have read that in ancient graves in the East they have found phials laid away with the dead—supposed to be those in which their mourning friends gathered their tears from the departed and treasured them up.

Whether the fact is literally true or not, it is symbolically true. From the time of the first death in the human family, there are few out of the myriads who have died who have not some person to mourn for them. A phial of tears has been put into every grave. Tell me, can you conceive of any statement so expressive of the infinite triumph of peace and blessedness as this: "And there shall be no more crying"?

**No more pain!** It is a pathetic fact, that just in proportion as we advance in refinement and culture, we become more and more susceptible of pain. The more perfectly the nerves are tuned, the more sensitive are they to discord, so that the difference between a saint and a savage is as the difference between a cremona violin and an Indian tom-tom. The latter, because it is discord itself, knows no discord; and so the savage has only a dull apprehension of the highest pain. But let the soul be tuned by the hand of God, and how sensitive it becomes to the suffering of our great humanity—how it thrills with pain at the anguish of the world! Therefore, instead of the Gospel lifting us *above* pain, it only brings us into accord with it. God must change the world, then, before He can blot out pain. And this He will do—wipe out the last vestige of sin and woe; then and then only will He wipe the tears from all faces.

**No more curse!** The earth, the man and the woman, this trinity of sufferers from the fall, lifted up into final and inseparable fellowship with God.

**No night.** "They that sleep, sleep in the night; and they that be drunken are drunken in the night." "Them also which sleep in Jesus will God bring with him" when He comes. The cemetery, the sleeping place, will be untenanted of all the saints when Jesus comes. Weeping endured for the night, but now it is morning, and joy cometh in the morning. No more night because . . .

**No more death.** All hope, all deliverance, all victory is contained in that word. We speak now of Christians dying a triumphant death. But such language is true only in a figure. It can be really true only when the trumpet shall sound and the dead shall be raised incorruptible. Now, when one dies, life is swallowed up in defeat. Now, death is the last ending; then will come our glorious Friend who shall pluck us out of his power. Not patient submission to the grave; not the disembodied state or the unclothed spirit is our supreme attainment. We wait the time when death itself shall die, and the grave shall be forever buried.

## God's City Fair

There is a river, the streams whereof
  Make glad God's City fair.
And trees of life all its banks adorn
  And fruit, each month, they bear.
Their leaves do heal all the pains and ills,
  There in God's City rare.

Ivory palaces, jasper walls,
  Pearl gates and streets of gold,
All gleaming bright in the light of God,
  And mansions, we are told
Prepared by Jesus for all His own
  In this Home of the soul.

Never a pain, nor a sigh nor tear
  But our God wipes away.
No death, no parting, no sad goodbys,
  For all things new are made.
And Christ, Beloved, Redeemer, King
  With us will be always.

Jesus is calling to all, Repent!
  Calling in mercy sweet,
Still off'ring all everlasting life,
  In Heaven loved ones greet.
A new heart yours and a Home above,
  And ev'ry need He'll meet.

Precious the blood that Heaven's door opens.
  Great is the Saviour who pardons our sin.
Sweet is the Gospel that offers redemption,
  Marvelous Grace that will take sinners in!

                                John R. Rice

# XIV.

# Heaven — How to Go There

## G. BEAUCHAMP VICK

The most stupendous thought that can occupy the mind of man is Heaven and how to go there. God has not left us to grope our uncertain way through a dark, starless night, with no light for our pathway and no guide for our faltering footsteps. We can shout with the sweet singer of Israel, "Thy word is a lamp unto my feet, and a light unto my path."

Yes, the Bible has much to say concerning Heaven and life after death. In fact, the Word of God was written to show us how to go to Heaven. How true, then, are the inspired words, "If in this life only we have hope in Christ, we are of all men most miserable" (most to be pitied).

In spite of that, most men are living in the opening words of that sentence—"In this life only." They plan for *this* life *only*. They work for *this life only*. They prepare for *this life only*. Oh, how true are the words of our Lord, "For what is a man profited, if he gain the whole world, and lose his own soul? or what shall a man give in exchange for his soul?" Therefore, my friend, you are making a foolish bargain if you have prepared for "this life only."

The only certain thing about this life is death. "The boast of heraldry, the pomp of power, all that beauty, all that wealth ere gave awaits alike the inevitable hour; the paths of glory lead but to the grave."

Sometimes when we have to stand beside the open grave over the earthly remains of one who is the dearest and the nearest of all earthly companions to us, we cover that mound with a blanket of flowers and water those flowers with our tears. Sometimes in our loneliness our hearts re-echo the words of the Lord Jesus as He hung upon the cross, "My God, my God, why?"

Does Jesus care when my heart is pained
Too deeply for mirth or song;
As the burdens press, and the cares distress,
And the way grows weary and long?

Does Jesus care when my way is dark
With a nameless dread and fear?
As the daylight fades into deep night shades,
Does He care enough to be near?

Does Jesus care when I've tried and failed
To resist some temptation strong;
When for my deep grief I find no relief,
Though my tears flow all the night long?

Does Jesus care when I've said goodby
To the dearest on earth to me,
When my sad heart aches 'til it nearly breaks —
Is it aught to Him? Does He see?

Oh, yes, He cares; I know He cares,
His heart is touched with my grief;
When the days are weary, the long nights dreary,
I know my Saviour cares.

Yes, my friends, we do have a Saviour who cares. "For we have not an high priest which cannot be touched with the feeling of our infirmities; but was in all points tempted like as we are, yet without sin." The Lord Jesus Christ, when He was here, was called the "man of sorrows, and acquainted with grief." He has drained to the bitterest dregs the cup of every human sorrow, suffering and woe. Therefore, He is able to help us when all human help is in vain.

## There Is a Heaven

Yes, there is a Heaven. The Bible says so, and all laws of logic demand it. Have you ever stopped to think that there is no instinct in animals, nor intuition given to man by the Creator that does not respond to a fact?

Who taught the newborn kitten, even before its eyes are open, to seek nourishment at its mother's breast? God the Creator placed that instinct in the kitten, and that instinct responds to a fact. It is a fact that nourishment has there been provided.

Who taught the birds to fly south in the autumn, then to return north in the spring? The Creator has given them an instinct—a response to a fact. Cold weather is coming; and they cannot endure the rigors of the northern winters, therefore must seek a warmer clime.

So God has also given man certain intuitions and desires, and everyone responds to a fact. God has given me eyes to see light; He has created light for the eyes. God has given me ears to hear sound; He has created sound for the ears. God has created me with a hunger; He has provided food to satisfy that hunger. He has created me with thirst; that thirst responds to fact, for He has created water to satisfy my thirst.

But deeper than any instinct in animal or intuition or desire given to man, there is a deeper longing in my soul, stronger than hunger for food or desire for water; there is a longing in my soul for something better than this old world can offer—for a better life, a fairer land. This longing too responds to a fact, for God has created that better land.

> **There's a land that is fairer than day,**
> **And by faith we can see it afar;**
> **For the Father waits over the way,**
> **To prepare us a dwellingplace there.**

The Lord Jesus Christ, the Son of God, has told us about that fair land. Listen to the immortal words of our Lord as recorded in John the 14th chapter, verses 1 to 6:

*"Let not your heart be troubled: ye believe in God, believe also in me. In my Father's house are many mansions: if it were not so, I would have told you. I go to prepare a place for you. And if I go and prepare a place for you, I will come again, and receive you unto myself; that where I am, there ye may be also. And whither I go ye know, and the way ye know. Thomas saith unto him, Lord, we know not whither thou goest; and how can we know the way? Jesus saith unto him, I am the way, the truth, and the life: no man cometh unto the Father, but by me."*

My friends, let's give urgent heed to these blessed words which fell from the lips of the Son of God. Listen to the opening verse:

"Let not your heart be troubled."

## He Has the Power and Authority

Only the Son of God has the right, the power, the authority to speak such words as those to a troubled world. Only He has power to speak such words as those to hearts that are bowed in sin and in sorrow and bereavement.

You remember that in the passage immediately preceding this, the Lord Jesus had just told His disciples that before long He must needs go away; that He was facing the cross upon which He would soon die, the Just for the unjust, that He might bring us to God. He told them that He was to be betrayed by one who professed to love Him.

And naturally the disciples, when they heard that the Master they loved so dearly was now so soon to go away, were heartbroken. They felt as sheep scattered without a shepherd. It was on that occasion that the Lord spoke these words of love and comfort and sustaining grace to them. But He also spoke those words for us and for those of all coming time who would face similar experiences of sorrow and trouble. "Let not your heart be troubled."

And then the next few verses give us a number of reasons why, even in the midst of sorrow and heartbreak and goodbys, the child of God can still have an untroubled heart. And the first reason He advances is, "Ye believe in God, believe also in me." In other words, He was showing us that the only basis for an untroubled heart is an individual, personal, vital, living faith in the Lord Jesus Christ as an all-sufficient Saviour.

If today you are trying to build your hopes for salvation and eternal life upon anything else than a vital faith in the crucified, buried and risen Lord, then you are building upon a false foundation; and one of these days you will awaken to the awful truth of the Scripture which says, "There is a way which seemeth right unto a man, but the end thereof are the ways of death."

Then in verse 2 the Lord Jesus gives us another reason why the child of God may have an untroubled heart even in the midst of sorrow and bereavement. He says, "In my Father's house are many mansions: if it were not so, I would have told you."

### It Means Home

My friend, I can never read or quote that verse of Scripture without reminding myself afresh that the word "house" there means "home." "In my Father's home are many mansions: if it were not so, I would have told you." Somehow the word *home* seems to make it a little sweeter to us, a little more personal and a little more real. "In my Father's home are many mansions." When I hear the word "home," I believe there are several reasons why the Lord Jesus in His sublime omniscience selected that word to best convey to us something of the beauty, of the wonders, of the glories of the eternal abiding place of His children.

When I say *home*, your mind goes back across the years, perhaps across hundreds of miles of intervening space to that spot which will forever be hallowed in your memories among all the places of earth. That place where you grew up as a boy or a girl, playing around the yard with brothers and sisters and neighbor children, sitting around the hearthside upon a winter's evening with Mother, Dad, and others in the family. You know there are several things about that old home place which are not true about any other spot on earth as far as you are concerned.

First, home is a place where love reigns supreme. I am talking about the old-fashioned Christian home, not one of these modern homes which is just a sort of glorified roominghouse where the members of the family meet each other in the halls occasionally on the way from one busy social engagement to another. Not a place where there is confusion, bickering, fussing and fighting, where the father and mother live like mad cats and where the children are anxious to get just as far away as possible, as soon as possible. Not that sort of a home. I am talking about the old-fashioned Christian home where the father can come home at the end of a busy day and there he can sit as the uncrowned king, honored, respected and obeyed. Where he can shut the world out with its mad business competition and strife. Where the mother is respected and honored and revered as the uncrowned queen. In such a home love reigns supreme, and perhaps that is the nearest approach to Heaven that earth knows anything about.

And so Heaven itself is a place where love reigns supreme, where peace shall flow like a river.

## Heaven Is a Place of Ample Provision

Second, home is a place of ample provision and room whenever the children arrive. Perhaps my experience has been duplicated by nearly everyone here. I have sometimes been away from my old home place yonder in Louisville, Kentucky, for years at a time. Because of the stress of my work, I have been unable to turn my steps homeward.

But after those years of absence, how wonderful it was to turn back homeward for an old-fashioned family reunion! I suppose I have arrived there most every hour of the day or night. Sometimes as twilight shades would gather I have driven up in front of the old home place. There I would see Mother sitting in her accustomed familiar place on the porch, and I would go in. After greeting the members of the family, we would go into the dining room and I'd sit down again at the same old place there at the table. The intervening years would seem to slip away into nothingness. I would seem just like a boy again.

Then I have arrived at the old home place in the wee small hours of the morning—two, three, four o'clock in the morning after driving many weary miles. Yet no matter at what unearthly hour I did arrive, I would walk up on the porch, ring the doorbell; and I could never imagine Mother coming to the door, opening it just a little crack and then saying, "Son, I am sorry, but all the beds are occupied; the house is full. Your brothers, your sister, and their families have already arrived; and there is no more room. You'll have to take your family and go to the hotel or somewhere else." No, my friends, I cannot imagine such a welcome or lack of welcome as that. Nor can you from your mother or from your home.

No matter how late the hour, no matter how many had preceded us, no matter if all the rooms were full and the beds occupied, Mother would always open wide that front door and open wide her arms of love and welcome; and she would bring us in. She could always spread another cover on the living room divan or make an old-fashioned pallet on the living room floor.

And, my friends, I give you my word that after driving hundreds and hundreds of miles, as I would stretch out on that old-fashioned pallet underneath the old roof tree where I had spent so many happy days in the long ago, it seemed to me that a quiet peace would pervade my soul, that the kinks would go out of the overwrought nerves, and that I would find a sweet rest there on that old-fashioned pallet on the floor that I have never been able to find on anybody's innerspring mattress, in anybody's expensive room in the most pretentious hotels.

So home is a place where there is always room, no matter when the children arrive. And so it is with the Heavenly Home above. I care not how soon or how late I shall gather there for God's great family reunion. I am not concerned about how many of God's children shall have preceded me, for there is ample provision for His own. For the Lord Jesus said, "In my Father's home are many mansions: if it were not so, I would have told you"; and He continues by saying, "I go to prepare a place for you."

Yes, friends, Heaven is a place just as real and definite as Detroit, Michigan, or any other of the cities of the earth.

## "Where Is Heaven?"

But somebody says, "But where is Heaven?" I cannot describe to you the geographic location of that fair land. I cannot tell you the longitude or latitude of that place, nor am I greatly concerned about that. After all, that is not what makes any place dear to our hearts. That is not what endeared your old family home in your memories. Heaven is sweet to us because of those who are there. And though I cannot tell you the longitude and latitude of that city, yet I think, after all, I can tell you just a little of where Heaven is. Heaven, to the believer, to the child of God, is but one step beyond that narrow veil which separates this world from the next, time from eternity.

Heaven to the believer is just one step beyond the end of this little life's pilgrimage. Not only so, but I think I can tell you something else about where Heaven is. Heaven is a place where Jesus is, for He says, "I go to prepare a place for you. And if I go and prepare a place for you, I will come again, and receive you unto myself; that where I am, there ye may be also." Yes, my friends, it is where Jesus is, and that is enough for me. I love the words of the old song, "Where Jesus is, 'tis Heaven there."

Not only so, but Heaven is a place where all of our loved ones who have died with their faith fixed unfalteringly in Jesus Christ as the all-sufficient Saviour have preceded us and where they await us. Heaven, therefore, is a place of grand and glorious and unending reunion.

## No "Goodby"

Have you ever stopped to think that the very word "goodby" is erased from the vocabulary of Heaven? Therefore, today to any lonely heart who mourns the Homegoing of some loved one whom you have loved long since and have lost awhile, may I say that if you and I could do the unthinkable, the impossible; if today we could call back our loved ones from yonder shore, it would be the height of selfishness for us to do so after they for this little while have tasted the joys which await the people of God on the other side. After they have experienced some of the unspeakable joys of the many mansions, it would be the height of selfishness for us to want them back here to endure and to undergo the sorrows and the heartbreaks which are the common portion of all mankind upon an old earth marred by sin.

Who of us would not gladly exchange Detroit, Michigan, or any other city of earth for that city which hath foundations, whose builder and maker is God? Who of us wouldn't gladly exchange an old city like this, with its sins and temptations, its filth, its bickerings, its imperfections, its tears, for that city built by God's own hand where nothing that destroys or mars or blemishes can enter? That, my friends, is the sure portion of the child of God.

Who of us wouldn't gladly exchange an old world like this that is torn by wars and rumors of wars for that beautiful place of ineffable joy where peace shall flow like a river?

Who of us wouldn't gladly exchange bodies like these, subject to heat and to cold, to hunger and to thirst, to pain and disease, temptations, sin, weariness, death itself, for bodies over which none of these things— heat and cold and hunger and thirst, pain and weariness and sin and temptation and disease and death—shall have no power? That I say is the sure portion of the people of God.

Who of us wouldn't exchange bodies like these, where the eye grows dim with the shedding of many salty tears, where the shoulders become stooped with the bearing of the burdens of years, where the footsteps become faltering, where the face is lined with the pen of time and etched upon our countenance is the story of every sorrow which besets us? Thank God, we will one day exchange these old bodies for bodies which are fashioned anew like unto the glorified body of our resurrected Lord!

Who of us wouldn't gladly exchange the companionships of earth, companionships with people like you and me, so imperfect, so quick-tempered, so apt to speak the hasty, thoughtless word that would wound even those we love best for the companionship and the fellowship with God's heroes of the faith, for patriarchs, prophets, priests and kings, for those children of God who have borne the burdens of life, who have fought its battles and have won the incorruptible crown? That, my friends, is the sure portion of the children of God.

No wonder the Apostle Paul says, 'I find a longing in my soul to depart and be with Christ which is far better.' No wonder that the same inspired apostle says, "To die is gain."

Now notice in verse 4 the Lord Jesus continues by saying, "And whither I go ye know, and the way ye know." Then Thomas, one of the twelve, interrupted the Lord with a question.

I have always been glad for that interruption and that question. It was a perfectly natural question, and the Lord Jesus Christ did not rebuke Thomas for that interruption. He answered that question for him and for us. I say it was a perfectly natural question, for Thomas said unto Him, "Lord, we know not whither thou goest; and how can we know the way?" In substance Thomas was asking a question which I believe has been re-echoed in the heart of every normal, thinking person from that day until now. Thomas was actually saying, "Lord, can a man be sure? Can we be certain of the way from earth to Heaven? Can we know beyond all shadow of doubt?"

My friends, Jesus answered that question for him and for us. The answer was so clear and unmistakable that no man need misunderstand.

Though nineteen hundred years have elapsed since the Lord Jesus answered this question so plainly, yet so hard is the heart of man, so encrusted with materialistic philosophies of life, that it seems that man is so stupid that he cannot understand the simple words of our Lord's reply. And if today, after these nineteen hundred years, I should ask the average adult audience of educated, refined, cultured people even in so-called Christian America, "What is your conception of the way from earth to Heaven?" I am afraid that we should be amazed at the many answers, the many varied answers, and the many wrong answers we should receive.

In this day when the Gospel is just as close to any man who wants to hear it as the television or radio dial in his living room, there is no excuse for any man groping in uncertainty and not knowing the sure, unmistakable way from earth to Heaven.

## How to Get There

What is your conception of the way to Heaven? I hear some man say, "Why, I believe the way to Heaven is to live a good life, to live upon a high moral plane, to be a good father, a good husband, a good citizen in the community, to live by the Golden Rule, to do unto others as I would have them do unto me."

My friends, these are wonderful virtues which should characterize the life of every child of God, but that is NOT the way from earth to Heaven. And if today you are dependent upon your own good works, your own moral life, your own good citizenship, or your own moral rectitude, you are building your hopes upon a false foundation. That is NOT the way to Heaven.

Some other man would say, "I believe the way to Heaven is to unite with the church, to be baptized, to submit oneself to the ordinances of the church, to be regular in attendance and faithful to the church's requirements."

Well, friends, these things, too, should be prominent characteristics of every Christian life; but that is NOT the way from earth to Heaven, for neither the Temple Baptist Church of Detroit with which I am affiliated, nor any church to which you may belong, has the power to forgive a single sin or to cleanse a single stain from your guilty, Hell-deserving soul.

That is NOT the way to Heaven.

What is it? Listen, as Jesus replied to Thomas' question, "How can we know the way?" Jesus answered him, "I am the way, the truth, and the life: no man cometh unto the Father, but by me." In other words, the Lord Jesus was telling us that all we need from a spiritual standpoint in time and in eternity, in this life and in the next, as far as salvation is concerned, is found in Him. "For neither is there salvation in any other, for there is none other name under heaven given among men whereby we must be saved."

Jesus said, "I am the way"—without the way there is no going. Jesus said, "I am the truth"—without the truth there is no knowing. Jesus said, "I am the life"—without the life there is no living. All we need is found in Christ.

Therefore, the words of I John, the 5th chapter, become all meaningful to us where we read, "He that hath the Son hath life; and he that hath not the Son of God hath not life."

I care not whatever else you may have—a good reputation, a good moral character, many lovable characteristics—if you do not have the Son of God as your Saviour, you do not have eternal life.

Years ago at the court of an oriental monarch one day there was much hurry and activity and bustle. The court jester, whose duty it was to while away the dull hours of the king with his witticisms, was sitting over on one side of the courtroom watching and listening as the king would issue his instructions and courtiers and servants would rush to do his bidding.

In a lull in the activity the court jester spoke up: "O king, why all this hurry and activity and confusion? Why are you going to such pains to issue these minute, detailed instructions?"

The king answered rather impatiently, "I thought you knew that on the morrow we begin a long journey of several days' duration. It lies across the burning sands of the desert. Therefore, every necessity of life must be thought of and provided in advance and carried with us. Food, water, clothing, bedding, shelter, tenting—everything must be provided, else this journey would be a very unpleasant one, even a very dangerous one."

The court jester nodded as he said, "Wisely said, O king, and certainly wisely done to thus prepare for this long journey of a few days. But now, O king, by your leave, one other question: There is another journey, Sir, upon which everyone of us must embark. It is the journey from this world to the next, from time out into eternity. Now this question, O king. Have you given any thought, any time, any attention to make sure that this journey, too, may be a pleasant and safe journey for you?"

The king dropped his head; and when he could control his emotions looked up, brushed a tear from his eye and said, "I suppose the court jester must have more sense than the king upon the throne, for I find that I have been so busy seeking pleasure where it may be found, so busy with business, the affairs of state, that I have given absolutely no thought, no attention to the proper preparation of that long, long journey from whence there is no return."

My friends, that is what the Lord Jesus Christ was talking about when He said, "For what is a man profited, if he gain the whole world, and lose his own soul? or what shall a man give in exchange for his soul?"

**When all the great plants of our cities,**
    **Have turned out their last finished work;**
**When our merchants have made the last bargain,**
    **And dismissed the last tired clerk;**
**When our banks have raked in the last dollar,**
    **And have paid out the last dividend;**
**When the Judge of the Earth says,**
    **"Closed for the Night!"**
**And asks for a balance—WHAT THEN?**

**When the choir has sung its last anthem,**
    **And the preacher has said his last prayer;**
**When the people have heard their last sermon,**
    **And the sound has died out on the air;**
**When the Bible lies closed on the pulpit,**
    **And the pews are all empty of men;**
**When each one stands facing his record,**
    **And the Great Book is opened—WHAT THEN?**

**When the actors have played their last drama,**
    **And the mimic has made his last fun;**

When the movies have flashed the last picture,
And the billboard displayed its last run;
When the crowds seeking pleasure have vanished,
And have gone into darkness again;
And the world that rejected its Saviour
Is asked for a reason—WHAT THEN?

When the bugle's last call sinks in silence,
And the long marching columns stand still;
When the captain has giv'n his last order,
And they've captured the last fort and hill;
When the flag has been hauled from the masthead,
And the wounded afield have checked in;
When the trumpet of ages is sounded
And we stand up before Him—WHAT THEN?

Several years ago an old engineer on the Baltimore and Ohio Railroad was retiring from active service. He was a great Christian and his testimony ran something like this:

I suppose it is perfectly natural that my mind should go back forty years or so ago when, just out of school, I got my first job on the old B. & O. I was the child of my parents' old age; therefore just as soon as I reached young manhood and was able to get a job, my father who was old had to retire from active work; and the sole support of the family fell on me.

All my life I had wanted to be a railroad man; but in those early days before many of the modern safety devices had been perfected, my mother seemed to live in a haunted dread and fear that one of these days I would be involved in a terrible railroad accident and would thus lose my life. Every morning when I would go out on the run, Mother, having prepared my lunch with her own hands, would put the lunch basket in my hands and place an arm about my shoulders; and I would kiss her goodby, and she would say, "O God, please watch over our boy today and bring him back home safe tonight." And I would go out on my run, climbing up on my engine with those words ringing in my ears, "O God, please watch over my boy today and bring him back safe tonight."

Then in the late afternoon as I was coming in from my run, when the old engine would round that last curve on the outskirts of our little town, I would look up on the hillside to a little vine-covered cottage; then I'd reach up and give one long blast of the old whistle; winter or summer a little whitehaired mother would always come over to the window and lean out and wave her handkerchief. The neighbors would tell me that she would always say, "Thank God, my boy is safe home at last!"

In the fullness of time Mother passed on and I had to get a hired woman to come and cook and keep house for my dad in his old age. While the hired woman would always fix my lunch, Dad took up where Mother left off and he would not allow anyone else to put that lunch basket in my hand. Every morning when I would go out on the run, he placed a trembling hand on my shoulder, and he, too, would say, "O God, please watch over and protect my boy. Bring him back home safe tonight."

Then just as of yore, when I would come in from my run in the late afternoon and the old engine rounded that last curve, I would reach up again and give a long blast of the whistle; and winter or summer, no matter how cold the weather, that old white-headed dad would totter over to the window, lean out and wave his handkerchef. The neighbors told me that he, too, would always say, "Thank God, my boy is safe home at last!"

Then in the fullness of time, my dad went on Home; and my life has been so lonely since then, living in boarding houses.

But he said:

Now boys, my hair, too, is white with the frosts of many winters; and it won't be long, according to the laws of nature, before I'll make my last long run.

When that time comes, I have always been so accustomed to riding up at the front end of the train that I am going to ask my Great Engineer to let me ride in the cab with Him on my final run on the old Gospel Train.

When the engine rounds the last curve and my eyes fall for the first time upon the gleaming lights and battlements of the City of God, just as we are about to glide into the Grand Central Station of the Skies, I want to reach up and give one long blast of the whistle. As I climb down from the cab on that last run and I walk into the station, I know that on either side of the Beautiful Gate there will be an old white-haired mother and an old white-haired dad; and the very moment the Gates of Pearl click upon my heels and my feet press for the first time the gold-paved streets of the City of God, I know that old white-haired mother and white-haired dad will throw their arms around me; and the first thing they'll say will be, "Thank God, my boy is safe home at last!"

## No Shadows There

No shadows There! They joyfully behold Him!
No cloud to dim their vision of His face!
No jarring note to mar the holy rapture,
The perfect bliss of that most blessed place.

No burdens There! These all are gone forever!
No weary nights, no long or dragging days!
No sighing There, or secret, silent longings—
For all is now unutterable praise.

No conflicts There! No evil hosts assailing!
Such warfare past—forever made to cease;
No tempter's voice is heard within those portals;
No foe lurks there to break the perfect peace.

No sorrows There! no sadness and no weeping!
Tears wiped away—all radiant now each face;
Music and song, in happy holy blending,
Fill all the courts of that sweet resting place.

J. Danson Smith

DWIGHT LYMAN MOODY
1837-1899

# ABOUT THE MAN:

D. L. Moody may well have been the greatest evangelist of all time. In a 40-year period, he won a million souls, founded three Christian schools, launched a great Christian publishing business, established a world-renowned Christian conference center, and inspired literally thousands of preachers to win souls and conduct revivals.

A shoe clerk at 17, his ambition was to make $100,000. Converted at 18, he uncovered hidden gospel gold in the hearts of millions for the next half century. He preached to 20,000 a day in Brooklyn and admitted only non-church members by ticket!

He met a young songleader in Indianapolis, said bluntly, "You're the man I've been looking for for eight years. Throw up your job and come with me." Ira D. Sankey did just that; thereafter it was "Moody will preach; Sankey will sing."

He traveled across the American continent and through Great Britain in some of the greatest and most successful evangelistic meetings communities have ever known. His tour of the world with Sankey was considered the greatest evangelistic enterprise of the century.

It was Henry Varley who said, "It remains to be seen what God will do with a man who gives himself up wholly to Him." And Moody endeavored to be, under God, that man; and the world did marvel to see how wonderfully God used him.

Two great monuments stand to the indefatigable work and ministry of this gospel warrior—Moody Bible Institute and the famous Moody Church in Chicago.

Moody went to be with the Lord in 1899.

## XV.

# Heaven — and Who Are There

### D. L. MOODY

*"Let not your heart be troubled: ye believe in God, believe also in me. In my Father's house are many mansions: if it were not so, I would have told you. I go to prepare a place for you. And if I go and prepare a place for you, I will come again, and receive you unto myself; that where I am, there ye may be also."* — John 14:1-3.

I was on my way to a meeting one night with a friend; and he asked, as we were drawing near the church, "Mr. Moody, what are you going to preach about?"

"I am going to preach about Heaven," I said. I noticed a scowl passing over his face, and I said, "What makes you look so?"

"Why, your subject of Heaven. What's the use of talking upon a subject that's all speculation? It's only wasting time on a subject about which you can only speculate."

My answer to that friend was, "If the Lord doesn't want us to speak about Heaven, He would never have told us about such a place in the Scriptures; and as Timothy says, 'All scripture is given by inspiration of God, and is profitable . . . .' "

There's no part of the Word of God that is not profitable, and I believe if men would read more carefully these Scriptures they would think more of Heaven. If we want to get men to fix their hearts and attention upon Heaven, we must get them to read more about it.

Men who say that Heaven is a speculation have not read their Bibles. In the blessed Bible there are allusions scattered all through it. If I were to read to you all the passages about Heaven from Genesis to Revelation, it would take me all night and tomorrow to do it. When I took some of the passages lately and showed them to a lady, "Why," said she, "I didn't think there was so much about Heaven in the Bible."

If I were to go into a foreign land and spend my days there, I would like to know all about it; I would like to read all about it. I would want to know all about its climate, its inhabitants, customs, privileges, its government. I would find nothing about that land that would not interest me.

## Heaven Is to Be Our Long Home: We Should Learn All We Can About It

Suppose you all were going away to Africa, to Germany, to China, and were going to make one of those places your home, and suppose that I had just come from one of those countries. How eagerly you would listen to what I had to say. I can imagine how the old, gray-haired men and the young men and the deaf would crowd around and put up their hands to learn something about it.

But there is a country in which you are going to spend your whole future and you are listless about what kind of country it is. My friends, where are you going to spend eternity? Your life here is very brief. Life is but an inch of time; it is but a span, but a fibre, which will soon be snapped, and you will be ushered into eternity. Where are you going to spend it? If I were to ask you who are going to spend eternity in Heaven to stand up, nearly every one of you would rise. There is not a man here, not one in Chicago, who has not some hope of reaching Heaven. Now, if we are going to spend our future there, it becomes us to go to work and find out all about it.

## Heaven Is a Real, Literal Place

I call your attention to this truth that Heaven is just as much a place as Chicago. It is a destination; it is a locality. Some people say there is no Heaven. Some men will tell you this earth is all the heaven we have. Queer kind of heaven this. Look at the poverty, the disease in the city! Look at the men out of employment walking around our streets, and then say this is Heaven? How low a man has gotten when he comes to think this way! There is a land where the weary are at rest; there is a land where there is peace and joy, where no sorrow dwells, and as we think of it and speak about it, how sweet it looms up before us.

I remember soon after I got converted, a pantheist got hold of me and tried to draw me back to the world. Those men who try to get hold of a young convert are the worst set of men. I don't know a worse man than he who tries to pull young Christians down. He is nearer the borders of Hell than any man I know. When this man knew I had found Jesus he just tried to pull me down. He tried to argue with me. I did not know the Bible very well then, and he got the best of me. The only way to get the best of those atheists, pantheists, or infidels is to have a good knowledge of the Bible. Well, this pantheist told me God was everywhere—in the air, in the sun, in the moon, in the earth, in the stars—but really he meant nowhere. The next time I went to pray it seemed as if I were not praying anywhere or to anyone.

## Heaven Is Not Far Away

We have ample evidence in the Bible that there is such a place as Heaven, and we have abundant manifestation that His influence from Heaven is felt among us. He is not in person among us, only in Spirit. The sun is about 95,000,000 miles from the earth, yet we feel its rays. In II Chronicles we read, "If my people, which are called by my name, shall humble themselves, and pray, and seek my face, and turn from their wicked ways; then will I hear from heaven, and will forgive their sin, and will heal their land." Here is one reference, and when it is read, a great many people might ask, "How far is Heaven away? can you tell us that?" I don't know how far it is away, but there is one thing I can tell you. He can hear prayer as soon as the words are uttered. There has not been a prayer said that He has not heard; not a tear shed that He has not seen. We don't want to learn the distance. What we want to know is that God is there, and Scripture tells us that.

Turn to I Kings 8:30 and we read, "And hearken thou to the supplication of thy servant, and of thy people Israel, when they shall pray toward this place: and hear thou in heaven thy dwelling place: and when thou hearest, forgive." Now, it is clearly taught in the Word of God that the Father dwells there. It is His dwelling place, and in Acts 7:55 we see that Jesus is there, too. "But he, being full of the Holy Ghost, looked up stedfastly into heaven, and saw the glory of God, and Jesus standing on the right hand of God." And by the eye of faith we can see Him there tonight, too. By faith we shall be brought into His presence, and we shall be satisfied when we gaze upon Him.

Stephen, when he was surrounded by the howling multitude, saw the Son of Man there. When Jesus looked down upon earth and saw this first martyr in the midst of his persecutors, He looked down and gave him welcome. We'll see Him by and by.

It is not the jasper streets and the golden gates that attract us to Heaven. What are your golden palaces on earth; what is it that makes them so sweet? It is the presence of some loving wife or fond children. Let them be taken away and the charm of your home is gone. And so it is Christ who is the charm of Heaven to the Christian. Yes, we shall see Him there. How sweet the thought that we shall dwell with Him forever, and shall see the nails in His hands and in His feet which He received for us.

## Jesus and Loved Ones Make Heaven Sweet

I read a little story not long since which went to my heart. A mother was on the point of death and the child was taken away from her in case it would annoy her. It was crying continually to be taken to its mother, and teased the neighbors. By and by the mother died and the neighbors thought it was better to bury the mother without letting the child see her dead face. They thought the sight of the dead mother would not do the child any good and so they kept it away.

When the mother was buried and the child was taken back to the house, the first thing she did was to run into her mother's sitting room and look all around it, and from there to the bedroom; but no mother was there. She went all over the house crying, "Mother, Mother!" but the child could not find her, and coming to the neighbor, said, "Take me back, I don't want to stay here if I cannot see my mother." It wasn't the home that made it so sweet to the child. It was the presence of the mother. And so it is not Heaven that is alone attractive to us; it is the knowledge that Jesus, our Leader, our Brother, our Lord, is there.

And the spirits of loved ones whose bodies we have laid in the earth will be there. We shall be in good company there. When we reach that land we shall meet all the Christians who have gone before us. We are told in Matthew, too, that we shall meet angels there, "Take heed that ye despise not one of these little ones; for I say unto you, That in heaven their angels do always behold the face of my Father which is in heaven." Yes, the angels are there and we shall see them when we get Home.

He is there, and where He is, His disciples shall be, for He has said, "I go to prepare a place for you. . .that where I am, there ye may be also." I believe that when we die the spirit leaves the body and goes to the mansion above, and by and by the body will be resurrected and it shall see Jesus.

Very often people come to me and say, "Mr. Moody, do you think we shall know each other in Heaven?" Very often it is a mother who has lost a dear child and who wishes to see it again. Sometimes it is a child who has lost a mother, a father, and who wants to recognize them in Heaven.

There is just one verse in Scripture in answer to this, and that is, "We shall be satisfied." It is all I want to know. My brother who went up there the other day, I shall see, because I will be satisfied. We will see all those we loved on earth up there, and if we loved them here, we will love them ten thousand times more when we meet them there.

## The Greatest Cause of Rejoicing: Name Written in Heaven

Another thought. In chapter 10 of Luke we are told our names are written there if we are Christians. Christ just called His disciples up and paired them off and sent them out to preach the Gospel. Two of us— Mr. Sankey and myself—going about and preaching the Gospel, is nothing new. You will find them away back eighteen hundred years ago going off two by two, like Brothers Bliss and Whittle, and Brothers Needham and Stebbins, to different towns and villages. They had gone out, and there had been great revivals in all the cities, towns, and villages they had entered. Everywhere they had met with the greatest success. Even the very devils were subject to them. Disease had fled before them. When the disciples met a lame man they said to him, 'You don't want to be lame any longer,' and he walked. When they met a blind man they but told him to open his eyes, and behold, he could see.

They came to Christ and rejoiced over their great success, and He said to them, "Notwithstanding in this rejoice not, that the spirits are subject unto you; but rather rejoice, because your names are written in heaven." Now there are a great many people who do not believe in such an assurance as this, "Rejoice, because your names are written in heaven." How are you going to rejoice if your names are not written there?

While I was speaking about this some time ago, a man told me we were preaching a very ridiculous doctrine when we preached this doctrine of assurance. I ask you in all candor, what are you going to do with this assurance if we don't preach it? It is stated that our names are written there; blotted out of the book of death and transferred to the Book of Life.

While in Europe I was traveling with a friend—she is in this hall tonight.

On one occasion, we were journeying from London to Liverpool, and the question was put as to where we would stop. We said we would go to the Northwestern, at Lime Street, as that was the hotel where Americans generally stopped. When we got there the house was full; could not let us in. Every room was engaged. But this friend said, "I am going to stay here; I engaged a room ahead. I sent a telegram on."

My friends, that is just what the Christians are doing—sending their names in ahead. They are sending a message up saying, "Lord Jesus, I want one of those mansions You are preparing; I want to be there." That's what they're doing. And every man and woman here who wants one, if you have not already gotten one, had better make up your mind. Send your names up now.

I would rather a thousand times have my name written in the Lamb's Book than have all the wealth of the world rolling at my feet. A man may get station in this world—but it will prove a bauble—"What shall it profit a man if he gain the whole world and lose his own soul?" It is a solemn question. Let it go around the hall tonight—"Is my name written in the Book of Life?"

I can imagine that man down there saying, "Yes; I belong to the Presbyterian church; my name is on the church's books." It may be, but God keeps His books in a different fashion than that in which the church records of this city are kept. You may belong to a good many churches; you may be an elder or a deacon, and be a bright light in your church, yet you may not have your name written in the Book of Life.

Judas was one of the twelve, yet he didn't have his name written in the Book of Life. Satan was among the elect—he dwelt among the angels, yet he was cast from the high hallelujahs.

Is your name written in the Book of life?

A man told me, when I was speaking upon this subject, "That is all nonsense you are speaking." A great many men here are of the same opinion; but I would like them to turn to Daniel, chapter 12, verse 1, ". . . and there shall be a time of trouble, such as never was since there was a nation even to that same time: and at that time thy people shall be delivered, every one that shall be found written in the book." Everyone shall be delivered whose name shall be found written in the Book. We find Paul, in the letters which he wrote to the Philippians, addressing them as those ". . . true yokefellow . . . my fellowlabourers, whose names are in the book of life."

Let us not be deceived in this. We see it too plainly throughout the Holy Word. In Revelation 21:27 we have three different passages referring to it and in almost the last words in the Scriptures we read, "And there shall in no wise enter into it any thing that defileth, neither whatsoever worketh abomination, or maketh a lie: but they which are written in the Lamb's book of life."

My friends, you will never see that city unless your names are written in that Book of Life. It is a solemn truth. Let it go home to everyone, and sink into the hearts of all here tonight. Don't build your hopes on a false foundation: don't build your hopes on an empty profession. Be sure your name is written there.

## Make Sure Your Children Are Ready for Heaven, Too!

The next thing after your own names are written there is to see that the names of the children God has given you are recorded there. Let the fathers and mothers assembled tonight hear this and take it to their hearts. See that your children's names are there. Ask your conscience if the name of your John, your Willie, your Mary, your Alice is recorded in the Book of Life. If not, make it the business of your life, rather than to pile up wealth for them; make it the one object of your existence to secure for them eternal life, rather than to pave the way to their death and ruin. I read some time ago of a mother in an eastern city who was stricken with consumption. At her dying hour she requested her husband to bring the children to her. The oldest one was brought first and she laid her hand on his head and gave him her blessing and dying message. The next one was brought and she gave him the same. One after another came to her bedside until the little infant was brought in. She took it and pressed it to her bosom, and the people in the room, fearing that she was straining her strength, took the child away from her. As this was done she turned to her husband and said, "I charge you, Sir, bring all those children home with you."

And so God charges us. The promise is to ourselves and to our children. We can have our names written there; and then, by the grace of God, we can call our children to us and know their names are also recorded there. That great roll is being called, and those bearing the names are summoned every day, every hour; that great roll is being called tonight, and if your name were shouted, could you answer with joy?

You have heard of a soldier who fell in our war. While he lay dying, he was heard to cry, "Here! here." Some of his comrades went up to him, thinking he wanted water, but he said, "They are calling the roll of Heaven and I am answering," and in a faint voice he whispered, "Here!" and passed away to Heaven.

If that roll were called tonight, would you be ready to answer, "Here!"? I am afraid not. Let us wake up; may every child of God wake up tonight. There is work to do. Fathers and mothers, look to your children. If I could only speak to one class, I would preach to parents and try to show them the great responsibility that rests upon them—try to teach them how much more they should devote their lives to secure the immortal treasure of Heaven for their children, than to spend their lives in scraping together worldly goods for them.

There is a man living on the bank of the Mississippi River. The world calls him rich, but if he could call back his first-born son he would give up all his wealth. The boy was brought home one day unconscious. When the doctor examined him he turned to the father, who stood at the bedside, and said, "There is no hope."

"What!" exclaimed the father, "is it possible my boy has to die?"

"There is no hope," replied the doctor.

"Will he not come to?" asked the father.

"He may resume consciousness, but he cannot live," said the doctor.

"Try all your skill, Doctor; I don't want my boy to die," replied the father.

By and by the boy regained a glimmering of consciousness, and when he was told that his death was approaching, he said to his father, "Won't you pray for my lost soul, Father? You have never prayed for me." The old man only wept. It was true. During the seventeen years that God had given him his boy he had never spent an hour in prayer for his soul. The object of his life had been to accumulate wealth for that first-born son. Am I speaking to a prayerless father or mother tonight? Settle the question of your soul's salvation and pray for the son or daughter God has given you.

But I have another anecdote to tell. It was Ralph Wells who told me of this one. A certain gentleman had been a member of the Presbyterian church. His little boy was sick. When he went home his wife was weeping and she said, "Our boy is dying. He has had a change for the worse. I wish you would go in and see him." The father went into the room and placed his hand on the brow of his dying boy and could feel that the cold, damp sweat was gathering there; that the cold, icy hand of Death was feeling for the chords of life.

"Do you know, my boy, that you are dying?" asked the father.

"Am I? Is this death? Do you really think I am dying?" questioned the boy.

"Yes, my son, your end on earth is near," replied the father.

"And will I be with Jesus tonight, Father?" asked the boy.

"Yes, you will be with the Saviour," comforted the father.

"Father, don't you weep, for when I get there I will go right straight to Jesus and tell Him you have been trying all my life to lead me to Him," said the boy.

God has given me two little children, and ever since I can remember I have directed them to Christ. I would rather they carried this message to Jesus—that I had tried all my life to lead them to Him—than have all the crowns of the earth; would rather lead them to Jesus than give them the wealth of the world.

If you have a child, go and point the way. I challenge any man to speak of Heaven without speaking of children. "For of such is the kingdom of heaven." Fathers and mothers and professed Christians ignore this sometimes. They go along themselves and never try to get any to Heaven with them. Let us see to this at once. Let us pray that there may be many names written in the Lamb's Book of Life tonight.

## *Beautiful Zion*

Beautiful Zion, built above!
Beautiful city that I love!
Beautiful gates of pearly white!
Beautiful temple, God its light!

Beautiful trees, forever there!
Beautiful fruits they always bear!
Beautiful rivers gliding by!
Beautiful fountains never dry!

Beautiful light, without the sun!
Beautiful day revolving on!
Beautiful worlds on worlds untold!
Beautiful streets of shining gold!

Beautiful Heaven where all is light!
Beautiful angels clothed in white!
Beautiful songs that never tire!
Beautiful harps through all the choir!

Beautiful crowns on every brow!
Beautiful palms the conquerors show!
Beautiful robes the ransomed wear!
Beautiful all who enter there!

Beautiful throne for God the Lamb!
Beautiful seats at God's right hand!
Beautiful rest, all wanderings cease!
Beautiful Home of perfect peace!

George Gill

CHARLES HADDON SPURGEON
1835-1892

## ABOUT THE MAN:

Many times it has been said that this was the greatest preacher this side of the Apostle Paul. He began preaching at the age of 16. At 25 he built London's famous Metropolitan Tabernacle, seating around 5,000. It was never large enough. Even when traveling he preached to 10,000 eager listeners a week. Crowds thronged to hear him as they came to hear John the Baptist by the River Jordan. The fire of God was on him as on the Prophet Elijah facing assembled Israel at Mount Carmel.

Royalty sat in his Tabernacle, as did washerwomen. Mr. Gladstone had him to dinner; and cabbies refused his fare, considering it an honor to drive for this "Prince of Preachers." To a housewife kneading bread, he would say, "Have you ever tried the Bread of Life?" Many a carpenter was asked, "Have you ever tried to build a house on sand?"

He preached in all the principal cities of England, Scotland and Ireland. And although invited to the United States on several occasions, he was never able to visit this country.

HOW GREAT WAS HIS HEART: for preachers, so the Pastors' College was founded; for orphans, so the orphans' houses came to be; for people around the world, so his literature poured forth in an almost unmeasurable volume. He was a national voice; so every national issue affecting morals, religion or the poor had his interpretation, his counsel.

Oh, but his passion for souls! You can see it in every sermon.

Spurgeon published thousands of poems, tracts, sermons and songs.

HIS MESSAGE TO LOST SINNERS WILL LIVE AS LONG AS THE GOSPEL IS PREACHED.

# XVI.

# *The Voice From Heaven*

## C. H. SPURGEON

*"And they heard a great voice from heaven, saying unto them, Come up hither."*—Rev. 11:12.

Waiving all attempts at explaining the text from its connection, I intend to use it as the voice of God to His people.

## I. A SUMMONS SENT TO EVERY SAINT

We shall regard it, first of all, as a summons sent at the appointed hour to every saint. When the time shall come, fixed by irreversible decree, there shall be heard "a great voice from heaven" to every believer in Christ, saying, "Come up hither."

### 1. A Joyful Anticipation

This should be to each one of us who be in Christ the subject of very joyful anticipation. Instead of dreading the time when we shall leave this world to go to the Father, we should be thirsting and panting for the hour that shall set our soul at liberty and give our spirit once for all its full discharge from an imprisonment of clay and from the bondage of "the body of this death."

To some Christians it will be not only joyful in anticipation but intensely delightful when it arrives. It is not true, as some suppose, that when death really appears it is necessarily a dreadful and hideous apparition.

> **Death no terrific foe appears;**
> **An angel's lovely form he wears;**
> **A friendly messenger he proves**
> **To every soul whom Jesus loves.**

I doubt not that many believers welcome the kind approach of death as the arrival of their best friend and salute their last hour with intense delight.

Witness the saint who has been for years bed-ridden. She is tossed to and fro as on a sea of pains, never resting at the anchorage of ease. She cries at night, *Would God 'twere morning!* And when the light of day affects her eyes, she longs for the returning darkness that she may slumber for a little season and forget her pains. Her bones have worn through her skin by long lying upon a bed made as soft as kindness can render it but still too hard for so weak and tormented a body. Pangs have shot through her frame as arrows piercing the foe. Every vein has been a river flushed with agony, every nerve a telegraph conveying messages of pain to the spirit.

Oh, how welcome shall it be when the voice shall cry from Heaven, "Come up hither!" No more weakness now! The joyful spirit shall leave all bodily pain behind. The last tear shall be wiped away by the Divine Father's hand, and she who was a mass of disease and decay shall now become an embodiment of intense delight, full to the brim with satisfaction and infinite pleasure. In that land where Jehovah-Rophi reigns, the inhabitant shall no more say, "I am sick."

With what joy will the voice from Heaven sound in the ear of the man wearied with labor! The world shall know of some of us when we die that we have not been idle but have served our God beyond our strength. He who finds the ministry an easy profession shall find the flames of Hell no pleasant resting-place.

There may be some of you in whose name I can speak now who have served God with throbbing brow and with palpitating heart. You are weary in your Master's service but never weary of it—springing to the collar when the load was far too heavy for your single strength. You are ready to labor or ready for fight, never putting off your armor but standing harnessed both by night and day, crying in your Master's name,

> Is there a foe before whose face
> I fear His cause to plead?
> Is there a lamb among His flock
> I would refuse to feed?

The time must come when age shall take away the juvenile vigor which for a while carried off weariness, and you shall be constrained to lament, "When shall the shadows be drawn out? When shall I fulfill as a hireling my day?" Happy for the minister, if in his pulpit he shall hear the voice, "Come up hither," and shall

**His body and his charge lay down,**
**And cease at once to work and live.**

Happy for you, fellow-laborers in the kingdom of Christ and in the tribulation of our common Saviour, if just when you think you can do no more,
your doing shall be ended and your reward shall come and your Saviour
shall say, "Come up hither," and you shall see the glory which you
have believed in upon earth.

Beloved, with what intense delight will death be hailed by the sons
of abject poverty; I mean "such as are of the household of faith." From
shivering in the winter's cold to the brightness of Heaven; from the
solitude and desolation of friendless penury to the communion and
fellowship of saints made perfect; from the table scantily furnished with
hard-earned bread; from famishing and want; from the poor emaciated
bones; from the form ready to be bowed down with hunger; from the
tongue that cleaveth to the mouth with thirst; from crying children and
a wailing wife—wailing for bread, crying that they may be fed—oh, to
be snatched away to Heaven!

Happy man, to have known so much of ill, that he may know the
better the sweetness of perfect bliss! Mansions of the blessed, how bright
ye are in contrast with the cotter's hut! Streets of gold, how ye shall
make the beggar forget the cold doorstep and dry arch! Paupers become
princes; pensioners are peers, and peasants are kings and priests. O
land of Goshen, how long before the sons of Israel receive thee for an
heritage!

Dear friends, I think I ought to add to this—with what seraphic joy
must this voice have been heard in the martyrs' ears! In caves and dens
of the earth where the holy wander in their sheepskins and goatskins,
what holy triumph must this message create!

Blandina, tossed in the Roman amphitheatre on the horns of bulls,
then seated in her red-hot iron chair and mocked while she is there
consumed before the jeering multitude—oh, how that voice, "Come
up hither!" must have cheered her in those horrid agonies which she
bore with more than masculine heroism.

The many who have perished on the rack—surely they have seen
visions like those of Stephen who, when the stones were rattling about
his ears, saw Heaven open and heard the Heaven-sent voice, "Come
up hither."

The multitude of our ancestors—our venerated predecessors who carried the banner of the cross before our day, who stood on flaming fag-

gots and bore the flames with patience, with their bodies consumed by fire till their lower limbs were burnt away and life just remained within a mass of ashes—oh, the joy with which they would leap into their fiery chariots, drawn by horses of fire straight to Heaven, at this omnipotent bidding of the Master, "Come up hither!"

Though yours and mine may never be the lot of protracted sickness, or abject penury, or excessive labor, or the death of martyrdom, yet let us still believe that if we are true followers of Christ, whenever death shall come, or rather whenever life and immortality shall come, it shall be a joyous and blessed time for us.

Seek not of the Most High to delay the time when He shall summon thee to the upper chamber, but listen every morning, with a heart desiring to hear it; listen for the royal message which saith, "Come up hither." An ancient singer sweetly words it—

> I said sometimes with tears,
>     Ah me! I'm loth to die!
> Lord, silence Thou these fears;
>     My life's with Thee on high.
>         Sweet truth to me!
>         I shall arise,
>         And with these eyes
>     My Saviour see.
>
> What means my trembling heart,
>     To be thus shy of death?
> My life and I sha'nt part,
>     Though I resign my breath.
>         Sweet truth to me!
>         I shall arise,
>         And with these eyes
>     My Saviour see.
>
> Then welcome harmless grave!
>     By Thee to Heaven I'll go:
> My Lord, Thy death shall save
>     Me from the flames below.
>         Sweet truth to me!
>         I shall arise,
>         And with these eyes
>     My Saviour see.

## 2. We Should Patiently Wait for the Voice From Heaven

While this should be the subject of joyous anticipation, it should also be *the object of patient waiting.* God knows best when it is time for us to be bidden, "Come up hither."

We must not wish to antedate the period of our departure. I know that strong love will make us cry,

**O Lord of Hosts the waves divide
And land us all in Heaven;**

but patience must have her perfect work.

I would not wish to die while there is more work to do or more souls to win, more jewels to place in the Redeemer's crown, more glory to be given to His name, and more service to be rendered to His church.

When George Whitefield lay sick and wanted to die, his black nurse who had prayed for him said, "No, Massa Whitefield, there is no dying for you. Many a poor Negro is yet to be brought to Christ, and you must live." And live he did.

When Melancthon lay very sick, Martin Luther said he should not die. And when his prayers began to work a cure, Melancthon said, "Let me die, Luther, let me die. Leave off your prayers." But Luther said, "No, man, I want you, God's cause wants you, and you shall not die yet." Then when Melancthon refused to eat or to take the necessary medicine because he hoped to be soon with Christ, Luther threatened him with excommunication if he did not there and then do as he was bidden.

It is not for us by neglect of means, or wanton waste of strength or profligate zeal, to cut short a life which may be useful. "Do thyself no harm"—the advice of the jailor to Paul—is not at all amiss here.

God knows the pace at which time should travel and how long the road of life should be. If it were possible for there to be regrets in Heaven, it might be that we did not live longer here to do more good. More sheaves, more jewels! But how, unless there be more work? True there is the other side of it—that living so briefly we sinned the less and our temptations were the fewer; but when we are fully serving God and He is giving us to scatter precious seed and reap a hundredfold, we would even say it is well for us to abide where we are.

An aged Christian, being asked whether she would rather die or live, said she would rather it should be as God willed it. "But if you might have your choice, which would you have?" Said she, "I would ask God to choose for me, for I should be afraid to choose for myself."

So be you ready to stay on this side Jordan or to cross the flood, just as your Master wills it.

### 3. All Should Make Sure of Salvation Now

As this "Come up hither" should excite joyous anticipation, tempered by patient waiting, so, beloved, it should always be to us *a matter of absolute certainty as to its ultimate reception.*

I would not give sleep to my eyes nor slumber to my eyelids if this were a subject of doubt personally as to whether at the last I should stand among the justified. I can understand a man being in doubt about his interest in Christ, but I cannot understand a man's resting content to be in these doubts. This is a matter about which we want absolute certainty.

Young man yonder, are you sure that the King will say to you, "Come up hither"? If thou believest in the Lord Jesus Christ with all thy heart, that call from the divine throne is as certain to meet thine ear as that other cry, of "Dust thou art, and unto dust thou shalt return." He that believeth on the Son of God hath everlasting life.

No "ifs" or "peradventures" ought to be tolerated in our hearts. I know they will come up like ill weeds; but it is ours to pull them, heap them together and set them on fire, as farmers do with the twitch in their furrows. The Devil loves for us to cast lots at the foot of the cross, but Christ would have us look unto Him and find a sure salvation.

We are not to be put off with guesswork here. My friend, can you be easy without infallible certainty? You may die tonight and be lost forever!

Man, I charge thee by the living God, shut not those eyes until thou art sure that thou shalt open them either on earth or in Heaven! But if there be this fear that thou mayest lift up those eyes in Hell, how darest thou sleep, lest thy bed become thy tomb and thy chamber become the door of Tophet to thee!

Brethren in Christ, let us seek to have the seal of God upon us, the infallible witness of the Holy Spirit bearing witness with our spirits that we are born of God, so we may both joyfully hope and quietly wait to see the salvation of God when the Master saith, "Come up hither."

### 4. With Joy Let Us Think About God's Call to Heaven

I think very often, besides joyfully anticipating, patiently waiting and being confidently assured of it, the Christian should *delightfully contemplate it.* Let every Christian now say, "I shall soon be dying: time swiftly speeds away."

I can paint the picture now. They have told me that I am very sick, but they have kept back from me till I asked them plainly the news that I must very speedily die. But now I know it and feel the sentence of death in myself.

Now for the joyous secret. In a few minutes I shall know more of Heaven than an assembly of divines could teach me. But how solemn is the scene around me! They are moving quietly about the room. Very silently they are catching each word uttered—treasuring it up.

Now saint, thou must play the man. Say a good word for the Master! Stir the deeps of Jordan with thy bold march of victory, O soldier of Jesus! Make its shelving shores resound with thy melodies now! Show them how a Christian can die. Now let thy full heart overflow with flood-tides of glory. Drink thou up the bitter cup and say, "Death is swallowed up in victory."

But, how is this that my mind seems fluttering as though about to take wing—

**What is this absorbs me quite—**
**Steals my senses—shuts my sight—**
**Drowns my spirit—draws my breath?**
**Tell me, my soul, can this be death?**

I cannot see; the film is forming on my eyes; it is the death-glaze. A clammy sweat is on my brow, the dew from the damps of death. The kind hand of affection has just wiped my forehead. I fain would speak, but there is a throttle in my throat which keeps down the word. This is the monitor to me of the silence of the tomb. I will strive against it.

**Joyful, with all the strength I have,**
**My quivering lips shall sing,**
**Where is thy victory, boasting grave?**
**And where's the monster's sting?**

The effort has exhausted the dying one. He must fall back again. They stay him up with pillows. Ah, ye may prop him up with pillows, but he has a better arm beneath him than that of the fondest friend. Now doth His beloved "stay him with apples, and comfort him with flagons," for while sick to death, he is also "sick of loves." His Master makes his bed in his sickness. His left hand is under his head, and His right hand doth embrace him. The Husband of that chosen soul is now answering the prayer for his presence which it delighted to offer, saying, "Abide with me." Now is the poet's prayer granted to the letter—

**Hold then thy cross before my closing eyes!**
**Shine through the gloom and point me to the skies!**
**Heaven's morning breaks and earth's vain shadows flee;**
**In life and death, O Lord, abide with me!**

We cannot paint the last moment—the rapture, the dawning glory, the first young flash of the beatific glory—we must leave all that. On earth the scene is far more sombre, yet not sad. See you yon friends gather round. They say, "Yes, he is gone. How placidly he slept! I could not tell the moment when he passed from sleep to death. He is gone."

They weep, but not with hopeless sorrow, for they mourn the body, not the soul. The setting is broken, but the gem is safe. The fold is removed, but the sheep is feeding on the hill-tops of Glory. Worms devour the clay, but angels welcome the soul.

There is general mourning wherever the good man was known; but mark ye, it is only in the dark that this sorrow reigns. Up there in the light, what are they doing? That spirit as it left the body found not itself alone. Angels had come to meet it. Angelic spirits clasped the disembodied spirit in their arms and bore it upward beyond the stars—beyond where the angel in the sun keeps his everlasting watch—beyond, beyond this lower sky immeasurable leagues.

Lo, the pearly gates appear and the azure light of the city of bejewelled walls! The spirit asketh, "Is yonder city the fair Jerusalem where they need no candle, neither light of the sun?" He shall see for himself ere long, for they are nearing the Holy City; and it is time for the cherub-bearers to begin their chorale. The music breaks from the lips of those that convey the saint to Heaven—"Lift up your heads, O ye gates, and be ye lifted up ye everlasting doors, that the blood-bought of the King of glory may come in!" The gates of pearl give way and the joyous crowds of Heaven welcome their brother to the seats of immortality.

But what next, I cannot tell. In vain the fancy strives to paint it. Jesus is there, and the spirit is in His arms. In Heaven, where should it be but in the arms of Jesus? Oh, boundless oceans of joy! I shall see Him! These eyes shall see Him and not another.

> **Shall see Him wear that very flesh**
> **On which my guilt was laid;**
> **His love intense, His merit fresh,**
> **As though but newly slain.**

> **These eyes shall see Him in that day**
> **The Man who died for me!**
> **And all my rising bones shall say,**
> **"Lord, who is like to Thee!"**

I could lose myself while talking upon this subject, for my heart is on fire. I wander, but I cannot help it. My heart is far away upon the hills with my beloved Lord. What will the bliss of Glory be? A surprise, I think, even to those who shall obtain it. We shall scarcely know ourselves when we get to Heaven, so surprised we shall be at the difference.

That poor man yonder is to be robed in all the splendors of a king. Come with me and see those bright ones: that son of toil who rests forever; that child of sin, washed by Jesus and now a companion of the God of Heaven; and I, the chief of sinners singing out His praise; Saul of Tarsus hymning the music of Calvary; the penitent thief, with his deep bass note, exalting dying love; Magdalen mounting to the alto notes, for there must be some voices even in Heaven which must sing alone and mount to higher notes where the rest of us cannot reach— the whole together singing, "Unto him that loved us, and hath washed us from our sins in his own blood, unto him be glory for ever and ever."

Oh, that we were there! Oh, that we were there! But we must patiently wait the Master's will. It shall not be long ere He shall say, "Come up hither."

## II. GOD'S VOICE, A WHISPER IN THE BELIEVER'S HEART

Now to a second part of the subject. We will take the text this time, not as a summons to depart but as a whisper from the skies to the believer's heart. There is a voice that sounds from Heaven tonight, not as a peremptory summons but as a gently-whispered invitation— "Come up hither."

*The Father* seems to say this to every adopted child. We say, "Our Father which art in heaven." The Father's heart desires to have His children round His knee; and His love each day beckons us with a tender "Come up hither." Nor will your Father and my Father ever be content till every one of His children are in the many mansions above.

And *Jesus* whispers this in your ear tonight, too. Hearken! Do you not hear Him say, "I will that they also whom thou hast given me be with me where I am, that they may behold my glory—the glory which thou hast given me—the glory which I had with thee before the world was"? Jesus beckons thee to the skies, believer. Lay not fast hold upon things of earth. He who is but a lodger in an inn must not live as though he were at home. Keep thy tent ready for striking. Be thou ever prepared to draw up thine anchor and to sail across the sea to the better port, for while Jesus beckons, here we have no continuing city.

No true wife hath rest save in the house of her husband. Where her consort is, there is her home—a home which draws her soul towards it every day. Jesus, I say, invites us to the skies. He cannot be completely content until He brings His body, the church, into the glory of its Head and conducts His elect spouse to the marriage feast of her Lord.

Besides the desires of the Father and the Son, all those who have gone before seem to be leaning over the battlements of Heaven and calling, "Courage, brothers! Courage, brothers! Eternal glory awaits you. Fight your way, stem the current, breast the wave, and come up hither. Without you we cannot be made perfect; there is no perfect church in Heaven till all the chosen saints be there; therefore come up hither." They stretch out their hands of fellowship; they look with glistening eyes of strong affection upon us; still again they say, "Come up hither."

Warriors who wear your laurels, ye call us to the brow of the hill where the like triumphs await us. The angels do the same tonight. How they must wonder to see us so careless, so worldly, so hardened! They also beckon us away and cry from their starry seats, "Beloved, ye over whom we rejoiced when you were brought as prodigals to your Father's house, come up hither, for we long to see you. Your story of grace will be a strange and wondrous one—one which angels love to hear."

**Stretch your wings, ye saints, and fly,**
**Straight to yonder worlds of joy.**

I have kept my pledge to be short on that point. You can walk in this meditation as in a garden when you are quiet and alone. All nature rings the bell which calls you to the Temple above. You may see the stars at night looking down like the eyes of God upon you and saying, "Come up hither." The whispers of the wind as they come in the stillness of the night talk to you and say, "There is another and better land; come away with us; come up hither." Yes, every cloud that sails across the sky may say to you, "Mount up beyond me into the clear ether which no cloud can dim, and behold the sun which I can never hide—the noon which I can never mar. Come up hither."

### III. A VOICE FROM HEAVEN CALLS EVERY UNCONVERTED PERSON

I shall want your attention to my third point for a few minutes, for

I think these words may be used as a loving invitation to the unconverted. There are many spirit voices which cry to them, "Come up hither; come up to Heaven."

I like to see so many crowding here on these dark, cold, wintry days. This huge place is just as crowded as though it were some little vestry. You press upon one another as did the throngs in the days of the Master. God gives a spirit of hearing nowadays in a most wonderful manner. And I would that while you are hearing, some living spark of divine fire may fall into your hearts and become the parent of a glowing fire.

If we ask any man whether he desires to go to Heaven, he will say, "Yes"; but his desires for Heaven are not strong enough to be of practical use. They are such sorry winds, that there is no sailing to Heaven with them. Perhaps if we can quicken those desires tonight, God the Spirit may bless our words to the bringing of men into the way of life.

Sinner, wanderer far from God, many voices salute thee. Albeit thou hast chosen the paths of the destroyer, there are many who would turn thee to the way of peace.

### 1. First, God Our Father Calls Thee

Thou asketh, "How?" Sinner, thou hast had many troubles of late. Business goes amiss. Thou hast been out of work. Thou hast tried to get on, but thou canst not do it. In thy house everything is out of order. You are always floundering from one slough into another; ye are growing weary of your life.

Dost thou not know, sinner, this is thy Father saying, "Come up hither"? Thy portion is not here; seek thou another and a better land. Thou hast built thy nest on a tree that is marked for the axe and He is pulling thy nest down for thee that thou mayest build on the rock. I tell you, these troubles are but love-strokes to deliver thee from thyself.

If thou hadst been left unchastised, I had had little hope of thee. Surely then, God would have said, "Let him alone; he will have no portion in the next life; let him have his portion here."

We heard of a godly wife who for twenty years had been persecuted by a brutal husband—a husband so excessively bad that her faith at last failed her. She ceased to be able to believe that he would ever be converted. But all this while she was more kind to him than ever.

One night at twelve o'clock, in a drunken debauch he told his friends he had such a wife as no other man had, and if they would go home with him, he would knock her up, but she should get a supper for them.

They came, and the supper was very soon ready, consisting of such things as she had prepared as well and as rapidly as the occasion would allow. She waited on the table with as much cheerfulness as if the feast had been held at the proper time. She did not utter a word of complaint.

At last, one of the company more sober than the rest asked how it was she could always be so kind to such a husband. Seeing that her conduct had made some little impression, she ventured to say to him, "I have done all I can to bring my husband to God, but I fear he will never be saved. Therefore, his portion must be in Hell for ever so I will make him as happy as I can while he is *here*, for he has nothing to expect hereafter."

Such is your case tonight. You may get some pleasure here, but you have nothing to expect hereafter. God has been pleased to take your pleasures away. Here, then, I have good hopes that, since He shakes you from the present, you may be driven to the future.

God your Father is making you uncomfortable in order that you may seek Him. It is the beckoning of His love-finger, "Come up hither." Those deaths you have had lately—all say, "Come up hither."

When your mother died—a saint indeed—do you remember what she said to you? "I could die happy if it were not for you and your brother. Oh, that I might have a hope that you may yet come to God."

Do you remember, man, how that little daughter of yours had been to Sunday school. She died so young! She kissed you and said, "Dear father, do give up the drunkard's cup and follow me to Heaven. Father, I am dying. Do not be angry because I said that. Father, follow me to Heaven." You have not yielded to that loving entreaty, so you are descending into Hell. All this was God beckoning to you and saying, "Come up hither." He has called and you have refused. Take care lest when *you* call, He should refuse you.

Besides, you have had a sickness yourself. It is not so long ago since you had a fever, or was it an accident? Everybody said you had a near escape for life. You had time for reflection when you lay in that hospital ward or in your own little room. Do you remember what Conscience said to you? How it rent away the curtain and made you look at your destiny, until you read in fiery letters these words, "Thou shalt make thy bed in Hell."

Oh, how you trembled then! You had no objection to seeing the minister. You could not laugh then at the Gospel of Christ. You made a great many vows and resolutions, but you have broken them all. You have lied unto the Most High. You have perjured yourself to the God of Israel and mocked at the God of mercy and of justice. Beware, lest He take you away with a stroke, for then a great ransom shall not deliver you. These things, then, have been beckonings of your Father's hand to you, saying, "Come up hither."

## 2. The Lord Jesus Christ Has Also Beckoned to You to Come

Thou hast heard that He made a way to Heaven. What does a way mean? Is not a road an invitation to a traveler to walk therein?

I have crossed the Alps and have seen the mighty roads which Napoleon made so he might take his cannon into Austria. But how shall we compare the works which men have made through the solid granite and over pathless mountains—mountains that before were pathless—with the road which Christ has made to Heaven through the rocks of justice, over the gulfs of sin, throwing Himself into the gaps, leaping Himself into the chasm to complete the way?

Now the way itself speaks to you. The blood of Christ, which made the way, speaks better things than that of Abel. This it says, "Sinner, believe on Christ and thou art saved."

By every drop of blood which streamed in sweat from Him in the garden; by every drop which poured from His hands and feet; by all the agony which He endured, I do beseech thee, hear the voice which crieth, "Go and sin no more." Trust thy soul with Him and thou art saved.

But, my dear hearer, have patience with me; give me thine ear.

## 3. The Spirit of God Strives With Thee and Cries, "Come Up Hither"

The Spirit of God wrote this Book, and wherefore was it written? Hear the words of Scripture: "These are written that ye might believe that Jesus is the Christ, the Son of God, and that believing, ye might have life through his name."

Here is the Book full of promises, perfumed with affection and brimming with love. Oh, wherefore wilt thou spurn it and put the voice of mercy from thee! Every time thou seest the Bible, think thou seest on its cover, "Go up to Heaven; seek eternal life."

Then there is *the ministry* through which the Spirit of God speaks.

I have often prayed my Master to give me a Baxter's heart to weep for sinners and a Whitefield's tongue to plead. I have neither; but if I had them, how I would plead with you!

But such as I have I give you. As God's ambassador, I do beseech you, sinner, turn from the error of your ways. "As I live, saith the Lord, I have no pleasure in the death of him that dieth, but would rather that he turn unto me and live."

Why will ye die? Is Hell so pleasant? Is an angry God a trifle? Is sin a thing to be laughed at? Is the right hand of God, when bared in thunder, a thing to be despised? Oh, turn thee! The Spirit bids thee flee to the refuge.

Moreover, does not *thy conscience* say the same? Is there not something in thy heart which says, *Begin to think about your soul; trust thy soul with Christ?* May grace divine constrain you to listen to the still small voice, that you may be saved!

And last of all,

## 4. The Spirits of Your Friends Departed Cry From Heaven to You

That voice I would you could hear saying, "Come up hither." Mother—unconverted woman—you have a babe in Heaven; perhaps not one or two, but a family of babes in Heaven. You are a mother of angels, and those young cherubs cry to you, "Mother, come up hither." But this can never be unless you repent and believe in the Lord Jesus Christ.

Some of you have carried to the tomb the most sainted of relatives. Your hoary-headed father at last went the way of all flesh, and from his celestial seat before the eternal throne he cries, "Come up hither."

A sister, sicklied by consumption, who has long since left your house for you to mourn her absence, cries, "Come up hither."

I adjure you, ye sons of saints in Glory; I adjure you, daughter of immortal mothers; despise not the voice of those who speak from Heaven to you. Were it possible for them to come here to speak to you, I know the notes of fond affection which would spring from your lips—"There's my mother." "There's my father."

*They* cannot come, but I am the spokesman for them. If I cannot speak as *they* might, yet remember, if ye be not converted when you hear the Gospel preached, "neither would you be converted if one rose from the dead." They could but tell you the Gospel; I do no less; that

Gospel is, "Believe on the Lord Jesus Christ, and thou shalt be saved."

"He that believeth and is baptized shall be saved," says the Evangelist. To believe is to trust Christ; to be baptized is not baby sprinkling—for *that* there is no warrant but in the inventions of man. To be baptized is to be buried with Christ in baptism after faith; for that which is done without faith, and not done of faith, is contrary to the Lord's command. Baptism is for saints, not for sinners: like the Lord's Supper, it is *in* the church, not *out* of it. Baptism does not save you; you are baptized because you are saved. Baptism is the outward recognition of the great inward change which the Spirit of God has wrought.

Believe, then, in Jesus. Flat on thy face before His cross cast thyself now; then rise and say, "Now will I confess His name, be united with His church and believe that at last, having confessed Him before men, He may confess me before my Father which is in Heaven."

Now I am clear of your blood—remember. I suppose there are seven thousand people here tonight who will be without excuse in the day of judgment. I have warned you as best I can. I have pleaded with you. Sinner, thy blood be on thine own head if thou refuse this great salvation.

O God the Holy Ghost, make them willing in the day of Thy power and save them this night for Thy name's sake. Amen.

## The Lovely Land

I soon shall see the beauty of the Lovely Land—
The country where the shining river flows—
The Paradise of love the Heavenly Father planned,
The Lovely Land where Heaven's Garden grows.

I soon shall hear the music of the Lovely Land—
The country where the singing river flows—
Redemption's anthem shall its euphony expand,
The wonders of salvation to disclose.

I soon shall go to dwell within the Lovely Land—
The country where the restful river flows—
No storm shall e'er destroy my homestead on that strand,
No foe assail, no enemy depose.

I soon shall see my Saviour in the Lovely Land—
The country where His peace forever flows—
Shall see His lovely face, shall touch His nail-scarred hand;
One glimpse, my restless spirit will compose.

                                        Paul Hutchens

HARRY J. HAGER
1899-1983

# ABOUT THE MAN:

Dr. Hager attended Hope College and later became professor of Bible and Biblical Literature there. He graduated from Western Theological Seminary as class valedictorian and graduated from Chicago University with a Ph.D. He did extensive research and traveled in Egypt, Palestine and other Bible lands from 1926-29.

Dr. Hager was pastor of Bethany Reformed Church, Chicago, from 1929-1975. In addition to his parish of some 3,000—the largest congregation of his denomination—he conducted several evangelistic campaigns and Bible conferences a year, directed America's largest summer DVBS and had a radio ministry of five hours weekly on two major Chicago stations.

Prior to his ministry at Bethany, he pastored a Presbyterian church in Volga, South Dakota, and a Reformed church at Forest Grove, Michigan.

Some of the other positions he enjoyed were: Bible conference speaker at Winona Lake and American Keswick, a speaker at the historic Congress on Prophecy at Calvary Baptist Church, New York City; a frequent speaker at the noonday meetings of the Chicago Christian Businessmen's Committee which broadcast over WJJD; was a frequent speaker on WMBI; a member of the Advisory Council of the World Christian Fundamentals Association, National Association of Evangelicals, and the International Child Evangelism Fellowship.

Dr. Hager crossed the Atlantic eleven times in the interests of worldwide evangelism. In 1949 he made a worldwide tour of foreign mission fields. In 1950 he made his third visit to the Holy Land. In 1952 he conducted a two-week evangelistic crusade in the Dutch language in Amsterdam under the auspices of Youth for Christ.

He is the author of *The Dutch School of Radical N.T. Criticism.*

He was a good friend of Dr. John R. Rice and the Sword of the Lord ministries. Many Sword of the Lord conferences on evangelism were held in his large church on the south side of Chicago.

Dr. Hager resigned his church in 1976 and died in 1983 in Holland, Michigan.

# XVII.

# *The City of God*

## HARRY J. HAGER

*"On the east three gates; on the north three gates; on the south three gates; and on the west three gates."*—Rev. 21:13.

You have often heard the statement that the New Testament is in the Old Testament contained, the Old Testament is by the New explained. We may well reverse the formula and say: The Old Testament is in the New contained, and the New Testament is by the Old explained. For there is no New Testament book that has in it so much Old Testament imagery as the one above.

This is particularly true of the passage which we shall study this evening. The entire description of the Holy City in this 21st chapter is both literal and symbolic. That is to say, we have here not merely a poem or a picture but a plan and a prophecy of the heavenly city with actual forms and measurements.

But we have here also a parable of the gospel fellowship, and for its understanding the encampment of the tribes about the Old Testament tabernacle and Ezekiel's vision of the New Jerusalem furnish us the keys.

These keys let us approach the gates of the heavenly city. Observe that there are twelve gates of the heavenly city. Observe that there are twelve gates always open, each bearing the name of a tribe with an equal number on each side facing the entire world.

From all of these details we glean the following parabolic truth: Through Jesus Christ, the fellowship of God's eternal society is available to every race, ample for every human diversity, accessible to every human condition.

## Catholicity of the City of God

It is unfortunate that the word "catholicity" has become passe; it is simply another accurate word for universal. Protestants do not like to use it because it suggests to them the church of Rome. Originally, however, that word connoted the very idea you have here in this passage of Scripture.

This city is a quadrangle; and it faces north, east, south and west. You have in this text the suggestion that the fellowship of the Gospel of Jesus Christ is of such a universal nature that upon the portals of this heavenly city are written these cheerful words: WELCOME ONE AND ALL. The gates on the east provide a welcome for China, Japan, Mongolia, Borneo, India and the islands of the sea. The northern gates are open to Lapland, Scandinavia, Siberia and Labrador. When we turn to the south, we think of Algeria, Ethiopia, South Africa, and Argentina. The Gospel is not only universal, but the heavenly city is catholic in its scope; and there will be multitudes from every nation, tongue and tribe in that Glad Day.

That is true for one reason only—there is a universal Christ. Jesus Himself is a manifold Saviour who makes an appeal to all races of men. We must protest against such statements, so popular these days, that, after all, Jesus was simply a Jew. The social, historical school of theology likes to confine Him to some little corner of Palestine, and stress such names as "The Galilean," "The Nazarene," "The Carpenter," as though Christ must be conceived only in terms of His immediate environment. Jesus Christ, according to the Scriptures, is "The Second Adam," "The Universal Man," not simply A man but THE Man, the Man Christ Jesus; and He makes an appeal to every type of human personality as represented by all of the different races and tribes of men. Out of Bethlehem arises the new humanity. At Calvary mankind got a new start.

What a picture this text suggests to us of the great day when all these people will begin to flow through the gates, multitudes from the east, multitudes from the south, great numbers from the west, and great hosts from the north, coming from all directions of the compass through the three gates on each side into that heavenly city. What a gathering that will be!

> **Oh that bright and golden morning when the Son of Man shall come,**
>   **And the radiance of His glory we shall see!**
> **When from every clime and nation He shall call His people home—**
>   **What a gathering of the Ransomed that will be!**
>
> **When the Bless'd who sleep in Jesus at His bidding shall arise**
>   **From the silence of the grave, and from the sea;**

**And with bodies all celestial they shall meet Him in the skies —**
**What a gathering and rejoicing that will be!**

**When our eyes behold the City with the many mansions bright,**
**And its River calm, and restful, flowing free —**
**When the friends that death has parted shall in bliss again unite,**
**What a meeting and a greeting there will be!**

Because the quadrangle has twelve gates and there are three gates on each side, we may be assured it will be the greatest of all convocations, a gathering from all generations and from all peoples that have ever populated this globe in all of the centuries and in all of the dispensations.

## Immensity of the City of God

Certainly the City of God must be an immense city if it has twelve gates for its people to pour through. That suggests its tremendous amplitude.

Ancient Babylon had one hundred gates; they needed them because it was a city of one hundred twenty furlongs. Thebes, the ancient Egyptian city, had one hundred gates. While this city has only twelve gates, we read that it was much larger than the city of Babylon, for the new Jerusalem is fifteen hundred miles square. It is almost beyond human imagination to conceive the length, breadth and height of that great City of God. It was beyond the imagination of a man like Augustine when in his great work, De Civitate Dei, the Celestial City, he was unable to compute its size and magnitude.

There is no stint or parsimony on the part of God when it comes to any work of creation.

When He makes stars, He makes them innumerable. When He fashions the jewels in the heart of the earth, He makes their supply inexhaustible. When He lays the deposits of coal in the earth, He deposits them in veins and strata immeasurable and incalculable. When God creates angels, He creates them by myriads and myriads, ten thousand upon ten thousands. When he creates the human race, He begins with a single pair; but He gives to them such power of multiplication that they too can hardly be numbered.

A city the building of which engages all the powers of God's recreative genius must be a city of stupendous size if it needs twelve different entrances that its people might have access to it.

And such a city ought to suggest to us the proportions of the Father's love. Nobody has ever measured the love of God. Paul longed that his readers might know the breadth and length and depth and height of the love of God. And when John wants to give some kind of measurement by which to compute that love, he says, "For God so loved the world, that he gave his only begotten Son, that whosoever believeth in him should not perish, but have everlasting life."

But if you want to know the length and breadth and height and depth of the love of God, go to the Celestial City and begin to measure its proportions. It has been built to house a great multitude that no one can number.

We are lead to another conclusion and a most solemn one. The Scriptures declare that God will have all men to be saved and to come to the knowledge of the truth, for He is not willing that any should perish but that all should come to repentance. He has created a city that is large enough, whose gates are wide enough, and ample enough for all to enter. "For without are dogs, and sorcerers, and whoremongers, and murderers, and idolaters, and whosoever loveth and maketh a lie." He has sent out His angel messengers with the behest, "Compel them to come in, that my house may be filled," and with the encouraging information, "yet there is room."

Hence, if you miss the gates of Heaven at last, it will be your own fault. If you are still "outside" it is not because God has not made ample provision. The city is big enough, the proportions large enough, the invitation broad enough—

> There's a wideness in God's mercy
> Like the wideness of the sea;
> There's a kindness in His justice,
> Which is more than liberty.

> For the love of God is broader,
> Than the measure of man's mind.
> And the heart of the Eternal
> Is most wonderfully kind.

## Multiformity of the City of God

Its multiformity matches our human diversity. You notice that each side has three gates. This suggests the multiplicity of Christ Jesus Himself which guarantees to us that every type sinner can find his way in by one of these twelve gates.

I read some commentator who was quite sure that Martin Luther went in by the third gate and Bishop Cranmer went in by the twelfth gate.

THE CITY OF GOD

I do not know how he figured it out, but we may be certain that there cannot be a sinner who has fallen so low or whose malady is so peculiar that he can lay before God as his reason for being lost that his strange case makes it impossible for him to find one among these twelve gates through which he can enter into the City of God.

We rejoice at this multiformity, for there are various motives that impel us to come to the cross of Jesus Christ.

*"The Spirit of the Lord is upon me, because he hath anointed me to preach the gospel to the poor; he hath sent me to heal the broken-hearted, to preach deliverance to the captives, and recovering of sight to the blind, to set at liberty them that are bruised, To preach the acceptable year of the Lord."*—Luke 4:18,19.

Our Saviour is a many-sided Redeemer. Some of us were first drawn to Jesus perhaps because of sickness, others because of poverty, still others because of temptation and defeat. Perhaps it was some other condition.

One comes to Christ impelled by a sense of duty. He has been trained in a Christian home, and he has been told all his life by his father and mother that the Christian life alone is worthwhile. He has a sense of Christianity's high principles and lofty ideals. He is aware that the standards of other religions and schools of thought cannot be compared at all with the stable concepts of Christianity. He hears the challenge to follow the gleam, to take up the Holy Grail. He responds,

> **I would be true, for there are those who trust me;**
> **I would be pure, for there are those who care;**
> **I would be strong, for there is much to suffer;**
> **I would be brave, for there is much to dare.**

From his sense of duty he gets his first glimpse of the Lord Jesus Christ in all His purity and perfection, and he says, "I will follow."

> **A still small voice in childhood,**
> **A beckoning hand in youth,**
> **An impulse prompting justice,**
> **A heart inclined to truth;**
> **A firm resolve to follow**
> **The path where saints have trod.**
> **Some of us call it conscience,**
> **And others call it — God.**

Here is someone else who comes to Christ driven by sorrow. This world is full of people who never once give a thought to Heaven and eternity and God and the cross until some little darling is taken out of the home. Then they begin to think, and think hard; and they go weeping to Calvary driven by one motive—a broken heart.

It is not sorrow for their sins first of all. It is sorrow for a lost loved one and the hope that she may be reclaimed in the great city beyond.

As they think of it they begin to look at themselves and see the blackness of their own sins. They cannot possibly go into the Celestial City unless they first go to Calvary's old humbling ground and plunge into the fountain opened for uncleanness. There is a gate that swings open for such in the Heavenly City.

Then there are some whose frustrations in life drive them to the Lord Jesus. Out of these frustrations come a sense of emptiness and a longing

> Like tides on a crescent sea beat
>   When the moon is new and thin,
> Into our heart's high longings
>   Come welling and surging in;
> Come from the mystic ocean
>   Whose rim no foot has trod—
> Some of us call it longing,
>   And others call it—God.

Oh, the multiple appeal the Holy Spirit has to the human heart! And when that appeal has been made, Jesus Christ is not simply one door, He is many doors into the kingdom, able to meet every human diversity. The Twelve Gates suggest to us the multiplicity of Christ.

But I believe He is also a multiple Christ in that He respects every diversity. There are some people today who are sure that we should not have any denominations. I am not quite so sure about that. "Many folds but one flock." We have one Shepherd, the Lord Jesus Christ; but this side of the grave He keeps us in many different folds. And that corresponds to the Heavenly City which has one House but many mansions, many dwelling places in the one Father's House, twelve gates by which we may enter into the city. Our human diversity is met by the great multiformity of this City of God.

And these gates are also a symbol of the many satisfactons of that great city—one satisfaction for this type and another satisfaction for that type.

> "What is Heaven?" I asked a little child,
> "All joy;" and in her innocence she smiled.
> I asked the aged, with her care oppressed,
> All suffering o'er, "Oh, Heaven at last is rest."

I asked the artist who adored his art —
"Heaven is all beauty," spoke his raptured heart.
I asked the poet with soul afire,
"'Tis glory," and he struck his lyre.
I asked the Christian waiting his release,
A halo round him, lo, he answered, "Peace."
So all may look with hopeful eyes above:
'Tis beauty, glory, joy, rest, peace, and love.

## Accessibility of the City of God

Our text says the gates are open day and night. This is most interesting because some commentators do not know what to do with a city that has a wall, yet whose gates are open.

One of them mixes metaphors, Gospel and prophecy and says these gates are going to be shut at a certain time, never to be opened again. This passage of Scripture says that they are never closed day or night.

One commentator suggests that the walls were meant to separate and exclude; hence, certain saints will get inside the city, but the rest will live outside in the fields. Only those who entered through the gateway of death with an "abundant entrance" into the everlasting Kingdom would actually go through those open gates into the city. The Gospel, however, does not tell us that there will be one class of saints inside the city and another class outside in the suburbs. The city has gates that are open all the time, and they never close day or night.

*"Therefore thy gates shall be open continually; they shall not be shut day nor night; that men may bring unto thee the forces of the Gentiles, and that their kings may be brought."* — Isa. 60:11.

What does this mean to us that the Heavenly City's gates are never closed? First of all, at from whatever point we may be standing, there is for each of us a straight line and a shortest distance to the nearest open gate of the City of God. There are so many who say, "I would like to come but I cannot find a way."

Paul found it, though he was a persecutor. Bunyan found it, though he was a blasphemer. John Newton found it, though he was a drunken sailor and a slave dealer. There is no point from which a sinner cannot find the shortest distance, a straight line, to an open gate into this Heavenly City.

Therefore, if you are not saved in the great day when the roll is called up yonder and the great procession comes marching home, it will not be because you have not been able to find the way, but because you started *too late*. Do not start too late; do not start tomorrow—take your first step now.

Take the matter of sin. It is a universal fact; so that wherever you go you will find sin and sinners. But you and I are not only interested in the universal fact of sin; I am concerned especially about my sin; you are concerned about your sin. I have to answer for my sin. You have to answer for your sin.

Jesus is the Universal Saviour not in the sense that everybody is going to be saved, but in the sense that His sacrifice is so sufficient and the gospel presentation so broad that no one need perish.

*"Then Peter opened his mouth, and said, Of a truth I perceive that God is no respecter of persons: But in every nation he that feareth him, and worketh righteousness, is accepted with him."*—Acts 10:34,35.

God can never be blamed if a man is lost. If a man is seeking God at all, he will find Him. God stoops to meet his condition. There is a gate by which he can enter.

Now, then, if your sin is a personal responsibility, do you not see that your salvation is also your personal concern; and if you are lost, it is your own personal loss? When we say that salvation is personal, we mean this: does it make any difference if thousands and hundreds of thousands have found Jesus Christ before I found Him? No, He is MY Jesus, my Saviour; and the salvation he gave me is thenceforth my salvation; and the gate through which I enter is *my* gate; and through the ages of ages I will never forget that gate by which I came into the gospel fellowship and entered into the City of God.

When Lafayette came back to this country to celebrate the victory of the Revolution, they put on one celebration after another. The man was too old and feeble to care about any of the things by which he was favored. Finally after they had exhausted all their ingenuity, the band began to play "The Marseillaise"; and they showed a tableau of his home city in France where Lafayette was raised as a little boy. That old warrior who with Washington had saved this country began to weep like a child. It was one chord that they could strike in the heart of the faded man. He longed for the homeland.

Down in your heart is there not that longing to enter into the City of God? It is the home of the human soul. Let that homesickness be a magnet to draw you.

There is a gate through which all of us *must* at some time pass—the exit out into the Great Beyond called "Death." When Livingstone was so feeble that his servants had to wait on him, they came to his tent one day and found him beside his cot, beside a little camp chair on his knees. He had before him a map of Africa that he himself had drawn. This great missionary-explorer was the only one who knew the African interior well enough to draw a map of it in those days. Tears had fallen on that map.

When his companions first looked in, they said, "The Master is praying. Let us not disturb him." They came back after a half hour; and he was exactly in the same posture, still praying, so they went away. Returning again and noticing he was still in the same position, the men drew near and found that he was no longer praying—he was praising! On his knees with his tear-stained map of Africa before him, David Livingstone, while praying that the hosts of Africa might follow him along the trail he blazed through the gates of the City of God, had himself passed out through the exit of death and through "his" gate into the Heavenly City.

Just as sure as you are living, YOU will go out through the exit of "Death" into eternity. Will the gates be standing open for YOU to enter into the City of God?

## There Is a Land

There is a land of pure delight,
  Where saints immortal reign;
Eternal day excludes the night,
  And pleasures banish pain;
There everlasting Spring abides,
  And never-with'ring flowers;
Death, like a narrow sea, divides
  This heavenly land from ours.

Sweet fields beyond the swelling flood
  Stand dressed in living green;
So to the Jews old Canaan stood,
  While Jordan rolled between;
Could we but climb where Moses stood,
  And view the landscape o'er
Not Jordan's stream, nor death's cold flood
  Should fright us from the shore.

                    Author Unknown

WILLIAM KENNETH McCOMAS
1929-

# ABOUT THE MAN:

William Kenneth McComas was born just prior to the Great Depression. Denied a formal education largely due to poverty, he completed only eight grades of school in Wayne County, West Virginia. A physical breakdown at fourteen was followed by a disease diagnosed as incurable.

He felt, at an early age, that God had called him to preach, so he entered the ministry and became remarkably successful as a pastor, author and evangelist.

God has given this self-educated man an incredibly retentive and photographic memory. His sermons are spiced with colorful, illustrative language. And he writes the way he preaches.

Dr. McComas began the Calvary Baptist Church, Rittman, Ohio, in 1960 with eight members; today it boasts a membership of several thousand.

Before going into full-time evangelism in 1976, in addition to pastoring this large church, he conducted revival campaigns, preaching in many great churches. Also, he often spoke on college campuses and to civic organizations.

His prolific pen has produced many books. Somewhere on his agenda, he also found time to record twenty long-play stereo albums of his messages. Two of his patriotic sermons have been read into the *Congressional Record*. He holds an honorary Doctorate of Divinity and an LL.D. degree for outstanding achievements.

Dr. John Rawlings said of him: "I consider Dr. McComas one of the strongest men spiritually I have ever known. He lives and practices what he believes with a dedication to God that sets him apart from others."

# XVIII.

# *Almost Heaven*

KENNY McCOMAS

Text: Revelation 21:1-17

*"And I saw a new heaven and a new earth: for the first heaven and the first earth were passed away; and there was no more sea. And I John saw the holy city, new Jerusalem, coming down from God out of heaven, prepared as a bride adorned for her husband."*—Rev. 21:1,2.

My subject this morning is "Almost Heaven."

Several years ago John Denver wrote a song about my native West Virginia entitled "Country Roads." It became the number one seller in this country and even in other countries. Although John had never been inside the state boundaries, he referred to West Virginia as being "almost Heaven." The phrase became very popular and was unofficially adopted as the state motto.

I became keenly interested in Heaven as a seven-year-old boy. It was when my mother moved to that place of mystery and such marvelous mansions that my interest grew so intent. But since then I have also become extremely interested in an area that is "almost" Heaven. And I do not refer to West Virginia when I refer to "almost" Heaven today.

I want to present four points of alliteration relative to Heaven:

Heaven's reality,
Heaven's residents,
Heaven's revelation,
Heaven's resemblances.

## Heaven's Reality

Let's consider briefly the reality of Heaven. It was in the far-famed Santa Clara Valley near San Jose, California, that the world's largest house was built. It was started in 1890 with very normal and ordinary dimensions; today that house covers more than fourteen acres.

It has a very curious and amazing labyrinth. It has many floors and many levels; it has winding stairs and upside-down pillars. It has blind doors and dead-end hallways. It has intricate passageways and literally thousands of windows. It has countless thousands of mysterious paintings, panelings and porches. If a visitor were to be left in the middle of that huge house, it would take him hours, possibly days, to find his way to liberty.

Mrs. Winchester, the original owner, labored under a very strange obsession. It was her belief that as long as she continued to build onto her house, she would never die.

But one evening at sunset, as the shadows of the mountains were cast out over the Pacific in Southern California, an uninvited and unwelcome visitor came into that huge house. Even though he had not been there before and did not have a guide, he found his way through the winding stair, through those strange, dark passageways, and finally found a room known as the blue room. In that room, lying upon her sickbed, was Mrs. Winchester.

The sad fate of his visit was: that grand, great, glorious house, as formidable and foreboding as it was, was now without an owner. Mrs. Winchester had died.

Perhaps my message will be more suggestive than it will be exhaustive. But I would like us to first consider two aspects of the reality of Heaven: number one—the topography of Heaven; two—the typography of Heaven.

Topography means that it is literal. That is exactly what our Lord said in John 14 to His disciples in the Upper Room, "Let not your heart be troubled: ye believe in God, believe also in me. In my Father's house are many mansions: if it were not so, I would have told you. I go to prepare a place for you." That word "place" has great and powerful dimensions.

The New Jerusalem has walls; it has gates; it has streets. Incidentally, they are paved with gold. How would you like to live in a city where gold is used for asphalt? The New Jerusalem has rivers. It has trees. And our Lord said it has "many mansions." He is saying that the dwelling places in the New Jerusalem are absolutely innumerable; they cannot be counted.

Mrs. Winchester's mansion, as great a giant as it is, is not worthy to be compared with the mansions of the New Jerusalem. The Word of God says the New Jerusalem, the Capital City of Heaven, is a four-dimensional city, which means it has the same measurements on all four sides.

There have been some deviation and variation among theologians as to the exact size. Some contend it is exactly 1,342 square miles. Others contend it is exactly 1,500 miles square. We do know, on the authority of God's Word, that it has ample space for us all. It would be somewhere in the area of the size of the eastern half of the United States—that is, one floor would be. But it is also somewhere in the area of 1,500 miles high.

Notice verse 1 of Revelation 21. Bear in mind that in order to measure any object, one has to have a starting and a stopping place. The New Jerusalem has to be literal, or it cannot be measured. Verse 1: "I saw a new heaven and a new earth." God is going to trade in the old model for a new one—a new Heaven and a new earth. When man sinned in the Garden of Eden a curse was placed upon this earth. God had not permitted any storm clouds in the skies up until that point. The choir sang this morning very beautifully, "Oh, they tell me of a land . . . where no storm clouds rise." Someday we will go back to a Paradise that will exceed the Paradise of Eden.

There were no storms, no wild convulsions in the elements of nature, no briers, no thorns, no thistles to disturb the ground.

But God said to Adam, "Because of this curse, you must earn your bread from this day forward by the sweat of your face. Because of this, all of these strange things are going to happen upon the earth."

Paul tells us in Romans, chapter 8, that "the whole creation groaneth and travaileth"; he said it is "waiting . . . for the redemption," to wit, waiting for the Lord to come.

This old earth has a lot of aches and pains. It is hurting. It is groaning.

There is no sadder sound in this universe than the storms at sea. Have you ever stood on a mountain and listened to the wind sigh with a broken heart through the pines? Did you ever see a big man stand with his shoulders shaking and the tears running down his face? Friend, this is a sad world.

Rosemary Cloony told reporters how she had stayed on top of the charts for twenty consecutive years: "I keep it simple, sexy and sad. The people want it that way."

Our record players, our radios and televisions have become nothing more than a mournful, sighing box of agony, presenting the sorrows, the sufferings, the pain, the travail of this world that Paul was speaking about.

Then John said that the new Heaven and the new earth are just slight deletions, not a great change. He mentioned two important major changes in the earth.

First, there will be no more sea. What did he mean by that? Ask a sailor who has spent some time out on the ocean. When I flew over to the Bahamas I saw thirty-foot waves on the ocean. Huge ocean liners were standing up on the end. I thought they were not going to right themselves. The sea presents storms, dangers and crises. Something out yonder is always a threat to the sailor's life.

Not only did he say there would be no more sea; he said, "There shall be no night there" (vs. 25). Days can be difficult, but nights can become literally unbearable. Seventy-eight percent of all crimes are committed during the dark hours. As brazen and as bold as the criminal is today, he still waits till night to do his dirty work.

John said here in Revelation, " I saw the holy city." A holy city—no night, no more seas. Won't it be something when the seas are removed from this earth! Oceans are nothing but huge septic tanks. Our health, our general well-being depends upon those oceans. And those tides are controlled by the moon. God put all the chemicals out there in the ocean to purify the pollutions of this world.

Seventy-five percent of this globe is covered with water. We will have a lot of parking space when He takes away all the water! There is talk about a shortage of space down here. In Southern California they are burying whole families in one grave. Well, there will be plenty of spaces on this globe then.

John said it was a *"holy city."* No night, no more seas, and it will have no crime. Never has there been a city that has not known murder, theft, rape, and all these other crimes. But John said in this holy city there are no crimes.

Friend, I have a mansion up there in that city! Do you?

Then as John looked and saw the holy city, the New Jerusalem, coming down from God out of Heaven, he said it was "like a bride adorned for her husband." I have never seen a bride who was not beautiful. I cannot say that for the grooms! When I was pastor and came out three, four or five times on a weekend and stood behind the pulpit, I didn't excite the congregation one bit. Those people were waiting for the bride to come out of that back room. This poor groom came and stood beside me. Both of us together couldn't impress anybody! They were watching for the bride. The New Jerusalem will also be ever so beautiful.

Now when you compare the holy city, the New Jerusalem, with the cities you have lived in down here, you will come to the same conclusion the Apostle Paul did: "For me to depart would be far better." Paul said, "If . . . our earthly house . . . were dissolved, we have a building of God . . . not made with hands, eternal in the heavens."

Stuart Hamblen in his once popular song, "This Old House," said, "This old house just groans and trembles when the night wind flings its arms." It gets pretty shaky sometimes. Paul said when the winds break in upon us, it is apt to crumble and fall apart. But if it does, he said, "We have a building of God, an house not made with hands, eternal in the heavens."

Now let's look at the typography of Heaven, which means it has style; it has design; it has visible glory. I wish I could describe Heaven to you, but I can't. Paul said, "I knew a man in Christ above fourteen years ago, (whether in the body, I cannot tell; or whether out of the body, I cannot tell: God knoweth;)." But he was caught up into the third Heaven, and he heard words that were not lawful for man to utter. In no generation of this world's history has man been able to enjoy heavenly things because we can't understand them. Everything God told us about Heaven was in the negative and in the language of accommodation.

John went on to say that in Heaven there are no tears. If I could announce this morning that there is a city where tears don't come, I have a notion we would form a long caravan and move in that direction before sunset. I have seen too many tears already; I would be happy to see no more.

An anthropologist wrote a new book some time ago, and only an anthropologist could say what he said: "Man is the only animal born without any ability to do anything for himself." He said, "The only thing a man can do when he is born is cry." He said, "Life, for humanity, is one long, loud and lasting cry." He said, "Man enters this world crying, he spends his time here crying, then makes his exit crying."

An agnostic said, "This life is a sad vale of tears." There won't be any tears there. John said there will be no more death. Death causes more tears than anything else. John said there will be no more morgues, no more funerals, no more hospitals, no more heartaches and heartbreaks. We can use our land for something else besides cemeteries, for there will be no more deaths.

## Heaven's Residents

Second, the residents of Heaven. The writer to the Hebrews said, "We also are compassed about with so great a cloud of witnesses . . . ." While we are performing down here in the arena of life, up yonder in the grandstands of Glory is a great cloud of witnesses watching us. When we do something pleasing to our audience, they probably stand up and cheer. Sometimes it seems I can almost hear them.

Way out yonder in the grandstands of Glory is Moses. And there are Joshua and Elijah and Gideon and Stephen; and James and John, the suns of thunder; and Simon Peter; and the Apostle Paul is up there, the man who could say at the end of the way, "I have fought a good fight, I have finished my course, I have kept the faith. I have made it Home!"

Look a little closer out yonder; by the eye of faith I think you can see some familiar faces. Not Old or New Testament saints who went out in centuries past, but those who have left your presence and mine. When I look I see some who are very dear and near to my heart. My mother is there. My dad is in that crowd. My old grandpa and grandmother also. I have a couple of little brothers up there. A lot of my loved ones are in that crowd.

They are up there, but they cannot tell us what they would like for us to know. We have to wait down here until our time comes to go to be with the Lord. But bear in mind: as the loved ones pass one by one and go down the valley, it makes the attraction over yonder a little brighter and the attraction here a little less behind us.

While taking a shipload of sheep from Scotland to Australia the ship was engulfed in great fog and had to anchor in and wait for days for the fog to lift. The sheep in that ship refused to eat. The caretaker thought they were all going to die. They wouldn't touch a bit of the food that had been prepared and brought on board.

Then one morning the fog lifted; and those sheep looked out and saw the green, grassy hills of Australia. Then the owner of those sheep understood. They were not about to eat that dry food on ship when they could smell the aroma of that green vegetation coming off those hills.

If you once get a glimpse of Heaven, you will say with Paul, "One thing I do, forgetting those things which are behind [I am not going to try to press any more satisfying juices out of this mundane world and the dry rocks down here] . . . I press toward the mark for the prize of the high calling of God in Christ Jesus."

## Heaven's Revelation

John Newton, on a slave ship, said, "When I get to Heaven, there will be three great surprises waiting me. First, I will be surprised to see some I didn't expect would make it. Then I am going to be surprised to find others missing that I thought would be there. But the greatest surprise of all is when I discover that John Newton is in Heaven for eternity."

**Amazing grace! how sweet the sound,**
**That saved a wretch like me!**
**I once was lost, but now am found,**
**Was blind, but now I see.**

You ask, "Are we going to know each other in Heaven?" O my friend, will we! Our very casual and brief passing acquaintance does not allow us to know each other down here. When we get out yonder in the vast expanse of this universe and are finally set at liberty and the fetters of the gravitation of this world are broken from us, we will discover that we have been locked up in a little darkroom down here and have finally been let out into the light of God's glory!

Tennyson caught a vision of that when he wrote his poem, "Let there be no moaning at the bar when I put out to sea."

When I was a boy in West Virginia, at all the funeral services the old preacher would talk about the loved ones being "anchored in" over yonder. My friend, that is not the case. When our loved ones leave here, they have just been cut loose from the harbor and are moving out into areas they have never known before.

It is very interesting to read what John said in Revelation 21 and 22 about God having a brand on all His people in Heaven. We wonder why He would do that.

The interesting thing is, through that big dish on the Mojave Desert, they have discovered there are literally millions of quasars burning out yonder many billions of times larger than our sun. They say they are so far out in space that it would take 400 billion light years for the light of those quasars (or suns) to penetrate the earth's atmosphere. Then they look at each other in amazement and say, "Isn't it strange they have been there all the time, and we didn't know there was space that far!"

We are prone to brag that man has gone to the moon. But we haven't gotten off the earth's back porch when we go to the moon. How about when we move on out into the galaxies? How about when men truly become astronauts and cosmonauts, when they ride in the cosmic atmosphere and among the stars that are millions of light years out yonder in space?

When we get out yonder, we will know some things we couldn't know down here. Now we see through a glass, darkly. The shades are pulled over the window, and everything is distorted; nothing is in its true perspective. But the one thing above all others that Heaven is going to reveal is the good things in people that we didn't see. Oh, we are so prone to find the strangeness and the eccentricities in others. We wonder, "What makes them do such silly things?" When we get up there, we are going to look at ourselves and wonder, *Why did we do that? Why did we do such silly things?*

Teachers are teaching in our schools that we are the apex of evolution's pyramid. They tell us we know all there is to know. They tell us that our ancestors came out of the deep freeze of dark and dismal ignorance. They tell us that through training and technological know-how, we are marching forward in seven-league boots and we have swept aside all ignorance—and we've got it!

But future generations are going to look at ours and say, "Strange that the little man in that day had to run off to the moon and try to learn to live up there before he could learn to live like a Christian down here." And they are going to say, "They thought they knew something, didn't they? Why, they were worse than cave men! They didn't know anything after all."

Like the Queen of Sheba of old when she came into the presence of Solomon, we are going to say up yonder, "We heard some things about this place down yonder in our native land; now that we have seen it with our own eyes, the half had not been told." We couldn't believe it then.

A preacher friend was telling me about following a couple through Carlsbad Caverns out in New Mexico. He said as they went through and all these amazing and wondrous stalagmites and stalactites kept coming into vision and focus, the lady, having gone through there at least once or maybe twice before, was holding onto her husband's arm. He said, "Honey, why didn't you tell me before about this beautiful place?" She looked at him and said, "I tried to, but I couldn't. I knew you would have to see it for yourself."

Christians have the mistaken idea that when they get to Heaven they are going to run over the New Jerusalem the first day they get there.

With all the modern means of travel, it still takes two weeks to look London over. It takes six weeks to look Rome over. It takes over three months to look over Tokyo, the largest city in the world. How long do you think it is going to take to look over the New Jerusalem, a city 1,500 miles or somewhere thereabouts in every direction?

I am adventurous by nature. I love to travel. If they were to announce that a rocket was leaving for the New Jerusalem today, I would say, "Save me a seat."

## Heaven's Resemblances

We look, last of all, at Heaven's resemblances. That which resembles Heaven most down here is when a lost soul comes to know Christ as Saviour. There is more rejoicing in the presence of the angels of Heaven "over one sinner that repenteth, more than over ninety and nine just persons, which need no repentance."

My friend, it is "almost" Heaven down here to know your family is all in the fold. It is "almost" Heaven down here to be able to take your family with you to church. It is "almost" Heaven down here to be able to sit down together with the Word of God, pray and have your devotions together and look forward to the time you will be eternally together in Heaven.

You can live in the suburbs of Glory here. But so many times the hustle and bustle of this wild, wicked world has taken its toll upon the Christian home and, instead of living in the suburbs of Heaven, we live in the suburbs of Hell. Many times husbands and wives have only a casual, passing acquaintance. What a shame, when God has provided so many wonderful things in His resemblances of Heaven down here!

There is another aspect of "almost" Heaven, and that is when those who stand on the very threshold of being saved turn, go out and never enter the Promised Land. Saying no to God may be saying goodby to God forever. "To day, if ye will hear his voice, Harden not your hearts." Why?

I spoke to a man one day who stood and trembled under the power of conviction. He admitted the Lord was dealing with his heart, but declared, "Nobody is going to push me! I'll get saved when I get ready."

He died suddenly, a young man in his thirties. His wife sat at the dining-room table, bit the blood out of her lips, pounded the table with her fists, and kept saying, "Preacher, tell me my husband is not in Hell!" I couldn't tell her that because the last thing the man said to me was, "Don't push me! I'll get saved when I get ready." I am afraid he let the Devil push him right into Hell. "Almost" to Heaven is a sad state.

Herod "almost" made it to Heaven. He went out to hear John the Baptist preach and was impressed. He saw those great throngs gathered in the Jordan Valley, and he went back again and again to hear John the Baptist. He was ready—as wicked and cruel and crusted as he was—to capitulate. But he chose instead that wicked woman. I looked at their caskets—hugh vaults of concrete with all their ancient, beautiful, architectural designs, when I was in the Holy Land. He had his great palace up on the hill and his huge theater in the backyard. Herod lived it up while down here. But as I stood there and looked at that hole over the top of his casket, I thought, *He has been dead now nearly two thousand years, and when two million years have gone by, Herod will be no closer to getting out of Hell than he is today!*

"Almost" Heaven can be Hell for eternity.

> "Almost persuaded" now to believe;
> "Almost persuaded" Christ to receive;
> Seems now some soul to say,
> "Go, Spirit, go Thy way,
> Some more convenient day
> On Thee I'll call."
>
> "Almost persuaded," come, come today;
> "Almost persuaded," turn not away;
> Jesus invites you here,
> Angels are ling'ring near,
> Prayers rise from hearts so dear,
> O wand'rer, come.
>
> "Almost persuaded," harvest is past!
> "Almost persuaded," doom comes at last!
> "Almost" cannot avail;
> "Almost" is but to fail!
> Sad, sad, that bitter wail—
> "Almost—but lost!"

# XIX.

# *Heaven*

## B. R. LAKIN

"And I saw a new heaven and a new earth: for the first heaven and the first earth were passed away; and there was no more sea. And I John saw the holy city, the new Jerusalem, coming down from God out of Heaven, prepared as a bride adorned for her husband. And I heard a great voice out of heaven saying, Behold, the tabernacle of God is with men, and he will dwell with them, and they shall be his people, and God himself shall be with them, and be their God. And God shall wipe away all tears from their eyes; and there shall be no more death, neither sorrow, nor crying, neither shall there be any more pain: for the former things are passed away."—Rev. 21:1-4.

The dictionary says that Heaven is the "abode" of God, and the Bible verifies this definition. In almost every book of the Old Testament, Heaven is mentioned as the abode of God. In Nehemiah 9:13 we read: "Thou camest down also upon mount Sinai, and spakest with them from heaven, and gavest them right judgments, and true laws, good statutes and commandments."

David recognized the existence of Heaven when he said: "The Lord looked down from heaven"; "He shall send from heaven, and save"; "O God . . . look down from heaven"; and "From heaven did the Lord behold the earth."

There is no religious doctrine so universally taught as the doctrine of Heaven. Practically all of the religions of the world teach that there is a Heaven to gain. Of course they differ in the methods and means of reaching that "desired haven," but they all agree that there is such a place.

But Christians invariably go to the New Testament in general, and to the utterances of Jesus in particular, for the corroboration of a doctrine, and we discover that Jesus verifies the utterances of the Old Testament writers in regard to the teaching of Heaven.

There is no doctrine more clearly taught by Jesus than the doctrine of Heaven. He said, "Lay up for yourselves treasure in heaven, where moth and rust do not corrupt and where thieves do not break through and steal." And, "When ye pray, say, Our Father which art in heaven." "Rejoice because your names are written in heaven." And, "Great is your reward in heaven."

Scores of times Heaven is mentioned in the New Testament, and it is always spoken of as a place, a definite location, the abode of God and His saints.

So that brings us to our first observation:

## I. HEAVEN IS A PLACE

Many people not versed in scriptural teaching consider Heaven a state of mind, or perhaps, if they believe in the hereafter at all, they say that it is a state of existence for the righteous dead.

Jesus asserted that it was a definite place when He said: "In my Father's house are many mansions [abodes]: if it were not so, I would have told you. I go to prepare a place for you. And if I go and prepare a place for you, I will come again, and receive you unto myself; that where I am, there ye may be also" (John 14:2,3).

Now Jesus Himself says that Heaven is a place, a prepared place, prepared by His own omnipotent hands. What a place it must be! It took God only six days to create the worlds, the firmament, and all of the wonders of the universe. But Jesus has been gone 1900 years preparing a place for us.

### 1. It Will Be a Place of Beauty

*"And the building of the wall of it was of jasper: and the city was pure gold, like unto clear glass. And the foundations of the wall of the city were garnished with all manner of precious stones. The first foundation was jasper; the second, sapphire; the third, a chalcedony; the fourth, an emerald; The fifth, sardonyx; the sixth, sardius; the seventh, chrysolyte; the eighth, beryl; the ninth, a topaz; the tenth, a chrysoprasus; the eleventh, a jacinth; the twelfth, an amethyst. And the twelve gates were twelve pearls; every several gate was of one pearl: and the street of the city was pure gold, as it were transparent glass."—* Rev. 21:18-21.

John the Revelator in describing the city he had seen, of course, had no words to adequately describe it, so he had to use the best words at his command to paint a picture of the beauty of the city. We are not to suppose that the beauties of that Holy City are limited to the existence of superb material splendor, described by the costly minerals described by John. This is the best he could do, with the vocabulary he possessed. One cannot describe spiritual splendor with material phraseology, but John was trying to give us a hint of the untold glory of the city that God had prepared. Paul, in thinking of the staggering glory that God has prepared for His own, said, "Eye hath not seen, nor ear heard, neither have entered into the heart of man, the things which God hath prepared for them that love him" (I Cor. 2:9).

## 2. Where Is Heaven?

We are not told the exact location of Heaven, but we are content in letting God alone know the whereabouts of our future abode. To know that it exists and that it is our final destination is enough for the trusting child of God.

In Deuteronomy 26:15 we read: "Look down from thy holy habitation, from heaven, and bless thy people." We read that Christ was "carried up into heaven," and that Stephen "looked up steadfastly into heaven." But the question comes to us, "How far up is Heaven?" Possibly not beyond the stars.

Come and go with me and we will take a little astronomical survey and see if we can find the "city foursquare." Let us take a journey from the sun and pass Neptune, our farthest planet, and we come to "Alpha Centauri" with its two suns and 26 times as much light as we have in our solar system, but we see no city there. Journeying on by the speed of light, we come to the Polar Star that is so far away that it takes light, traveling at the speed of 186,000 miles per second, 46 years to reach the earth, but we find no city. We come next to Vega, which has 440 times as much light as our solar system, and yet we find no Heaven. We hurry on to Alcyone, with 12,000 times as much light as our solar system, but we find no city.

Perhaps Heaven is not so far away as all that. We read in God's Word that it is so close that Jacob's ladder could reach up to it. It was so close that the angels came instantly to the side of Daniel to protect him from the ravenous jaws of the lions. It was so close that the angels descended immediately and delivered Peter from prison in answer to the prayers of the saints. It is so close that the vilest sinner, living on the brink of Hell, is just one step from it—that single step being the step of faith in taking the Lord Jesus as his Saviour. Jesus said: "I am the way."

### 3. It Is a Place of Definite Dimensions.

*"And the city lieth foursquare, and the length is as large as the breadth: and he measured the city with the reed, twelve thousand furlongs. The length and the breadth and the height of it are equal."*—Rev. 12:16.

Twelve thousand furlongs makes 1500 statute miles. The Holy City will be a cube 1500 miles long, 1500 miles wide, and 1500 miles high. The walls of the city were 144 cubits, or 216 feet thick.

Such a city would dwarf all of the great cities the world has ever known. Ancient Alexandria was only 30 furlongs in length. Jerusalem was 33 furlongs; Babylon was 120 furlongs; New York City measures 400 furlongs, and London, England, 325. The base of such a city would reach from Maine to Florida, and from the Atlantic Ocean to Pike's Peak in Colorado. It would cover all of Great Britain, Ireland, France, Italy, Spain, Germany, Austria, Poland, European Turkey and half of European Russia taken together.

Paul spoke of the "third heaven," and we have other hints in the Scripture that there will not be just one level of abode in Heaven. We, in our glorified bodies, will not be limited to the ground as we are here. The city could be subdivided into 1500 sections a mile high and 1500 miles wide and 1500 miles long. We can readily see that there will be plenty of "elbow room" in the City of God.

There will be twelve gates made of solid pearl. A gate in proportion to the size of such a wall should be about 100 miles wide. So, we will have an abundant entrance to that city, as there will be 50 miles of elbow room as we go through those gates of pearl. This thought inspired the song of F. H. Lehman:

> **Where the gates swing wide,**
> **On the other side;**
> **Where the flowers ever bloom.**
> **On the right hand, on the left hand—**
> **Fifty miles of elbow room.**

### 4. It Will Be a Place of Joy

*"And God shall wipe away all tears from their eyes; and there shall be no more death, neither sorrow, nor crying, neither shall there be any*

*more pain: for the former things are passed away."* —Rev. 21:4.

Tears, death, sorrow and pain came to the human family because of the fall. But God through the ages has been executing His plan of complete redemption of the race, and Heaven will be the "commencement day" of the saints of God. It is not the end of life for the Christian, but the "beginning of days."

> **Now our eyes are often dimmed,**
> **Tear-stained with the trials of life!**
> **But we know in that "long home,"**
> **We'll know no blighting pain and strife.**
>
> **Saddened then by dear ones lost;**
> **Taken from this earthly fold.**
> **O! What joy 'twill be up there,**
> **To meet them on the streets of gold.**

Because of the absence of the things that make sad, there will be unbounded joy and limitless Glory. "And they shall bring the glory and honour of the nations into it" (Rev. 21:26).

## II. HEAVEN IS A HOME

*"Behold, what manner of love the Father hath bestowed upon us, that we should be called the sons of God. . . . Beloved, now are we the sons of God, and it doth not yet appear what we shall be: but we know that, when he shall appear, we shall be like him; for we shall see him as he is."* —I John 3:1,2.

*"But as many as received him, to them gave he power to become the sons of God, even to them that believe on his name."* —John 1:12.

A home is for a family, and one must be born into a family. When Nicodemus inquired the way to Heaven, Jesus said, "Ye must be born again."

There are several denominations who doggedly insist that if one does not belong to their "man-made sect," that one will not go to Heaven. But no place in the Word of God are we told that we must affiliate with any particular religious group in order to gain admission to that "city foursquare."

Every Christian should belong to some sane, sound, and aggressive religious organization, but membership in a man-organized church group will not fit one for Heaven.

There is only one true church, and that is the New Testament church of the first born. This invisible church is comprised of all those who have trusted in Christ for salvation, regardless of their church affiliation.

*"But ye are come into mount Sion, and unto the city of the living God, the heavenly Jerusalem, and to an innumerable company of angels, To the general assembly and church of the firstborn, which are written in heaven, and to God the Judge of all, and to the spirits of just men made perfect."* —Hebrews 12:22,23.

Heaven is a home for those who have properly met the qualifications for citizenship in Heaven. "Now therefore ye are no more strangers and foreigners, but FELLOWCITIZENS with the saints, and of the household of God" (Eph. 2:19).

Heaven will be more than a house. A home is a house where love abides. The love of God will hallow that city, and a spirit of heavenly unity and harmony will fill the hearts of the citizens of that fair haven.

There will be no cause for discord, because the Devil and all his cohorts will be cast in the lake of fire where they shall be tormented day and night "for ever and ever."

*"The fearful, and unbelieving, and the abominable, and murderers, and whoremongers, and sorcerers, and idolaters, and all liars, shall have their part in the lake which burneth with fire and brimstone."* —Rev. 21:8.

Notice, the "unbelieving" will receive the same condemnation as the murderers, liars and whoremongers. "He that hath the Son hath life; and he that hath not the Son of God hath not life."

God does not classify sinners as we do. We say, "He is not a bad fellow." But God judges men according to their relationship to His Son. If we are not members of the heavenly family through faith in Christ, no matter how good we may be morally, we will be lost and will have our part in the lake of fire with the murderers, abominable and liars.

The members of this heavenly family will possess certain Christlike characteristics which will fit them for life in the eternal city of God. Even now do we have an "earnest of our inheritance":

*"For this cause I bow my knees unto the Father of our Lord Jesus Christ, Of whom the whole family in heaven and earth is named, That he would grant you according to the riches of his glory, to be strengthened with might by his spirit in the inner man; That Christ may dwell in your hearts by faith; that ye, being rooted and grounded in love,*

*May be able to comprehend with all saints what is the breadth, and length, and depth, and height; And to know the love of Christ, which passeth knowledge, that ye might be filled with all the goodness of God."*—Eph. 3:14-19.

Heaven will be the final abode of all those who through faith in Christ have become like unto their Heavenly Father in love, glory, and the fulness of His Spirit.

### III. HEAVEN WILL BE ETERNAL

*"For here we have no continuing city, but we seek one to come."*—Hebrews 13:14.

Life upon this earth is transient and changing. The sun may be shining today, but tomorrow may bring the tempests of sorrow, death, pain and heartache. The fond relationships of life are often broken, and our hearts bend beneath the weight of human bereavement. But Heaven will be the place where we will reap the reward of "everlasting life."

There are several "everlastings" in God's Word that apply to our eternal abode in Heaven.

### 1. Everlasting Joy

*"And the ransomed of the Lord shall return, and come to Zion with songs and everlasting joy upon their heads: they shall obtain joy and gladness, and sorrow and sighing shall flee away."*—Isa. 35:10.

In this life we are born crying and die sighing. There is little of permanent joy in this life. But joy and gladness will be eternal in Heaven. No moments of discouragement and depression, but righteous bliss throughout the endless ages of eternity.

### 2. Everlasting Light

*"Thy sun shall no more go down; neither shall thy moon withdraw itself: for the Lord shall be thine everlasting light, and the days of thy mourning shall be ended."*—Isa. 60:20.

*"And the city had no need of the sun, neither of the moon, to shine in it: for the glory of God did lighten it, and the Lamb is the light thereof."*—Rev. 21:23.

The light of the sun is the source of all life on this earth. Without light, there could be no life. Christ, the Light of the world, is the source of all spiritual life. "I am the light of the world: he that followeth me shall not walk in darkness, but shall have the light of life."

Christ, who is the source of our spiritual life, will be our Light throughout eternity. No more shadows. No more loathsome valleys. No more dread hours of loneliness in the night. But we will have the presence of the "Sun of Righteousness" throughout all eternity.

### 3. Everlasting Salvation

*"But Israel shall be saved in the Lord with an everlasting salvation: ye shall not be ashamed nor confounded world without end."*—Isa. 45:17.

*"And I give unto them eternal life; and they shall never perish, neither shall any man pluck them out of my hand."*—John 10:28.

A man once dreamed that he constructed a ladder from earth to Heaven. When he did a good deed, his ladder went up two feet. When he did an unusually good deed, his ladder went still higher. After a while it went out of sight, and he expected at death to step off the top rung of his "ladder of good works" into Heaven. But, in his dream, there came a clap of thunder and a bolt of lightning, and his ladder crumpled to the ground, and he heard a voice saying: "He that . . . climbeth up some other way . . . is a thief and a robber." When he awoke, he realized the mistake he had made, and sought salvation by grace through personal faith in Christ.

*"The wages of sin is death; but the gift of God is eternal life through Jesus Christ our Lord."*—Rom. 6:23.

This gift of eternal life will not lose its luster and glory throughout the eons of eternity.

A sainted mother in Israel dreamed that she had died. The guardian angel was showing her around in Heaven. Down the gold-paved streets they walked, past the tree of life bearing its twelve manner of fruits, and on to the expanseless rows of mansions of the saints.

Presently they came to an imposing celestial edifice, and the angel said, "This is yours." The sainted lady stood there in speechless wonder, drinking in the lavish beauty of the scene. The angel allowed her to gaze in awe upon her possession for some time, but finally said: "We must go now!" But the redeemed one said, "O must I leave, it is so beautiful?" The angel said, "Yes, we must go around in front now; you're only looking at the back yard."

> The stars look up to God,
>     The stars look down on me,
> The stars shine over the earth,
>     The stars shine over the sea.
>
> The stars may shine a million years,
>     A million years and a day,
> But Christ and I shall live and love,
>     When the stars have passed away.

**HEAV'N!** . . . *You take—*

> The lustre in the eye of the babe,
> The rose in the mother's cheek,
> The smile on the father's face,
> And you have a bit—just a wee bit—
> Of the SPIRIT of Heav'n!

**HEAV'N!** . . . *You take—*

> The yellowish gleam of gold,
> The red of the rose,
> The blush of the violet,
> And you have a bit—just a wee bit—
> Of the BEAUTY of Heav'n!

**HEAV'N!** . . . *You take—*

> The twinkle of the stars,
> The glow of the moon,
> The brightness of the noonday sun,
> And you have a bit—just a wee bit—
> Of the MAJESTY of Heav'n!

**HEAV'N!** . . . *You take—*

> The sparkle of the dewdrop,
> The brilliant hue of the diamond,
> The glory of the rainbow,
> And you have a bit—just a wee bit—
> Of the WONDER of Heav'n!

**HEAV'N!** . . . *You take—*

> The ripple of the babbling brook,
> The murmuring of the pine,
> The music of the sweetest songbird,
> And you have a bit—just a wee bit—
> Of the VOICE of Heav'n!

**HEAV'N!** . . . *You take—*

> The loyalty of a Jonathan for a David,
> The fascination of a laddie for a lassie,
> The devotion of a mother for a baby,
> And you have a bit—just a wee bit—
> Of the LOVE of Heav'n!

DRUIE ANSELM McCALL
1895-1959

## ABOUT THE MAN:

Dr. D. A. (Scotchie) McCall was for eleven years Executive Secretary and Director of Evangelism for some 1,500 Baptist churches in Mississippi. He preached around the world, in some 35 foreign countries.

His consecrated energy, his buoyant, radiant, happy Christian faith, his wholehearted love for people, along with solid and holy convictions concerning God, Christ, the Bible and the saving Gospel of a crucified Saviour, made him wonderfully useful.

In Mississippi, soul winning among Baptists reached an all-time high under his leadership. The denominational work, bogged down with a million-dollar indebtedness, was brought out to a solvent, triumphant place of united support. Gifts through denominational causes multiplied seven times over under his leadership.

Before called to this Secretaryship of Baptists in Mississippi, he had triumphant pastorates at Lyon-Jonestown-Cohama, Philadelphia and Jackson, Mississippi.

He had two years of blessed ministry in Tabernacle Baptist Church, Chicago.

He was also for two years full-time Minister of Revival Promotion for Sword of the Lord Foundation.

Dr. McCall was not a dry and technical preacher, but his heartwarming, easily-read sermons blessed thousands.

## XX.

# *The Language of Heaven*

### D. A. McCALL

What is the language of Heaven? There must be some language of Heaven. We are told that twenty-seven hundred languages and dialects are spoken by the people of the earth. What is the language of Heaven?

In Revelation, chapters 2 and 3, we see Jesus in the midst of His churches talking to each church. What language does He employ? How does He speak to His churches today?

We note a brief verbal discourse in Heaven as found in Revelation 5:8-14:

*"And when he had taken the book, the four beasts and four and twenty elders fell down before the Lamb, having every one of them harps, and golden vials full of odours, which are the prayers of saints. And they sung a new song, saying, Thou art worthy to take the book, and to open the seals thereof: for thou wast slain, and hast redeemed us to God by thy blood out of every kindred, and tongue, and people, and nation; And hast made us unto our God kings and priests: and we shall reign on the earth. And I beheld, and I heard the voice of many angels round about the throne and the beasts and the elders: and the number of them was ten thousand times ten thousand, and thousands of thousands; Saying with a loud voice, Worthy is the Lamb that was slain to receive power, and riches, and wisdom, and strength, and honour, and glory, and blessing. And every creature which is in heaven, and on the earth, and under the earth, and such as are in the sea, and all that are in them, heard I saying, Blessing, and honour, and glory, and power, be unto him that sitteth upon the throne, and unto the Lamb for ever and ever. And the four beasts said, Amen. And the four and twenty elders fell down and worshipped him that liveth for ever and ever."*

What language is used? Let us read John 13:34,35:

*"A new commandment I give unto you, That ye love one another; as I have loved you, that ye also love one another. By this shall all men know that ye are my disciples, if ye have love one to another."*

The manner and measure of our love for each other is to be as the love of Jesus for us.

### Love, the Sign of Recognition

When Jesus got ready to choose a sign of recognition for His followers, He carved it not out of costly woods, neither precious stones, but in love one for another. He gave it not in gold, nor silver, but love one for another. Yet, how many Christians, churches, or denominations do you know who are characterized by love one for another?

Look at these precious Scriptures:

*"If ye love me, keep my commandments. He that hath my commandments, and keepeth them, he it is that loveth me: and he that loveth me shall be loved of my Father, and I will love him, and will manifest myself to him. Jesus answered and said unto him, If a man love me, he will keep my words: and my Father will love him, and we will come unto him, and make our abode with him."* — John 14:15,21,23.

*"But God commendeth his love toward us, in that, while we were yet sinners, Christ died for us."* — Rom. 5:8.

*"For God so loved the world, that he gave his only begotten Son, that whosoever believeth in him should not perish, but have everlasting life."* — John 3:16.

*"For this is the message that ye heard from the beginning, that we should love one another. Not as Cain, who was of that wicked one, and slew his brother. And wherefore slew he him? Because his own works were evil, and his brother's righteous. Marvel not, my brethren, if the world hate you. We know that we have passed from death unto life, because we love the brethren. He that loveth not his brother abideth in death. Whosoever hateth his brother is a murderer: and ye know that no murderer hath eternal life abiding in him. Hereby perceive we the love of God, because he laid down his life for us: and we ought to lay down our lives for the brethren."* — I John 3:11-16.

*"Beloved, let us love one another: for love is of God; and every one*

*that loveth is born of God, and knoweth God. He that loveth not knoweth not God; for God is love. In this was manifested the love of God toward us, because that God sent his only begotten Son into the world, that we might live through him. Herein is love, not that we loved God, but that he loved us, and sent his Son to be the propitiation for our sins. Beloved, if God so loved us, we ought also to love one another. No man hath seen God at any time. If we love one another, God dwelleth in us, and his love is perfected in us. Hereby know we that we dwell in him, and he in us, because he hath given us of his Spirit. And we have seen and do testify that the Father sent the Son to be the Saviour of the world. Whosoever shall confess that Jesus is the Son of God, God dwelleth in him, and he in God. And we have known and believed the love that God hath to us. God is love; and he that dwelleth in love dwelleth in God, and God in him. Herein is our love made perfect, that we may have boldness in the day of judgment: because as he is, so are we in this world. There is no fear in love; but perfect love casteth out fear: because fear hath torment. He that feareth is not made perfect in love. We love him, because he first loved us. If a man say, I love God, and hateth his brother, he is a liar: for he that loveth not his brother whom he hath seen, how can he love God whom he hath not seen? And this commandment have we from him, That he who loveth God love his brother also."* —I John 4:7-21.

What a galaxy of inspiring Scriptures! And all hammering away at one thing!

This thing Jesus speaks about works. It is the most practical thing in the world.

*"A new commandment I give unto you, That ye love one another; as I have loved you, that ye also love one another. By this shall all men know that ye are my disciples, if ye have love one to another."* —John 13:34,35.

An illustration: I went to a field as pastor and found a great church in the aftermath of tragic strife and division. One after another told me they were to blame, thus further suggesting the great spirit that really characterized them. Lest I forget it later, allow me to say that I saw that great church so welded in harmony and love that if there was one case of breach of fellowship, I did not know of it. Well, there was a deacon in the church, who, by the way he looked, gave me the idea he just did not like the new preacher. Maybe he didn't. I couldn't blame him—for at times I do not like myself. Occasionally I stand myself up beside the wall and say things to myself I would not readily take from another. You do not amount to much unless you treat yourself the same way.

I did like the deacon and set out to let him know as much. One day at his place of business, he said, "Preacher, I have been wanting to see you." Here it was about to come off, so I thought. Well, it seemed we had as well have it out; and as good Christians try to put the pieces back together after it was all over, so I said truly, "I am glad to see you." At once he said, "I want to resign as Sunday school teacher and deacon."

I knew then he did not like the new preacher—but still felt we together should make the best of it; so I asked, "Would you mind telling me why you want to resign as deacon and Sunday school teacher?" "Not at all," said he, "I have got to go into bankruptcy."

My "feathers fell." There I had been misjudging one of the best men I ever knew. Again I said some things to myself I needed to hear! Then I asked, "Would you mind telling me why you must go into bankruptcy? Is your business all right morally and legally?" He straightened up and with a manly flash said, "Yes, sir! My business is straight. I simply have not been able to come back from the depression. It seems I must go into bankruptcy."

I will tell you what I told him, without apology, then and now. Said I, "If your business is all right—and I believe it on your word—I will never vote for your resignation as a deacon and Sunday school teacher."

As for myself, away with fair-weather friends! If they cannot be my friends when I am down, I care not for so-called friends only when I am up. Thank God for Mary, the mother of Jesus, the wife of Cleophas, and others with John, who stood by Jesus while He was dying.

*"Now there stood by the cross of Jesus his mother, and his mother's sister, Mary the wife of Cleophas, and Mary Magdalene. When Jesus therefore saw his mother, and the disciple standing by, whom he loved, he saith unto his mother, Woman, behold thy son!"* —John 19:25,26.

I saw to it that some good businessmen heard of our brother's plight. Instead of being glad a competitor was falling, they gathered around him. They counseled with him, advising him to give up part of his business, retaining part of his business. Today he is a successful businessman. He did not resign from Christian service. He has a fine Christian family and is one of the best of friends to this preacher.

Christianity works! The Gospel of the Lord Jesus Christ is the most practical thing on this earth today. The tragedy is, too many of the professed people of Christ have not really tried it.

What is the language of Heaven? Some might think Hebrew, the language of the Old Testament, the language of patriarchs and prophets, to be the language of Heaven. I think not.

Others might think the language of Heaven to be Greek, that most expressive language, the universal language when Christ came in the flesh. I think not.

Still others would cry out that surely the language of Heaven is English, our own mother tongue. I have read magazine articles predicting English would become the one world language. From experience I know of from traveling around the world, as long as you follow the main avenues of travel, whether in Cairo, Marseilles, Jerusalem, Bombay, Shanghai, Rio, Buenos Aires, Antifogasta, Barranquilla, or elsewhere, one will rather readily find speakers of English. I know at the same time if one swerves a few blocks to the right or left, he will be among a people speaking to him a strange language. As long as selfishness dominates men, we will have no one world language on this earth.

*"And the Lord said, Behold, the people is one, and they have all one language; and this they begin to do: and now nothing will be restrained from them, which they have imagined to do. Go to, let us go down, and there confound their language, that they may not understand one another's speech. So the Lord scattered them abroad from thence upon the face of all the earth: and they left off to build the city. Therefore is the name of it called Babel; because the Lord did there confound the language of all the earth: and from thence did the Lord scatter them abroad upon the face of all the earth."*—Gen. 11:6-9.

I do not think English to be the language of Heaven.

You now may be ready to urge us on with the question, "Well, what IS the language of Heaven?"

## Love Is a Language

I am daring to say that LOVE may be the language of Heaven. Immediately someone asks, "But is love a language?" Turning to the dictionary, I find language to be "any means or method of conveying or communicating ideas." And I am sure that love fulfills every requirement of that definition at every step of the way. Let us remember that languages are not always verbally delivered or organized. The cry of a baby is a language known and understood by mothers the world around. Let one shake his fist in the face of another, backing it with a scowl on his own face, and he is speaking a language known and understood around the world. Business is about to pick up. Somebody is about to be whipped. Somebody had better be able to "back it up." A hen's cackle means the same thing around the world. It says we are fixing to have bacon and eggs, provided we have the bacon. Boy Scouts have their sign language, as the Indians had theirs. The military of this country have their signs and emblems—all meaningful to those who know and understand.

I further dare to say that in love, which I am pleased to call the language of Heaven, one may say in one moment of time more than may finally be said in any and all of the twenty-seven hundred combined languages of this earth.

Let me illustrate. A schoolteacher who loves teaching, who loves boys and girls, who revels in growth and learning and development in Christian character; a country doctor going miles and after midnight to see a suffering patient; or, a minister, before daybreak, standing beside the dying—each is speaking, without a spoken word, this language I am pleased to call the language of Heaven. May I ask when have you ever heard or read adequate praise spoken or written about such loving service?

Again, a mother bends over her baby, meeting his needs as only a mother can. That baby already knows there is a relationship between him and anyone else. That mother delivers no verbal dissertation upon the love of a mother for a baby. But in the tenderness of her touch, in every loving caress, and in the constancy of her care, she in one moment of time is saying more of the love of a mother for a baby than you have ever read in the finest book apart from the Bible, and more than the finest orator might picture in an hour of time. Oh, yes, love is a language, if language is "any means or method of conveying or communicating ideas."

A patriotic celebration is taking place. Orators have received meager rounds of applause as they have declared their love for "Old Glory," as they have stated their patriotism and love for country. They are about ready to dismiss for "dinner on the grounds." The master of ceremonies has noted all the morning a veteran of the last war standing on crutches and a lower limb, the other limb missing. Quick to sense a dramatic situation, he asks the veteran to come to the platform. This the veteran hesitantly does. With briefest greeting they speak. Then the veteran hobbles to the corner of the platform where the flag majestically drapes itself about the flagstaff. As tenderly as a man might, he reaches over, catches by the tip the flag, raises it to his lips, kisses it, turns it loose, and it again drapes itself about the flagstaff.

There arises from thousands of lips such cheering as all the orators of all the morning have not received. Why? They were just talking about their patriotism. This veteran has delivered no verbal declaration of patriotism. His body "speaks his piece." It says he put his body between the enemy and home saying, "Only over my dead body." He offered his life, he shed his blood, he suffered, he sacrificed for his country. When have you heard oral language properly describe that sort of patriotism? Again I say, Love is a language. It says more than any or all of the combined languages of this earth!

That very thing is illustrated in the great fifth chapter of Revelation. They are looking for one worthy to take the book and break the seals. They have to pass by angel and archangel, patriarch and prophet, cherubim and seraphim. Finally, they look upon One who has not said a word so far as the record goes. His name is Jesus. Yet they look upon Him and begin to sing and say,

". . .Thou art worthy to take the book, and to open the seals thereof: for thou wast slain, and hast redeemed us to God by thy blood out of every kindred, and tongue, and people, and nation; And hast made us unto our God kings and priests: and we shall reign on the earth."— Rev. 5:9,10.

In His body He speaks the language of Heaven. On His countenance He speaks the language of Heaven. In His life He speaks the language of Heaven.

Yes, love is a language. I gladly call it the language of Heaven.

## Love Speaks Strangely

If love is a language, how does it speak? It speaks strangely to folks who are not in love. The Word of God says of it:

"Love suffereth long, and is kind; love envieth not; love vaunteth not itself, is not puffed up, Doth not behave itself unseemly, seeketh not her own, is not easily provoked, thinketh no evil; Rejoiceth not in iniquity, but rejoiceth in the truth; Beareth all things, believeth all things, hopeth all things, endureth all things. Love never faileth: but whether *there be prophecies, they shall fail; whether there be tongues, they shall cease; whether there be knowledge, it shall vanish away. For we know in part, and we prophesy in part. But when that which is perfect is come, then that which is in part shall be done away. When I was a child, I spake as a child, I understood as a child, I thought as a child: but when I became a man, I put away childish things. For now we see through a glass, darkly; but then face to face: now I know in part; but then shall I know even as also I am known. And now abideth faith, hope, love, these three; but the greatest of these is love."* —I Cor. 13:4-13.

Did you ever note a young couple in love? Of course you have. They like to be together. They sometimes hold hands. They try to please one another. They look at one another in that "soulful, mournful, come hither" way. They tell me young people have changed. I do not believe it. Now, as in the days of yore, they go around not three by three, nor five by five, but two by two. Some, having gotten away from those sweetheart days, look at them and say sophomorically, "Ain't they silly!" They are not one whit more silly than you and I were when we were at that stage. We had as well be honest and admit it.

I have always really put my heart into anything I tried to do. I will never forget my last year at the university. I played varsity football and basketball; stood twenty-one examinations; worked my way in the university store; did YMCA work; did literary society work; preached every Sunday, and courted nearly every night. It paid—I got her. Many students thought it strange that we were together so much. Not strange at all. I was dead in love with her. She gave me pretty good reason to believe she reciprocated.

Oh, the world thinks it strange that Abraham loved God so much he would offer his only son in sacrifice at the word of God. The world does not love as Abraham loved (Gen. 22).

The disciples were so filled with love for Jesus and the power of the Spirit on Pentecost, they were accused of being drunk (Acts 2:13) — maybe intoxicated with very love for Jesus. The world does not love Him as they loved Him, so these lovers acted strangely in their sight.

Paul is so in love with Jesus; as he tells of meeting Jesus, a Roman governor accuses Paul of madness (Acts 26:24). No! Paul is not mad—but desperately in love with Jesus. He loved Jesus so much that hardship and suffering did not stop him witnessing and working for Jesus.

*"In labours more abundant, in stripes above measure, in prisons more*

*frequent, in deaths oft. Of the Jews five times received I forty stripes save one. Thrice was I beaten with rods, once I was stoned, thrice I suffered shipwreck, a night and a day I have been in the deep; In journeyings often, in perils of waters, in perils of robbers, in perils by mine own countrymen, in perils by the heathen, in perils in the city, in perils in the wilderness, in perils in the sea, in perils among false brethren; In weariness and painfulness, in watchings often, in hunger and thirst, in fastings often, in cold and nakedness. Beside those things that are without, that which cometh upon me daily, the care of all the churches. Who is weak, and I am not weak? who is offended, and I burn not?"* —II Cor. 11:23-29.

Look at what love and faith caused heroes and heroines to do:

*"And what shall I more say? for the time would fail me to tell of Gideon, and of Barak, and of Samson, and of Jephthae; of David also, and Samuel, and of the prophets: Who through faith subdued kingdoms, wrought righteousness, obtained promises, stopped the mouths of lions, Quenched the violence of fire, escaped the edge of the sword, out of weakness were made strong, waxed valiant in fight, turned to flight the armies of the aliens. Women received their dead raised to life again: and others were tortured, not accepting deliverance; that they might obtain a better resurrection: And others had trial of cruel mockings and scourgings, yea, moreover of bonds and imprisonment: They were stoned, they were sawn asunder, were tempted, were slain with the sword: they wandered about in sheepskins and goatskins; being destitute, afflicted, tormented; (Of whom the world was not worthy:) they wandered in deserts, and in mountains, and in dens and caves of the earth. And these all, having obtained a good report through faith, received not the promise: God having provided some better thing for us, that they without us should not be made perfect."* —Heb. 11:32-40.

Yes, they acted strangely to those not in love with Jesus. Thank God, multitudes who love Him understand why they acted as they did.

Cold, carnal Christians (if they are Christians) say, "Don't get excited about it." God's Word by deed and word teaches us to get stirred up, get excited about things Christian.

## Love Speaks in Action

How does love speak? It speaks in action! The Word of God says so. Jesus says as much:

*"If ye love me keep my commandments. He that hath my command-ments, and keepeth them, he it is that loveth me: and he that loveth me shall be loved of my Father, and I will love him, and will manifest myself to him. Jesus answered and said unto him, If a man love me, he will keep my words: and my Father will love him, and we will come unto him, and make our abode with him."* —John 14:15,21,23.

Jesus emphasizes that relationship with Him is primarily 'hearing the word of God and doing it.'

*"Then came to him his mother and his brethren, and could not come at him for the press. And it was told him by certain which said, Thy mother and thy brethren stand without, desiring to see thee. And he answered and said unto them, My mother and my brethren are these which hear the word of God, and do it."* —Luke 8:19-21.

*"Jesus answered and said unto them, This is the work of God, that ye believe on him whom he hath sent. And Jesus said unto them, I am the bread of life: he that cometh to me shall never hunger; and he that believeth on me shall never thirst. And this is the will of him that sent me, that every one which seeth the Son, and believeth on him, may have everlasting life: and I will raise him up at the last day. Verily, verily, I say unto you, He that believeth on me hath everlasting life."* —John 6:29,35,40,47.

Here we see that the work of God is to believe on Christ, and the will of God is to believe on Christ! It is not talking about Jesus, nor arguing about Jesus, nor quoting Scripture, but **accepting** the Lord Jesus Christ. Love speaks in action!

We are admonished,

*"My little children, let us not love in word, neither in tongue; but in deed and in truth."* —I John 3:18.

God loved a lost world and He headed that way.

*"For God so loved the world, that he gave his only begotten Son, that whosoever believeth in him should not perish, but have everlasting life."* —John 3:16.

*"Thanks be unto God for his unspeakable gift."* —II Cor. 9:15.

*"Not every one that saith unto me, Lord, Lord, shall enter into the kingdom of heaven; but he that doeth the will of my Father which is*

*in heaven. Many will say to me in that day, Lord, Lord, have we not prophesied in thy name? and in thy name have cast out devils? and in thy name done many wonderful works? And then will I profess unto them, I never knew you: depart from me, ye that work iniquity."* — Matt. 7:21-23.

You may tell if you love a lost world. Are you headed that way — to the lost man across the street, or to the lost around the world? You may tell if you love the Word of God. Are you headed that way? You may tell if you love His church. Are you headed that way?

Love sends "her" flowers. It does not merely take her by the garden where she may smell them. Love sends candy. It does not merely take her to the store to admire the pretty boxes. Love does something about it!

About the oldest story I know illustrates this point. Back in the horse-and-buggy days, in a section of a state, people had never seen a two-story building. Many did not believe it could be done. But word got out that a crossroads storekeeper had erected a two-story building. A gala day was to mark the opening. People were coming from miles around.

A boy made a date with his very best girl. He was driving her in the buggy to see this sight. As the "tall skyscraper" came into view, they were awestruck. Coming down the one road that ran through the village, they stopped across the road from the building. He dropped the lines on the dash, and together they were all athrill and filled with questions. "My, it is high up!" "How in the world did they slip that second story up on that first story?"

The proprietor, just to make the day a complete success, had imported a brand new popcorn popper and peanut parcher. The fragrance and aroma of all that drifted across the street and fell against the young lady's olfactory nerve. (I think that is the right one.) Her nose and lip twitched.

He noted it and said, "Do you like that?"

"I sure do," she replied.

He gathered up the lines, drove down the road, made a complete turn, and came back as closely as he could get the buggy to that popcorn popper and peanut parcher, stopped the horse, dropped the lines on the dash, and remarked manfully, "Now you can smell it better."

He could have done better than that! He was a cheapskate. He could have pulled out his last Indian head nickel saying, "This is the last nickel I have in the world. You are my best girl. I am going to buy you a bag of popcorn or peanuts; furthermore, I am going to let you decide which it shall be." He didn't do it! "Now you can smell it better," was his best because of what he was.

Love speaks in action. Love does something about it. A mine has fallen in, entombing several miners. Rescuers quickly gather. A crossroads storekeeper hears his son is one of those caught in the disaster. A mere church member might have said to two customers in the store at the time, "Do you hear that? My boy is down there. He was a good boy. I tried to be a good Daddy to him. How many pounds of salt meat do you want? What size sack flour did you say you wanted?"

Church members may act like that but not Daddies. Here is the way a daddy acts: "Do you hear that? My boy is down there! I must go! You understand—you will come back!" All the while he is gently but steadily pushing them to the door.

He locks the door. Away he goes to the scene of the disaster. When he gets there, he does not join the crowd of the curious; only some church members would do that. He rushes up to a tired rescuer who has been digging away, sweat-covered; almost rudely, the daddy takes the pick from his hands, saying, "Let me relieve you. My boy is down there." That daddy begins to turn rock and dirt. He is headed in the direction of his boy. Love is speaking in action. Love is doing something about it.

Oh, that God would show us how we are just "playing church." Oh, that God would show us how we are just playing at revival! Oh, that God would show us how we are just playing at winning the lost!

Oh, that God would teach us we are not fooling anybody unless it be ourselves! We talk about the lost but do so little about them. We talk about a lost world but are not headed that way. We talk about His Word but read everything else.

All along the way in the Word of God, Genesis through Revelation, God is headed toward the human family He has created, acting in their behalf, doing something about them.

*"For God so loved the world, that he gave his only begotten Son, that whosoever believeth in him should not perish, but have everlasting life."* —John 3:16.